A Bateman  Family Novel

4

SEEING Jess

JENNY GLAZEBROOK

*To the Broekman Family
I love the way you live for Jesus
heart, soul, mind and strength.
You're an inspiration.*

CHAPTER ONE

Jessica Cardelle smoothed her skirt and stepped into her office. One more appointment to go. She ran her finger down the list of names on the clipboard and stopped at the last one. Tim Bateman. The man involved in the awful train disaster a year ago. She drew in a deep breath and sank into her leather office chair. She forced herself to skim his file again. Amputee. Twenty-four years old. Close to the age Toby would be if he'd survived the crash. She took another deep breath. She didn't want to see this patient. The one who'd survived, when her brother hadn't.

Lauren hadn't given her much choice. 'He's going to end up seeing you when I leave the practice, anyway. Might as well start now.'

Jess's chest felt tight. She'd become a physiotherapist to help people and then added O.T. to her training because Lauren needed support in her role. But life hadn't turned out the way she imagined it would. She'd never been given a chance to help Toby. In an instant he was gone.

'Jess, you here?' The front door banged open and Jess smiled as

Milla charged through. Her fifteen-year-old sister was like a cyclone the way she flew in and out, her curly brown hair looking like it had been swept up in a storm.

'I'm in here.'

Milla spun around the corner, pony-tail bouncing, hazel eyes sparkling behind her glasses. She threw her school backpack onto the floor beside Jess's desk. 'I've decided what I'm going to be when I leave school.'

Again? Jess held her tongue. What would it be this time? She could always count on her little sister to come up with random, outrageous ideas.

'I'm going to be a truck driver,' Milla said. 'I'm going to drive one of those big livestock transporters.' Her hands went to her hips. 'Riley reckons a woman can't handle it. Not strong enough. Ha. I'll show him.'

Jess chuckled. 'You can't decide on a life-long occupation just to prove someone wrong. It has to be something you want to do.'

And yet hadn't she chosen to become a physio not because it was her dream, but because she believed her hometown of Barrawi needed allied health professionals? It had been the perfect solution. Work here during work hours and help out on the family farm in her spare time. It was the best of both worlds.

Milla settled onto Jess's desk, pushing aside a file to make room. She crossed her legs and leaned over Jess's patient list. 'Are you done yet?'

Jess moved the list away from her prying eyes. 'Confidentiality, remember? And no, I've got one more patient to go.'

Milla pulled a disappointed face then giggled. 'Leave it. Wag the afternoon. We could sneak out together. Wouldn't that be fun?'

'If only I could.' Jess meant it to come out lighthearted, but something in her tone alerted Milla because her face fell.

'What's wrong?'

Should she tell her? Milla should be allowed to be young and carefree. And yet, not telling her would imply she didn't trust her to understand. She looked into Milla's concerned eyes. 'My next patient was in the train accident.'

Milla released a drawn out 'oh' sound. In it was a world of understanding. She bit her lip and tilted her head, curls sliding across her forehead. 'But Jess, maybe this is your chance to make something good come of it? Remember, Toby wouldn't want us to stop living because *he* has. You couldn't help Toby, but you can help this person.'

Jess nodded. Milla was right. Her brother had lost his life in that train disaster and this man had lived for a reason. God was in control. Just because grief and loss had hit so close to home, didn't mean she should stop believing God cared.

So, guide me, Lord. Give me strength.

And yet the prayer felt empty; ritualistic. So much spiritual talk and reasoning from so many people, including herself. She believed it all, but it didn't take away the empty, lost feeling deep inside.

The front door to the practice opened. Her client had arrived. Milla gave her arm a quick squeeze. 'You'll be fine. I've got fire cadet training now, but Mum said you can take me home?'

'I can. I'll pick you up after I see this patient.'

Milla grinned and jumped off the desk, grabbed her school bag and shrugged it onto her shoulder. 'See you then.' She hesitated, looked back and captured Jess's eyes. 'You've got this.' Then she bounced out the back door of the practice.

The bell on the counter rang and Jess heard Kelly, the new receptionist, greet the patient. She'd need to have a quiet word with her. Kelly should know to acknowledge a patient the moment they entered the office, not wait for them to ring the bell.

'Good afternoon.' Thankfully, Kelly sounded cheery and professional. 'You must be Tim Bateman.'

'Yes, I'm here to see Lauren.'

The voice was deep. Almost a low, rumbling growl.

Kelly hesitated. 'Ah, yes, actually, there's been a change and you're seeing Jess today.'

'I don't think so. I've been booked in with Lauren.'

'Yes, well, Lauren had something urgent come up.' Had gone home early more to the truth. 'If you'd like to just take a seat ...'

A deep, mirthless chuckle came from the man. 'Really? I came with my own in case you haven't noticed.'

Jess took a deep breath and stepped into the waiting room. Time to intervene and go into damage control. She needed to put Toby out of her mind and do her job. She turned to the patient and stopped. For the first time since the accident, her own pain was forgotten. There, facing Kelly in a wheelchair sat a young man with dark, attractive features. His hair was neatly cut with slight waves on top and his strong jaw was clean shaven. Even sitting down, she could see he was tall. But what struck her was the heaviness that enveloped his being. There was a solemn sorrow that overshadowed him.

Tall, dark and handsome, she thought, then put those thoughts aside. There was no place for romance in her life. She was an independent, successful young woman with a loving, supportive family. She was practical and she'd known from the time she was five years old that she was not the marrying kind. There was no excuse for appreciating, let alone dwelling on the good looks of a stranger who would never be more than a client.

The client turned to her and those inky black eyes were expressionless. In them was a complete absence of light or joy.

It's like he has a heart of stone, she thought, recalling a verse she'd read in Ezekiel a couple of days ago. What did it say? Something about God promising to replace a heart of stone with a heart of flesh.

Something stirred within. She couldn't hold herself aloof or put protective walls around her heart. This man was in need and only God could help him.

She smiled. 'Tim?' He didn't respond. She held out a hand for him to shake. 'I'm Jessica Cardelle. I'm a therapist here.'

He stared back and the anger and resentment oozed from him, almost a physical force. She braced herself against the intensity of it and managed a smile. 'I hear you need—'

'I don't need anything.'

She started at the crack of his harsh, expressionless voice. 'That's ... that's ... I didn't mean ...'

'No. Nobody *means* anything, do they?'

'Um ...' Jess licked her suddenly dry lips, confidence racing out the door. 'I was of the understanding you are my new patient.'

His eyes narrowed. 'Were you? I was told I'd be seeing Lauren. And your name badge says you are a physiotherapist, not an O.T.'

Jess nodded. 'It's true I usually see the physio patients, but I am also a qualified O.T. You will probably need both, so we thought ...'

Tim raised a hand and whipped it down like a lash. 'You thought, did you? I was told it was all to be discussed and negotiated. I'm sick of people telling me what I need and what I have to do. I might not approve of you. Had you thought of that?'

She hadn't, but she wouldn't dare say so. Everybody in town knew Jessica Cardelle and they liked and appreciated her. She was the smart one, the caring one, the extraordinarily gifted, all-together Christian girl whose resume consisted of outstanding achievement after outstanding achievement. Tim didn't know that, being a stranger to town, but his harsh words threw her.

His eyes drilled into her. 'Just because I've lost my foot doesn't mean I've lost my right to choose.'

'Tim ... I, well do you want my services?'

He chuckled, but there was a coldness to it that sent shivers down her spine. He looked her up and down as though considering his answer. Then he crossed his arms and she noted they were strong and muscular, unlike his legs. She quickly assessed the situation. The physio in her knew the trauma his body had been through; knew the struggle but also how to strengthen and rebuild those wasted leg muscles. The O.T. in her knew he needed purpose. Something to work toward.

His eyes narrowed as though he knew she was analysing him. 'It doesn't matter what I want. I can't do much about it, can I? Unless you're such a brilliant therapist you can grow me back a foot.'

'I can help you find the right prosthetic foot. I can get you back on your feet and as fully able as you were before the accident. If you really want something, there is always a way to get it.'

'Confident, aren't you? What if I want something you're not willing to give?'

What was he insinuating? She avoided his eyes. She knew she wasn't attractive. Unruly, reddish-brown hair, freckles and plain features didn't amount to being pretty. She knew it. Everyone knew it. All she had was her personality and her achievements, and Tim hadn't had time to discover either.

He ran a hand through his dark, wavy hair. 'You can't make me into a whole man again, can you?'

She gritted her teeth. She had to remain professional and polite. Why was he baiting her? She must remain cool, calm and collected. 'You are no less a man now, than you were before you lost your foot.'

His lips twisted in a sneer. 'Lost it? It wasn't lost. It was mangled beneath a pile of metal, torn to shreds like my strength, my identity, my purpose in life. It's gone. If I had my way, I would have died in that accident, but this stupid heart keeps beating.'

He tapped his chest and she felt the blood drain from her face. Okay, so he was angry, resentful, possibly even suffering survivor's guilt, but she didn't need to put up with this. Wasn't going to. He was being cold and heartless. And he was here, resenting the gift of life he'd been given while her brother who loved life had been given no choice. Without another word, she turned, marched back into her office and closed the door behind her.

He was a crude, angry young man and she didn't have to tolerate his abuse. He might be in pain, but it wasn't her job to be his punching bag. He was hurting, but so was she. Let Lauren deal with him.

She sat down at her desk. Her hands were clammy with sweat. What was wrong with her? She was usually the placid, calm one. She prided herself in her patience, but she'd lost it out there. Maybe she wasn't patient at all. Maybe it was just that nobody had ever pushed her buttons to this extent. She hated that Tim Bateman had managed to rattle her so completely. She bit her lip. His dark eyes haunted her. He was in pain and she knew the only One who could ever help him.

'What do I do, Lord?' Tim Bateman made her want to run and hide, but God was her hiding place. Her refuge and rock. He would shelter her from the storm in Tim Bateman's heart. And so, standing tall, taking a deep breath, she reached for her clipboard again. She would go back out there. God would be her refuge.

God, help me. Keep me calm. Help me love him as you love him.

She opened the door and stepped back out into the waiting room. He was still there, his expression stony. She studied him, waiting, gathering strength, clipboard clasped to her chest.

He raised his head and a tight smile, if it could be called that, pulled at his lips. 'Can I help you?' Sarcasm seeped through every syllable as he tilted his head, mocking her own words from earlier.

'I don't think so.'

His expression changed ever so slightly at her renewed composure.

'I don't know what your problem is,' she continued, lowering the clipboard. *Confidence, Jess.* She stepped towards him. 'I can tell you're bitter, but that doesn't mean you have a right to take it out on me.' She stood taller. 'I hate it when I have to report a patient as non-compliant. I feel like we've both failed. But I really don't think you're the type to give up before you've even started. So, do you want to wait to see Lauren, or are we going to give each other a chance? Show each other some respect?'

When he didn't answer, she gave him her fiercest glare. 'I take it that's a yes?'

He gave that hard, dry smile again. 'If you say so.'

She didn't ask if he'd like to be wheeled into the consult room. That would be asking for trouble. 'This way.'

He wheeled himself in and she left the door open. Just in case. Part of her had hoped he wouldn't follow, but he did, and she had a job to do.

He answered her questions like a sulky child and she wanted to tell him to grow up, but she persisted with her friendly, professional manner. She didn't touch his leg or the stump where his foot was once attached. She didn't want him to feel the way her hands were clammy and realise she was nervous. Just an assessment was more than enough for today.

She ran her finger down the final paperwork. 'You've written down that you are a vet.'

'Yes.'

So, he was a professional. 'Currently working?'

'I've just finished study but there's a position waiting for me.'

'What kind of position?'

'Livestock work.'

Her head jerked up. He couldn't manage livestock in a wheelchair. And possibly not even once she arranged for a prosthesis. Her father was a strong, steady man and yet a bull had knocked him completely off his feet.

Tim's jaw jumped and he stiffened. 'You think I can't do it.'

'I didn't say that.'

'I might be a cripple, but my eyes and mind still work. Your body language shouts skepticism. But you're underestimating me.'

Jess stepped back from him, allowing herself to meet his piercing eyes. 'And you're underestimating me, too.'

His mouth curved up in a sardonic smile. 'I doubt it. I mean, are you even old enough to have a degree?'

She held in a sigh. She didn't need to explain to him that she'd finished school early and was the youngest person in her course to complete a masters, that she'd worked with Lauren while completing her studies so she could be qualified sooner.

How was she going to put up with him every day? It was clear he had no respect for her. All his harsh, cryptic comments showed he was not impressed by her position, profession or even her personality. Usually her friendly, open manner won over the grumpiest of patients. But Tim was beyond grumpy. He was so absorbed in his own pain and darkness that he shied away from the light.

'God,' she muttered, 'Give me strength.'

Because God's supernatural strength was the only thing that would get her through this.

CHAPTER TWO

Milla Cardelle did up the last of the press studs on her bright orange fire cadet overalls and tried to put Jess out of her mind. Her sister would be fine with her new patient. If anyone could help him, Jess could. She was the strong, understanding one. The smart one in the family who always had it together. It freaked her out a little bit sometimes, the way Jess looked at her as though she could see right into her heart and mind. She always seemed to know exactly what others were thinking and feeling and what they needed.

'Focus!'

Milla started at Zac's voice. She turned to fake glare at him, then stopped. He'd taken her glasses from where she'd sat them down on a tree stump while she got her fire gear on. He now wore them and was peering at her with a half grin on his familiar face. Normally she would laugh and snatch them back, but he looked so different. So … so much older. More mature and manly. How could one pair of glasses make such a difference? Her heart did a funny jump and she forced herself to playfully slap him.

'Give them back, Zac!' How fickle was she? One pair of glasses wasn't going to make her feel any different about her closest childhood friend and neighbour. The Buckley's were practically family. He was a brother to her and nothing more.

Zac took off the glasses and held them out. She reached for them but he snatched his hand away at the last minute. He tilted his head at her. 'Say please.'

'Hah! I'm not going to ask politely for something I already own.'

The fire captain called for attention.

Zac grinned and handed Milla her glasses. 'You're lucky I'm a polite thief then. Most of us don't return stolen items at all. Ever.'

The chainsaw roared to life, cutting off Milla's comeback. 'You'll keep,' she mouthed at him. He grinned.

The noise and power of the saw drew her attention back to the fire captain and the chainsaw. She itched to hold that machine herself and slice through the thick branches of the ironbark gum. Neil continued demonstrating the cuts and angles needed to slice through the tough wood.

Zac nudged her with his elbow and spoke into her ear above the noise. 'Going to be selling firewood this winter? Great pocket money.'

She hadn't thought of that. A slow smile crept across her face. There was plenty of wood on their property. Old, dead trees Dad hadn't cleared away yet. But would Dad let her? What if Zac helped her? She reckoned she could convince him to. And it was his suggestion, after all.

Neil stopped the machine and stepped back, setting it carefully on the ground. 'Now, no heroics. As firefighters we only do what is necessary in the moment. It will be the job of the arborists to come in after the fire and work out which trees are safe and which need to be felled. If a tree has blocked the road, fair enough, cut it up and toss it aside to get through.' He looked around the group. 'Who wants to have a go?'

Milla shot her hand into the air at the exact same time Zac did.

He grinned and pushed her hand down with one hand while still holding up the other. Milla fought against him, biting back a laugh. He was not going to get in before her.

Except he did.

'Zac.' Neil pointed at him. 'Get your safety gear on. Chaps, helmet, earmuffs, gloves.'

Zac shot a triumphant look at Milla and did as he was told.

She stuck out her tongue and his eyebrows shot up. 'Really, Milla? You think you're mature enough to use a chainsaw but you resort to that?'

She tried to glower at him and failed. He patted her shoulder, peering at her through his face shield. 'Now, no sulking. I'll be back in a minute. Then maybe, if you're a good girl, you can have a turn too.'

She swiped at him as he bounced over to the chainsaw looking way too eager to operate the dangerous piece of equipment. He handled it with skill, but he'd done it many times before. His dad was the local SES controller. Not that Barrawi had many emergencies that required the State Emergency Service, but they still had weekly meetings and training events. Zac had attended most of them with his dad since he was a little boy and his mum had left.

He wasn't a little boy anymore, though. She watched him easily slice through the ironbark. She couldn't believe how much he'd grown in just the last couple of months. It was disconcerting. He now towered above her and their competitive games were completely uneven. She pretended she didn't notice. She didn't want to grow up. Didn't want him to grow up. Growing up meant pain. Experiencing the cost of life. Losing people you loved. Change was something she fought against, heart and soul.

He came back to her side, pulling off his gloves and helmet. 'How'd I do?'

'As well as can be expected when you have the advantage of having done it a hundred times before.'

He chuckled and put his arm around her. 'Ah, now you're just being a bad sport.'

She shoved her hip against him, forcing him to lose balance and take a step sideways. 'Am not.'

Neil called her forward. Throwing Zac a triumphant smile, she donned the safety gear and headed to the chainsaw lying on the ground, begging to be brought to life. Only, the cord was a lot harder to pull than she'd expected. Zac had made it look so easy. She gritted her teeth, trying not to show the effort it took to pull the cord. Twice, she failed and the cord dropped dead and slid back into the machine. No one spoke. She was aware of the eyes of the rest of the group on her.

God, please help me.

Maybe God was testing her. Taking her strength to show her how stupid her pride was. Maybe she deserved to be humbled this way.

Finally, the machine roared to life. She lifted it but her arms were so weary. The machine didn't look this heavy. Not the way Zac had lifted it with such ease. What was wrong with her? She forced herself to keep going. Her forehead glistened with sweat and she gritted her teeth. She managed, but it was hard. So hard.

'Well done,' Neil said when she shut off the noise and pulled off the earmuffs.

But she knew it wasn't well done. Especially when Zac didn't tease her, but instead looked at her with concern. He'd had that same look when news of Toby's death had come. That look that said he wanted to comfort her but wasn't quite sure how to when she'd always been the strong, competitive, cheerful one.

Maybe she needed to help Dad out around the farm again to build up her strength. Since Toby's death she hadn't felt like it. Everything was different. Dad laughed less. Mum cried a lot. Jess tried harder than ever to please everyone and stop them hurting even though they all knew this was something she couldn't fix.

Laying on her bed reading or looking at social media on her phone kept her mind off the emptiness she felt inside. Chatting with friends about menial, everyday things helped. And filling the rest of the time with soccer training or fire cadets kept her busy enough not to become lost in grief.

Noises behind caught her attention. A new girl had joined the group today. She'd seen Kirra Hurley at school, but she was quiet and didn't speak much. She hung around with the more academic girls and Milla definitely wasn't one of them.

'Reckons she's indigenous,' she heard Riley snicker. 'She's whiter than a sheet.'

'Just wants the government payouts,' Cheyanne agreed with him.

Milla frowned and tensed. Why did everyone have to pick on those who were different? Or in this case, pick on them because they weren't?

'Leave it,' Zac said, and she knew he'd also heard the comments. But if he heard, Kirra would have, too.

She met Zac's gaze. 'I can't.'

'Why?'

'Micah six verse eight.'

Zac looked at her. 'Remind me.'

'What does the Lord require of you? To do justly, to love mercy and to walk humbly with your God.' Humbly. Hmm, she hadn't been doing that part so well. 'They're being unjust.'

Zac's mouth curved in something close to a smile. 'You want some backup?'

'Nope. I'm fine.' Humble. 'Actually, some support might be nice.'

He followed her over to the group who were still muttering about Kirra. Riley had a stick with a couple of leaves on the end. He flicked it into Kirra's hair. She jumped, swiping at what she must have thought was an insect or spider. Milla grabbed the stick from Riley, broke it in half and threw it to the ground, glaring at him.

He glared back. 'Keep out of it, four eyes.'

Did he really think such a childish taunt would hurt? She shook her head. 'I can't. You're being a bully.'

'You don't even know what the word means. You think everyone's a bully. Think you have to step in and save the day like some big hero. Couldn't save your brother though, could you?'

She reeled back, his verbal slap stunning her. Then she let loose, marching forward until she was nose to nose with Riley. 'I'll have you know that indigenous people have many shades of skin, just like us. And they have a right to every bit of money they get from the government and more.'

'Why? So they can drink and bludge and sponge off us?'

Now she was seething, fire fueled by his ignorance and prejudice. 'Haven't you been listening in history? Our people stole their land, Riley. You and I live well today because our ancestors took what was theirs and made it ours. We wrecked their lives. We try to force them to follow our culture. All these fires we are trying to fight, it's because we didn't listen to them. They know how to care for this land better than we do!'

Kirra had turned, eyes wide, and was staring at her.

She felt a calming hand rest on her shoulder. Zac. Why did he have to do that just when she was getting started? She needed to vent this frustration, this anger, this …

Neil strode over. 'What's going on?'

Milla drew in a deep breath, ready to tell him exactly what was going on but suddenly felt like a sink draining of water. All the energy seeped from her body and to her own mortification, she began to cry. Big, fat tears rolled down her cheeks and no words would come. This was humiliation of the worst kind. How would she ever live this down? Riley was never going to forget. And neither were his mates. If she were old enough she'd leave school now, get her truck license and go out on the roads. Out where she could enjoy the scenery of this amazing country. The scenery the aborigines had fought and died for.

'What's her issue?' Riley demanded. 'All I did was made a comment and she lost it.'

Neil turned on him. 'I doubt that.'

Riley crossed his arms, his chest coming out. 'It's true. She just over-reacts to everything these days.'

Maybe he was right, but some days Milla couldn't work out which way was up and which way was down. It was as though every bit of grief she'd ever felt in her life; every sad memory, picked this moment to drown her in its pain. She knew that today she was fighting as much for Alan as for Kirra. Alan had worked on their family farm for years and she'd grown to love him. Had loved the unique sound of his voice as he sang and worked. But then he'd left to take on another job. She'd only been six years old but she'd been heartbroken. He was a wanderer, her parents had said. He never stayed in one place for long. She wished she could be the same.

Neil looked around the group. 'How about we focus on chainsaw safety, hey? I want you two to separate – Riley, you over there. Milla, you over that side. Zip your lips and listen. We're about saving lives, not attacking each other.'

Milla let her shoulders fall, but gratefully moved as far away from Riley as she could. Zac followed her, staying by her side, a silent support. Finally, parents began to arrive and Jess pulled up alongside them. Milla sighed with relief, avoiding everyone's eyes. Escape at last. She wanted to curl up in bed and go to sleep.

'Grab Zac too,' Jess called out the window. 'Pierce texted and asked me to drop him home.'

Milla turned back. Zac waved a hand to show he'd heard. He grabbed his equipment bag and rushed to catch up, then threw himself into the back seat, squeezing his long legs in behind Milla's seat. Soon he wouldn't fit. Milla moved her seat forward to give him more room.

'Either of you up for a walk?' Jess asked, as they headed out of town and toward their farms, side by side along Gable Road. 'I need to work off some steam.'

Milla laughed. 'Don't fall for it, Zac. She's started powerwalking. It's nothing like a normal walk.'

Jess screwed up her nose. 'It's better for you. Lower impact but still good cardio. You have no idea how many people end up with shin splints and stress fractures from running. It puts too much strain on the joints.'

Milla shook her head and reached behind to pat Zac's leg. 'Don't do it, Zac. She makes it sound all good and professional, but there's no way anyone can keep up with her the way she charges up and down the hills.'

Zac grinned. 'As much as I'd like to take up the challenge, I'd better get dinner on. Dad's going to be home late and Pierce has a work meeting.'

Milla glanced back at him. Getting a meal ready was a normality for Zac on the days he didn't come over and eat with her family. He never complained, but Milla wondered if he sometimes resented his mother leaving. He never spoke about it if he did. But then, her own mother had taken him and his older brother Pierce under her wing. And now that Toby was gone, she asked them over for meals more often, almost as though she needed to fill the empty place Toby had left at the table.

'Have dinner with us,' Milla told him. 'Mum said you have to come around more, remember?'

Zac frowned. 'I don't want to be an inconvenience.'

'Don't be stupid. You know Mum loves you.' She leaned around the seat to poke his sweaty leg.

He grinned, pushing her finger way. 'Yeah, okay. I'll come.'

'So, you can both come with me, then?' Jess was now looking across at Milla, a question in her eyes. Come where? What had Jess asked a moment ago?

Jess's brow furrowed in a concerned way. 'You coming for a walk with me?'

Milla shook her head. 'Not today.' She saw the way Jess's shoulders slumped and guiltily recalled that Jess had been having a rough time when she'd dropped in on her before cadets. Some patient? Trouble with the receptionist? Why was her mind so fuzzy? She closed her eyes, resting her head back against the car seat.

CHAPTER THREE

Tim wheeled himself up the ramp to the front door of his home. His wheelchair friendly home. How had it come to this? Every dream for his life had been stripped away in one cheap train ride. He should have driven his own car into the city that day.

The old lady in the unit next door waved, but he pretended he didn't see. He didn't want her pity. He breathed hard at the effort of the last slope of the ramp and relaxed as his wheelchair settled on the verandah.

He'd faced every trial head-on his whole life and let it strengthen him and build his character. The loss of his dad, his mother's emotional distance, the rebellion and mischief of his younger siblings, the loss of his grandfather … he'd been able to keep strong, be resilient, force himself to keep going. But he could not separate himself from this loss – the loss of a part of himself. And even more so, the loss of his independence. Yet still, he fought. Not just against this loss, but against the whole world. A shooting pain made its way up his leg and he bit his lip.

His phone rang. He glanced at the screen and read, NDIS LAC.

How was it that an acronym he'd never heard until a year ago was now burned into his brain? His National Disability Insurance Scheme Local Area Co-ordinator was helpful, but he hated everything she represented. He turned his phone over and ignored the call. He was supposed to be running around the countryside doctoring livestock by this time in his life, not navigating a health scheme for the disabled. He'd loved his vet training. He'd loved using his intelligence and natural ability to understand science. He'd loved being fit, healthy and capable. He'd thrived on it.

Now he struggled to get out of bed in the morning. He refused contact with his family. He closed off his heart because it had been bruised one too many times and now lay bleeding, dying in a gutter somewhere.

Tim juggled his keys and leaned forward to open his front door. The lock had been set lower to make it easier for him to reach in his wheelchair. He'd taken being tall for granted. He pushed the door open. Bluey let out an excited bark and skidded around the corner, tail wagging and making loud thumping sounds against the wall.

'Hey, Blue.' He reached out and affectionately rubbed the dog's ears. 'What would I do without you, hey?'

Bluey grinned up at him, pushing his wet nose into Tim's hands, his front paws on the footrest of the wheelchair.

His phone rang again. NDIS LAC. She wasn't going to give up. With a frustrated growl, he answered. 'Tim here.'

'Tim, it's Natasha your LAC.'

'I know.'

She was used to his gruff manner and rushed on, her tone cheerful and professional. 'Your family have asked for special permission to contact you.'

'No.'

'I think you might want to let them, this time.'

'Is someone injured? Dying?' Guilt nudged through his sarcasm and his shoulders tensed. What if they were? He remembered the time his little sister, Beth, had witnessed the murder of a friend. He'd been busy studying in the city. If he'd been there, he would have helped her; stopped her developing the depression and anxiety she now battled. Instead she'd turned to faith—the false hope, the crutch he most despised. She'd been brainwashed by all those ridiculous Christian platitudes. And there was nothing he could do about it now. They all saw him as the one who needed help; a crutch. He would prove otherwise.

'No, they're fine,' Natasha reassured him.

His shoulders relaxed. Hopefully that murderer who ruined his little sister's life had died in jail. What was his name? Joel Elliot. The name left a bitter taste on his tongue. 'Well, if they're fine, they don't need to contact me, do they?'

'They have good news they want to share with you.'

'Well it can wait,' he snapped. He'd learned that what his family considered good news, was not always good news. Like when Beth was brainwashed into becoming a Christian, just like Clare. 'I'll contact them when I'm ready.'

Natasha hesitated, then sighed. 'I'll let them know.'

Tim ended the call. Why did they have to push? Couldn't they see that they weren't helping? Contact with them brought back all the bad memories.

His mother's face came to his mind and he tried to push it away. Why had he let her talk him into a kidney transplant? To prolong the half-life he was now living? The life that was taken away as he lay, helpless in hospital, knowing that life as he knew it was over. Pain was so intense, so all-consuming that he wished for relief in any way it could be found. But the morphine they fed into his veins could only take away his physical agony and make way for the emotional knife to twist into his heart.

He closed his eyes, remembering the doctor's words that day. 'We may need to amputate and you urgently need a kidney.'

Bluey pushed his nose into Tim's hands and he gave his head

an affectionate pat. But not even Bluey could distract him from the memories.

'I will donate a kidney,' his younger brother, Dan had said — the brother he had been commissioned to protect and care for from the day their father had been killed. There was no way Tim was going to let his little brother give up a kidney for him.

Especially when a voice that had haunted him as a child returned.

How was it that his kindergarten teacher still turned up to trouble him at every turning point in his life? The old woman was probably long dead, but her thoughts infiltrated his mind as though her voice was right against his ear.

'I knew you were weak,' her raspy voice had mocked him.

But the worst had been at his father's funeral. Only eight years old, he'd wanted to run when he saw her in the church. Why Ms Schneider had even been at his father's funeral was beyond him. She'd hated him from his first day of school. Bullied him, he now recognised as an adult looking back. Her abuse of power would have had her in big trouble had she been caught, but he'd never spoken a word and neither had his classmates. Not when she'd torn up their artwork because they hadn't written their names neatly enough on the back, not when she'd screamed at them for mispronouncing her name, not when she'd grabbed him by the scruff of his shirt for being so slow and shoved him into line. Not when she'd thrown his friend's lunch into the bin because he was too slow eating, or when she'd mocked Tim for bringing his favourite teddy bear in for Show and Tell.

'You're too old for teddy bears now,' she'd laughed, the raspy sound grating on his young ears and causing his face to burn. 'What are you, a baby?' She'd turned to face the class. 'Do you think we need to put Timmy in a nappy for today? Maybe give him a dummy?'

Some children listened in wide-eyed horror as hot tears of

humiliation spilled down Tim's cheeks. Others laughed and called him 'Teddy-baby.'

He'd grown up that day. No teddy bears for him. No more comfort toys, not even a nightlight.

'I don't like kisses,' he'd told his mother when she'd come to say goodnight. 'I can tuck myself in.'

She didn't seem to mind. She was busy enough with his younger siblings and baby Beth.

When Dad came to his room with a story book, Tim tried to send him away. 'I can read to myself. I'm a big boy now.'

Dad grinned and ruffled his hair. 'That's great. How about you read to me, then?'

Tim wriggled away. 'Okay. But you have to sit over there. On the chair.'

With a shrug, Dad complied, but he brought the chair so close he might as well have been sitting on the edge of the bed. Then he tried to put his arm around Tim, but Tim shoved him away.

'Don't. I don't like hugs.'

Dad gave him that affectionate, half amused look he gave Mum when she was being demanding. 'Can I at least kiss you goodnight?'

He might have caved in had he not remembered Ms Schneider's mocking voice at that moment. 'No!'

'Why not?' Dad still looked amused rather than offended.

'Because I'm grown up now.'

'But I'm grown up too, and I still like hugs and kisses.'

He had a point, but Tim didn't back down.

And then three years later Dad had been killed in a car accident. How Tim regretted not accepting those hugs. He regretted all the times he could have snuggled under his father's arm, hearing his deep voice read him bedtime stories. But time wasn't something you could snatch back. It was gone.

The funeral went from bad to worse when Ms Schneider came and rested a hand on his shoulder. It was her fault he hadn't made the most of all those years with Dad. Her hand burnt through his shirt and into his heart. He wanted to shake it off, to tell her exactly what she'd done, but instead he froze and forced himself to hold her gaze. She hadn't changed. He saw the mocking challenge in the tilt of her chin, in her hard gaze.

'God needed your dad as an angel,' she said. 'You need to step up and be the man of the family now.'

And he'd heard what she was really saying. 'Grow up and stop being a whingy little boy who needs a teddy bear.'

And how could God need Dad as an angel? Mum had said it, too.

'We know Ben is looking down at us from heaven,' she agreed absently with Ms Schneider.

And Tim felt something tight and hard go around his heart. It tightened the more the people in that church talked about his dad.

'His faith in God was an example to us all.'

'He's so much better off now. He's happy and free from the burdens of this earth.'

'He's up there with the angels, where he was always meant to be.'

'God needed him more than we do.'

He kept his eyes down, didn't let anyone see the fury in his expression. If God needed Dad more than a grieving eight-year-old boy, then God was either a weakling, hard hearted, or not even real. And if Dad preferred to be with God than his own children, then God was nothing more than competition. And if Ms Schneider believed in God, then Tim would do the opposite. No great loss. Dad had taken him and Clare to church on occasion, but it had been boring. So many religious rituals, expectations, and empty sounding words. Church was a place of death and God was a cold-hearted being who took loved ones from their families.

That was the main reason he accepted the kidney transplant when Mum came to plead with him in hospital the day of the accident.

'We can't lose another family member,' Mum had said, her eyes sparkling with tears.

No. They couldn't. He wouldn't let God take him from his family. He wouldn't give people the chance to speak empty platitudes at his funeral about how God needed him as an angel in heaven. But neither would he allow himself to be a burden on his family. He would not be weak and needy. He left the hospital and moved away from anyone who knew him. He cut off all contact with his family apart from allowing his LAC to assure them he was fine. They had their own lives to live while he found a way to live his. If there was a way.

He let his head fall into his hands. If only Dad were here now. To ruffle his hair. To draw him into a hug. To tell him it would all be okay. Bluey nudged him with his nose, but Tim couldn't make himself move. If he did, the tears would start. And if they started, he knew they'd never stop.

CHAPTER FOUR

Tanner Elliott followed the prison guard along the corridor. 'I'm here to see my brother, Joel Elliott,' he said.

The guard would know exactly why he was here, but it helped Tanner's confidence to say it. He didn't need to be ashamed of Joel. His brother didn't belong here. He was too intelligent. Too powerful.

The guard led Tanner to the visitor's room. Tanner lifted his shoulders, masking his expression. The prison walls threatened to close in on him. He kept his eyes ahead, took control of his mind and focused.

The supervised visiting room was set up with four tables, each with two chairs seated across from one another. Two prison wardens stood side by side, stance alert and watchful.

Tanner's eyes went straight to his brother. Joel was at one end of the tables, his hands resting calmly on the surface of the table. He contrasted with the other inmates who sat wringing their hands, on edge, either nervous or excited. Joel had never shown nerves or excitement in his life. He was always in control. His eyes glittered dangerously, the only hint of softening being the moment they connected with Tanner's.

'Hello little brother.'

Tanner reined in his smile. Joel wouldn't appreciate it. Instead, he gave a brief nod and pulled out the chair across from Joel. He needed to prove to Joel that he had this. He could do this and he would. The drone of voices began around them while the brothers sat in silence, just looking at one another, communicating through their eyes. Tanner was relieved to see the control still in place. Joel was not worried. As always, he had a plan.

'I'm missing home,' Joel said, his eyes darting a glance to the prison warden supervising the visits.

Tanner nodded. Joel wanted him to decode his words. They'd never had a home. Not really. Moving around as children, switching from their mother's house to their father's every month didn't equate to having a home. When their father became completely absorbed in his casino work, they relied on his money and each other. Then when he was convicted and jailed for fraud, they only had each other.

Joel twisted his lips into a wistful expression. 'Kamira Creek was beautiful. I wish I hadn't thrown away my chances there. Rod Green did so much to bring the program together and help the state wards.'

Again, Tanner nodded, while Joel rubbed the left side of his chest. The place he normally kept valuable items. So, there was something of value at Kamira Creek.

'I would send them a letter, but it's not the same as actually being there, seeing a place in person.'

'No,' Tanner agreed, picking up on the message. Joel wanted him to go there. He needed more information. 'Nothing like actually being in a place,' he said. 'But what do you miss the most? The place? The people?'

'The main house. It's a beautiful farmhouse. White trims, that feeling of age but value and character. And probably Rod Green, too. He didn't live there, but he might as well have. He kept all his things there.' Joel gave a low laugh. 'Even his mail ended up there a lot of the time.'

It clicked. Tanner gave a nod to show he had it. Joel wanted him to go to the Cairns' farm in Kamira Creek and find all the records he could. Find any useful information.

Joel sighed. 'Sometimes I wish I could change things, you know. I wish I could be someone else. But I don't know if I can ever change who I am, deep down inside.'

Tanner got it. Joel wanted to change his identity again. He wanted Tanner to prepare another alias for him. Clearly, he was planning an escape. Easy done. Tanner met Joel's eyes. 'I miss you, bro. Can't wait to have you around again.'

'Won't be for a while, but visit any time you can, hey?'

'I will.'

'Been working hard?'

Tanner smiled, then. 'Always. Doing an online computer course.' Code for researching more about hacking into computer systems. 'So much to learn.'

'I know you can do it.'

'Thanks bro. It helps that you believe in me.'

Joel's hard expression softened as he nodded, but Tanner knew there was no affection there. Just a knowing that he could count on Tanner, because if he couldn't, it would cost Tanner his life.

THE CAIRNS' farm was quiet on Sunday morning. Everyone went to church, which was an open invitation in Tanner's thinking. The cow in the front yard made him nervous before he realised it was more interested in the grass than in him. The back door was unlocked. Such trust. Misplaced trust. The house smelled much better than the yard, though he did catch a whiff of cut grass or something else unsavoury. He kicked a farm boot out of his way.

The office wasn't hard to find. Directly off the lounge room, easily the smallest room in the house. Tanner glanced around, taking in the desk top computer, the printer and an old laptop. These people obviously weren't very up with technology, country farmers that they were. A tall filing cabinet stood in the corner of the room and he made his way to it. He'd check out all the computers once he had everything he needed from the files.

It took less than half an hour to complete his job. Satisfied he had all the passwords and information he needed, he glanced once more around the room in case he'd missed something. There. A package sat on the shelf looking as though it was ready to be posted. He turned it over. It was addressed to someone by the name of Toby Cardelle but wasn't yet sealed. He'd seen plenty of packages like this in his lifetime and instinct led him to peek inside. A wad of fabric met his eye and he pulled it out. Just a sports jacket. A very nice one. He reached further in to pull out a note. He squinted, trying to make out the scrawled writing.

HEY TOBES MY MAN, I STILL HAVE YOUR JACKET FROM THAT DAY YOU LOANED IT TO ME AT THE FOOTY. FIGURED YOU SHOULD HAVE IT BACK, BUT I HAVEN'T BEEN ABLE TO CONTACT YOU. HAVE YOU CHANGED YOUR PHONE NUMBER AND EMAIL ADDRESS? I'VE ALSO INCLUDED THE RECEIPTS FROM YOUR LAST DONATIONS TO THE CAUSE. THANKS SO MUCH! ROD.

So, not likely to find any bags of tablets or white powder in here, but sometimes information was of greater worth. Tanner unfolded the receipt and whistled. This Toby Cardelle was quite the contributor. He was obviously well off. And generous, too. Worth looking into. In fact, Joel was sure to be interested in all this information. But not yet. First, he would prove to Joel that he could work some things out for himself. He didn't need to depend on his brother's brilliant mind. He had a sharp mind of his own and he didn't want to always be a pawn in someone else's game.

He slid his arms into the jacket and closed his eyes. Imagine what it would be like to be this Toby Cardelle. Well off. Generous. A good friend who would loan his valuable jacket to another. Obviously not powerful like Joel, and yet there was a kind of strength in being Toby Cardelle that warmed his veins.

He ran his hands down the front of the jacket, then stopped. Something hard was in the inside of the jacket. He reached his hand inside to find a hidden pocket. He pulled out a sports watch. Rod must have missed it there. Tanner fingered the watch and a plan began to form. He smiled. His next step would be to find Toby. He had his address and that's where he'd start. It should be easy.

Only it wasn't. Back in his apartment just blocks from the prison, Tanner traced every digital trail he found but all ended up dead. Until one.

Death Certificate. Toby John Cardelle. Cause of death, multiple injuries.

Tanner started at the wave of emotion that passed over him. What was wrong with him? He didn't even know this guy. And this was good news. Joel would say it was great news. Identity theft was so much easier once someone had died. No double ups in identification. And maybe he could convince Toby's family to make more donations to Rod Green's program ... only the new bank account details he would provide would send them straight to Toby Cardelle, AKA Joel Elliot.

The plan was brilliant. Even Joel would be impressed. If it were possible to impress Joel.

Tanner read back over the certificate. The date clicked. The train accident. Toby must have been in that train accident. He just needed to find the right records, hack into the right systems and he'd have all the information he needed.

Then he would make sure the Cardelle family received this letter from Rod Green. But attached to it would be new receipts, a new bank account number, a new email address. All indirectly coming to him with a trail that would be impossible to chase. Too easy. He wasn't born smart and trained up under the best manipulator and con artist in the world for nothing.

CHAPTER FIVE

Jessica's feet beat a steady rhythm in time with the swing of her arms. She forged her way up the hill, processing the day. She thought of Tim Bateman and shook her head.

'God, please soften his heart.' She frowned. 'And please help me be a good Christian witness to him.'

Why was it so hard to pray for him? Maybe she should get others in the church praying for him. Her heart lightened at the thought. She couldn't give them his name or specific details, but God knew.

Her mind went to Milla. Something must have happened at cadets. Milla hadn't said anything – and that was what had her worried. Once Milla would have talked the whole way home. She didn't talk as much anymore. Everything had changed since Toby died.

She rounded the corner to the house and smiled. Maybe not everything. A farm truck with a huge bull in the back was parked out the front of the house. It didn't look like it belonged to the neighbours. Who had Dad invited home for dinner this time?

The bull snorted as she strode past and she eyed it warily. She didn't trust the creatures. This one looked very much like the one-ton bull that had knocked Dad down and damaged his back ten years ago. That bull was the reason she'd given up her dream of being a farmer. The physio Dad saw had encouraged him to get back on his feet and helped him regain his strength. But he'd had to travel over an hour for his appointments. The noble thing for Jess at the time had been to promise she would become a physiotherapist and give back to the town she'd grown up in. After all, God had given her good brains and good health. She needed to use them for God and others.

But she hadn't been able to help her own brother. Physios couldn't help someone who was dead, could they? Neither could an O.T. and when it came down to it, helping people rebuild their muscles and manage their day to day lives wasn't enough. She sighed, slowing her pace as she came around the side of the house to the back door. Whoever was here, she didn't want them seeing her hot and sweaty and out of sorts.

She slipped out of her shoes and quickly changed, smiling at the sound of Milla's lively voice in the lounge room. Milla must be okay after all. Milla could brighten the darkest day.

'I can be a truck driver if that's what I want,' Milla was saying to her audience. 'I can be whatever I want to be!'

'What about a fairy?' That was Zac's voice, and everyone laughed.

Jess entered the loungeroom to add to the conversation. 'Or a donut,' she said, giving Milla a sideways glance. She nodded at the visitor in greeting. Ed Callum. The farmer she'd worked with when he'd lost his leg below the knee in a farming accident. It could have been saved if he'd gone to hospital straight away. But Ed was one of those farmers who had to be dying before he sought medical help. Too self-sufficient by far.

Milla screwed her nose up at Jess. 'Why do you always have to bring that up?'

Jess grinned unrepentantly and explained to Ed. 'When Milla

was two, she was watching Wiggles on TV and she told us, "I be big red car when I donut." We finally worked out she meant "grown up", not "donut". And she wouldn't believe us when we told her she couldn't actually become a car.'

Ed chuckled. 'Ah, a bit of a dreamer, I see.'

'You'd better believe it,' Dad called from where he sat at the dining table, part of the open plan living room. 'Next, she planned to be a brumby, and if she couldn't be a brumby, she decided she'd be a stockman like our indigenous friend, Alan.'

Ed smiled affectionately at Milla the way everyone did. Milla had been a charmer from the moment she was born. She wasn't aware of it, but that was part of her appeal.

'And now a truck driver, hey?' Ed asked.

Milla nodded, hands going to her hips. 'I'd like to see someone stop me!'

'Careful,' Dad warned. 'That sounds like a challenge. Don't forget to keep God at the centre of your plans.'

Jess's heart sank. She loved Milla's enthusiasm for life; her dreaming, the way she saw the world as something to conquer, not something that would drag her down. Would God really step in and take that away?

And yet he had when he took Toby. And he'd taken Tim Bateman's dreams, too. She didn't believe he would ever be able to work with large animals. Certainly not like the bull she saw out the front.

'Would you like to have dinner with us?' Mum asked Ed from where she stood at the stove.

'No thanks, Lydia.' He twisted the Akubra hat in his hands. 'I just dropped by to see if Charlie can help me unload this bull I've got on my truck. I need to get him into the holding yard to give him a shot before I put him in with the cows.'

All eyes shot to Ed. Jess bit her lip. Of course Ed couldn't manage that bull on his own, but Dad … he'd almost lost his life at the mercy of a bull just like that one. And yet God had spared him. That time.

'I'll help,' she said.

Zac jumped up. 'Me too.'

'And me.' Milla grinned around at them, then looked at Dad. 'You can come to give directions.'

Ed chuckled. 'Teamwork. I like it. It shouldn't take long.'

Mum took the saucepan off the stove and turned off the gas. Jess grinned. Mum was used to working with interruptions. Mum caught her look and smiled, then winked. She'd told Jess only yesterday that she'd prefer to have to work around interruptions from a husband and children than to not have them at all. She was the most flexible, skilled hostess and cook Jess had ever known.

Milla raced to Ed's truck. 'Can I do the reversing when we get to the holding yard? I know I can do it.'

'No, Milla,' Dad called out from behind.

Ed chuckled. 'Sorry Milla, but we gotta listen to your dad. Get in.'

Zac and Milla piled into Ed's truck while Dad and Jess took the family car.

'I don't like the look of that bull,' Jess admitted to Dad as they followed behind Ed's truck. It was stomping and swaying, looking very unsettled.

Dad took one hand off the steering wheel to pat Jess's arm. 'It'll be right. We're experienced now.'

It was true. Still, her heart rate insisted on its unruly speed as they pulled into the Callum's farm gate ten minutes later and headed to the holding yard. If only they had another vet in town. One who could manage the livestock and not have all their time taken up with the domestic animals.

Her mind flew to Tim Bateman. No, he wouldn't be able to manage. Not the way he was now. Would he ever allow her to help him become independent again, or would he continue to be stubborn and difficult?

Zac was already working with Ed to direct the bull into the holding yard. Milla held the gate open, clearly enjoying the thrill of handling the huge creature. To Jess's relief, Ed kept a safe distance as the bull stomped down the ramp, its hoofs pounding against the metal and striking the gate on its way out.

It tried to back out of the holding yard. 'Milla, shut the gate,' Dad called.

'I'm trying!' Milla huffed, her face red. Jess went to help, shoving the gate against the bull's behind and moving him in.

'Thanks.' Milla's voice was quiet and held a slight tremor.

Jess studied her. 'You okay?'

Milla nodded, but she looked pale and a sheen of sweat glistened over her upper lip. And Jess watched as she bent down to rub at her leg as though she had a cramp. Fear coursed through her. She reached a hand to touch Milla's arm. Clammy. What was wrong with Milla? Most days she was her normal fifteen-year-old extroverted self, full of life and energy. But Milla had definitely lost some of her bounce these past few months. What if her only remaining sibling was sick? Seriously sick? No, she had to be imagining it. Could grief be having an effect on her? She knew from experience that grief could have strong, lasting effects on a body and Toby's death had hit them all hard.

IT TOOK Jess a long time to get to sleep that night. The day the bull knocked Dad down had been traumatic. They hadn't known if his back was broken; whether he'd ever walk again. Her job now was to make people walk again. To restore them, or to at least help them reach their potential. She would do it with everything she had. She couldn't do it for Toby, but she'd do it for Tim Bateman. With renewed determination, she drifted off to sleep.

And dreamed.

Toby smiled at her, that familiar, cheerful, care-free smile.

'Smile,' he said and reached his hand out to her.

And she beamed. Because her big brother was there. Just like he had been from the moment she was born. Her protective, fun-loving brother who was proud of her every achievement. Who understood her. Loved her.

He wrapped his arms around her in a brotherly hug and she leaned her ear against his chest. His heart beat strong and sure in her ear.

'Toby', she whispered. 'You're alive.'

'Always,' he said. Warmth and security filled her. To know and be known was a gift she had taken for granted.

She looked up at him, then pulled back. It wasn't Toby. She was looking into someone else's eyes. Brown, not blue like Toby's. But they were full of love and life and hope. And they knew her.

With a sigh of contentment, she leaned back in and heard that strong, solid heartbeat again. Toby's heartbeat. But in someone else.

Jess woke and blinked. The dream had felt so real. She still felt loved and at peace. Even though Toby wasn't here. Warmth surrounded her as she dressed for work. She was loved. So completely loved.

And then she glanced at herself in the mirror and reality hit. Toby wasn't here. Nor the other man in her dream – the one with the caring brown eyes, who loved her the way she longed to be loved.

But the mirror shouted out the truth. She wasn't pretty or physically desirable. She was the only one in her class and Uni group who had never had a boyfriend. No one had ever shown real interest in her. They respected her and liked her, but she wasn't the type anyone could fall in love with.

She remembered her friends in kindergarten. They were playing weddings. Each one had a turn at being the bride. But when it came time for Jess's turn, Naomi shook her head.

'No Jess, you can't be the bride.'

'Why not?'

'You have to be pretty.' She shook out her long, blonde hair. 'See, like this.'

All her friends had nodded in agreement.

'You can be the minister,' Naomi had said to placate her. And so Jess took her place in front of the miniature bride and groom and talked about love and Jesus and told them they were now married, just the way she'd seen it happen at Aunty Lil's wedding.

Jess's eyes slid shut as she now tried to block out the image in the mirror and return to the feeling she'd had in her dream last night. It had felt so real. The person had looked at her with a depth and compassion she had never imagined possible. She had known that he understood her intimately, loved her, would help her be the best person she could possibly be.

Who was it? Jesus? Or someone else? Maybe God was trying to tell her Toby's heart really did beat in someone else's chest. He'd been an organ donor but Jess had tried not to think about it. She didn't know how she felt about someone else having Toby's heart. In fact, she didn't know how she felt about anything anymore.

When Toby was alive, all had been right with the world. Now everything was confusing and she couldn't make sense of it no matter how hard she tried.

CHAPTER SIX

Jess knew everyone expected her to go to the church prayer meeting tonight. Maybe it was a good thing. God knew she needed to make sense of everything going on in her heart and mind. Maybe praying it out would help. She'd tried telling Tim Bateman about the way Ed Callum managed well with just one leg and a bit of help, but Tim wasn't interested. It seemed that teamwork wasn't his thing. Surprise, surprise.

She sighed, slipped on her walking shoes and picked up the hand weights she'd added to her routine. She wasn't keen to go to the prayer meeting if she was honest. Public prayers irked her. The drone of voices, people praying for great Aunty Mary's hip or asking God to be with Graham Jones … There was nothing more irritating than hearing people ask God to 'be with them' when God was the one who said he was there in the first place. She had better things to do with her time. And when they 'claimed promises from the Word' that no harm would befall them, well, harm had befallen her brother, hadn't it? He had believed in God and lived for him. So why had the 'promises' not worked for him? So many questions. God was not the god of happy endings she'd once convinced herself he was. She still hadn't quite worked out exactly who he was, but she knew she had to believe and trust. That was what was expected of her. Her past faith was all she had left to cling to. She couldn't let doubts creep in. What would people think? If she, the town's upstanding Christian girl, were to turn away from God it would have a devastating impact. She needed to cling to her faith, no matter how shaky it was right now.

She looked up at the sky. 'Where else would I go if I didn't have you?' she asked God aloud. She thought of the disciples of Jesus. Life had become hard and Jesus asked them if they wanted to leave. 'Where else would we go?' Peter had asked. 'You have the words of eternal life.'

Jess drew in a deep breath, pushing her body forward. 'Lord, you are all I have. There is nothing else worth holding onto. Help me hold on!'

She continued up the farm's main hill, watching kangaroos spread across the grass like locusts, hopping just far enough away to clear her path and stare steadily back at her, noses twitching. They were destroying the crops and eating all the grass for the cattle, but as Dad said, they were here first. He would just work with them as best he could. At least the drought had broken and the winter rain had brought a fresh spread of green across the paddocks.

Maybe a good dose of rain was what her heart needed. It felt dry. Empty. Perhaps she needed the prayer meeting more than she'd thought.

JESS WAS PREPARED to be met by little old ladies as she entered the church hall for the prayer meeting, but instead she was met by one person. Pierce Buckley. Zac's older brother and Toby's best mate. Pierce was dressed in his work suit, looking every bit the professional he was. Jess had prayed he would get the tech support job with the local council but hadn't counted on how much he'd look the part once he did. No more farm clothes and jeans. He was now all professional suits.

He gave Jess a quick salute. 'Looks like it's just me and you,' he said.

Jess smiled but she hoped not. 'Where is everybody?'

Pierce sat down carefully, pulling at his suit pants. 'Pastor Hanbrook's away. He gave me the keys to open up. Maybe everyone thought it wasn't on because he's away.'

Pierce picked up a stray bulletin left over from Sunday's service and opened it. Jess studied him. He was nice looking. Neat and carefully groomed. He smelled of whatever classy deodorant he used, making her suspect he had doused himself only minutes before. He was the complete opposite to his father and brother, almost as if he deliberately worked to be that way.

'Your dad's not coming?'

Pierce looked up from the bulletin. 'Nah. He's fishing.'

Jess smiled. That man spent almost every spare moment fishing. Or volunteering for the SES. It was no wonder he had trouble keeping the farm afloat.

'Good day at work?' she asked next, to fill the silence.

Pierce nodded. 'Busy but good.'

She waited, but he didn't say anything else; didn't even ask her the same question in return. But she'd brought that on herself. A person who came across as all together, didn't need anyone to check up on them, right?

She pushed the thought aside. It wasn't Pierce's fault she had set the precedent. Everyone expected Jess, the nice girl, the friendly, smart, intelligent girl to lead the conversation. They couldn't know that sometimes it felt too hard. *Come on, Pierce. Your turn.*

He looked up, probably surprised by her silence. He swallowed and she knew he was trying. She'd give him that. Finally he spoke. 'You going to be a leader for the youth camp this year?' He sat back, looking triumphant that he'd thought of something else to say.

'No.' There was no way she could handle sitting around a campfire without Toby. No way she could hold her emotions in check as some other youth leader took out a guitar and replaced him. She looked at Pierce. 'You?'

He jiggled his leg, avoiding her eyes. 'Maybe. I've been asked to.'

Of course he had. Some of the teenage girls in the church were infatuated with Pierce Buckley.

'Not keen on the idea of sleeping rough?' Jess asked with a smile. She recalled the last camping trip the Buckley's and Cardelles had shared. Pierce hadn't wanted to go. Felt he was beyond camping. But Toby had convinced him to come along.

'We need you, mate. You know how rowdy and out of control they get without you.'

Pierce had grunted, unimpressed. 'I'm not the adult. Let the parents sort them out.'

Toby had thrown his head back and laughed. 'You know it's Dad and Buck who need sorting, not the kids.'

He was right. Dad and Mr. Buckley were crazy when they got together. It was as though their childhood returned in full force and they belly-laughed late into the night, pulled pranks, told stories and let go of all responsibility for a few days. Jess didn't blame them. Zac was only two years old and Pierce eight when Mrs. Buckley left. Buck blamed it on mental illness but Mum and Dad said she was just plain selfish. They were the ones who stepped in, helped Buck care for the house, the farm and the children. Pierce and Zac began calling Jess's parents Mum and Dad and their father was just 'Buck'.

The sound of feet crunched on the gravel outside. Jess looked up. Pierce raised his eyes questioningly and Jess shrugged. The door opened and closed and footsteps sounded in the foyer. Not the steps of an old lady, or the pastor, but light, energetic steps. Those steps slowed as soon as the newcomer stepped into the room. Sasha Leroy. Her beautiful face fell before it forcibly brightened.

'Pierce, Jess ... how are you?' She glanced around. 'I thought there was a prayer meeting?'

'Yes. This is it.'

Sasha's eyes darted back to the door as though she wanted to escape. 'Where's Pastor Hanbrook?'

Pierce pulled a chair out for Sasha. 'He's away. We'll wait a few more minutes in case anyone else turns up and then start.'

Sasha bit her lip but sat down.

Pierce cleared his throat, then gave Sasha his steady look. 'How's your day been?'

She cast him a grateful look and her shoulders relaxed. 'Busy today. A man from out of town needed all his business suits dry cleaned. He must have had about twenty of them.'

Jess studied Sasha. This was the woman who would have been her sister-in-law had Toby not been killed. Sasha was attractive. Her shiny blonde hair and shapely figure left Jess feeling plain. And to top it off, Sasha Leroy's skin was perfect. It was a creamy peach colour with rosy, healthy cheeks. Not once had Jess seen a pimple or freckle blemish that skin.

'I never thought you'd go for her type,' she'd teased Toby one day. 'I thought you'd look for more than a pretty face.'

To her surprise, Toby had glared at her. 'Take a second look,' he'd snapped. 'You should be smart enough to know that just because someone is beautiful on the outside, doesn't mean they can't be the same on the inside.'

And for the first time in her life, Jess had known what jealousy felt like. Sasha now came first in Toby's life. Before his family, before her. He'd been so protective or her and Milla in the past. Now it seemed he felt he needed to protect Sasha from *her*.

It was her own fault. She shouldn't have spoken about Sasha

that way. But when Jess had befriended the new girl working at the dry cleaners in town and invited her home for dinner, she'd never dreamed Toby would fall in love with her. She'd expected him to want someone with greater career prospects. She'd thought he'd be smart enough to see beyond a sweet, pretty face and look for someone who challenged him, who kept him thinking, kept him on his toes. She's doubted Sasha had an IQ high enough to do that.

'Well, I think we might be it,' Pierce said after a few moments of uncomfortable silence. 'Shall we pray?'

Jess nodded and Sasha folded her hands together. The diamond shining from her ring finger pierced Jess's heart. Sasha Leroy was the reason there were issues with Toby's estate. If she hadn't lured Toby into pooling their assets into one account before they were married, it would have been clear cut.

That wasn't fair and Jess knew it. She sighed. *God, why can't I be nice? Help me be nice to Sasha.* She was tired of this pain. Tired of the reminders, the empty, aching hollow deep inside.

She tried to focus on Pierce's prayer. Why did she feel distant from the God who was supposed to be her refuge? She couldn't feel him; couldn't see him. There was too much pain and turmoil in the way. She'd come here planning to ask for prayer for Tim Bateman. To pray that God would use her to help him. But how could she help him when she couldn't help herself?

Tyres crunched in the gravel and Jess held her breath. Please God, could more people be arriving? She felt exposed in this near empty room with Sasha's poise and grace screaming across the space between them.

She peeked up to see Mr. and Mrs. Tammerin walk in. She breathed a sigh of relief as the couple quietly took seats to form a circle. Mr. Tammerin began to pray as though he had been in the middle of a conversation with God and was taking it up with him again. He probably had been.

'Lord Jesus, please wrap your arms around those who are

grieving. May they feel your presence, Lord Jesus, may they see your face, your love, your plan, Lord Jesus. Hold them up, Lord Jesus.'

Jess frowned. He used the name of Jesus like a comma. He always had, so why did it bother her tonight?

'Lord Jesus, we pray for those here tonight. We pray for dear Sasha as she walks this journey of grief. And we pray for Jessica. We pray for strength in her weakness, for calm in her fear.'

The words jarred Jess like a physical blow. What weakness did Mr. Tammerin mean? What fear? What made him think she was no longer the calm, in control, Christian girl she'd always been in the eyes of the church people? She bit her lip, indignation forcing her to plan a prayer that proved she was okay. It needed to be well-presented and theologically correct. She needed to reassure them she was still the intelligent, capable Jess Cardelle.

She managed the prayer. It was perfect even to her own ears. Just the right amount of passion and compassion. The correct words, not overly academic, but well spoken. Trusting. Spiritual. Insightful.

But then Sasha cleared her throat and it threw Jess. She went blank, desperately searched for words to fill the silence. Any words would do.

'Lord,' Jess prayed, hoping she didn't sound as lost as she felt, 'we ask that you will open the eyes of the people in this town to your love. Open their eyes to see you.'

See God? She winced. That was too abstract. If she'd been praying from her heart she'd be begging God to see her; to see Jess Cardelle and love her even though she'd become invisible to Toby once Sasha came on the scene. To care about what she was going through.

Where had that thought come from? Of course God loved her. She'd known and believed that all her life. She scrambled for more words to finish her prayer. She needed it to end smoothly.

'And Lord, we thank you for the rain. Please be with the

farmers as they battle the effects of the drought we've had for so many years.' Argh! What a hypocrite she was. God said he was with people. And God knew the drought had gone on for years. She didn't need to tell him. Why did the words she judged other people for, roll so easily off her own tongue? She should have kept quiet rather than bring her own judgements down on herself.

'Thank you for your goodness, in Jesus name Amen.'

It was an abrupt finish, but surely she'd satisfied them?

Sasha prayed next. It was a simple, stilted prayer. Poor Sasha. Speaking in public was not one of her strong points. You could be forgiven for thinking she was nervous, but some people just weren't good at putting words together.

Jess peeked through her fingers. Sasha twisted the engagement ring on her finger as she fought for words. The engagement ring Toby had spent thousands on for a girl who stopped visiting his family once he died. Proof that Sasha was shallow. She had been infatuated with Toby but she clearly hadn't loved those Toby loved. She accepted all the love and sympathy offered her at the funeral and then she turned her back on Toby's family. It devastated Mum and that on its own was enough to anger Jess. Her family had been through enough without the pain of Sasha's rejection.

Sasha's deceptively sweet tone was hesitant as she searched for words. 'Lord, we lift up to you all those who are hurting.'

Jess bit the inside of her lip. Lift up? Sasha was petite. There was no way those arms could lift up the number of heavy hearted in this church. She pictured her trying and a smile peeked through. She glanced over at Pierce beside her. Pierce might manage. He had strong, muscular arms. Not quite as strong as Tim Bateman's – she cut off the errant thought. Why couldn't she focus the way she used to? Losing brain cells was her greatest fear. If she didn't have her intelligence, what did she have?

Mr. Tammerin finally brought the meeting to a close and Jess opened her eyes, blinking in the light. She glanced across at Pierce who stretched, raising his arms up above his head. He caught her looking and smiled in that serious way of his.

'You okay?' he asked.

She nodded, picking up her phone and car keys. 'Yeah, just had a big day at work. I'll head home now.'

Sasha stood. 'Me too.'

Pierce glanced between them. Was that disappointment she saw in his eyes? Surely Pierce hadn't developed feelings for Sasha? Did it go both ways? She needed to know.

'Sasha, did you walk? Maybe Pierce could drop you home.'

Sasha spun to face her, pretty blue eyes wide with shock. Then her mouth hardened into a tight line. 'No, thank you. I'm fine.'

'I can do it,' Pierce said, glancing at Jess, then back to Sasha. 'Your place is on my way.'

'I said, I'm fine.' Sasha turned and barrelled out the door, but not before Jess caught a glimpse of her quivering lip and the sheen of tears.

Mr. Tammerin frowned in concern. 'What was that about?'

Pierce shrugged. 'I have no idea.'

'I'll go after her.' Mrs. Tammerin disappeared out the door, followed by her husband.

Jess drew in a deep breath, then let it out slowly. Sasha clearly wanted attention and now she had it. Good on the Tammerins.

Pierce stepped closer. 'You sure you're okay?'

She painted on a smile. 'Yeah. Just tired.'

'I'll walk you out.' He picked up his notebook and pen, collected his suit jacket from the back of the chair and walked by her side. She waited while he locked the hall door. She was about to walk down the steps when he stayed her with a hand on her arm.

'Do you remember the day I gave my life to God? Here.'

'Yes.' How could she forget? It was not long after his mother left. Dad had brought them all to Kid's Club together and she and Toby had sat Pierce between them, trying to make the shy boy feel comfortable. And then, when the leader invited children to come out the front if they wanted to give their heart to Jesus, Toby had jumped up and almost dragged Pierce down the front. Jess had worried Toby pressured Pierce into it, but the more the years passed, the more it was clear that Pierce's faith was genuine. Steady and strong like he was.

'I'm glad you were there that day,' Pierce said and there was a nostalgic tone to his voice she'd never heard before.

She smiled. 'Me too.'

'I'd lost my mum but God gave me a new family.'

'I know. And there's nothing better than being God's child – you've got a new family now.'

A look of surprise passed over his face before he nodded. 'Oh. Yeah.'

Clearly that wasn't what he had meant. Maybe he'd meant that her own family had taken him in. It was true. Pierce and Zac practically lived at the Cardelle's house.

Pierce cleared his throat. She waited. He had never been good with words like Toby, but she'd learned that if she waited he would make the effort to communicate.

He swallowed hard, then fiddled with his tie. 'From when I was really little, all I wanted was to be a *real* member of your family.'

A threatening lump came to her throat. 'I know,' she said softly. 'And we love having you as part of our family. At first I thought you needed us, but we needed you, too. Especially now that Toby's gone. I need a brother more than ever.'

Pierce's shoulders slumped and he looked away. What had she said?

'I'll see you Sunday.' He didn't meet her eyes as he turned and strode toward his car.

She hated that she'd hurt him somehow. There was enough hurt in this world without her adding to it.

'Pierce!'

He turned back. She raced to catch up with him.

'I'm sorry.'

He glanced away, his eyes settling on the hall where he had made his commitment. 'For what?'

Good question. She wasn't sure.

'You mean the world to me, Pierce. I don't want to hurt you.'

His serious gaze intensified. 'Really? Do you mean that?'

'Of course. We grew up together. You know me better than any other living person. We were here for each other when I lost my brother and you lost your best mate. At Toby's funeral, well, having you there helped me through. I know just about everything about you. That you're sometimes a bit too serious, that you were deaf until you were five years old and had grommets put in your ears so you were slow learning to speak, that you are now sparing with your words and careful where you tread. That you refuse to make the same mistakes your father made, that you prefer barbeque sauce to tomato sauce ...' She smiled. 'Just about everything, see?'

He tilted his head, a soft look coming to his eyes. 'And I know that you speak twenty thousand more words than I do in a day – that it's your way of dealing with things.'

She slapped playfully at his suited chest. 'Twenty thousand you reckon?'

He caught her hand and held it to his chest. 'Yes. And that is why we belong together.'

Her heart missed a beat. What was he saying? She tried to step back, but his long fingers held hers in place.

'Because ... because I speak twenty thousand words a day?'

He smiled. 'No. Because we know each other so well. It makes sense. Everyone knows it.'

What made sense? What was he saying? 'Everyone?' She was stalling, trying to get her thoughts together. Oh no, oh no, oh no. *God, no.*

His hand tightened on hers. 'If I married you, I could really be a part of your family.'

She wanted to pull back from him, but she didn't want to hurt him. And yet she knew she was about to hurt him more than she ever had before. If Pierce knew her so well he'd know she wasn't the marrying type. Yes, she was practical, but she didn't want to marry because it was practical. Pierce was a good man, but that wasn't enough. If she ever married, it would have to be for love and the truth was, she didn't love Pierce. Not that way.

She cleared her throat. 'Pierce, I'm not really the marrying type.'

A shuttered expression came over his face. 'What makes you say that?'

As she tried to piece together words to make him understand, he stepped toward her. 'You are my type, Jess. I know you.'

Not enough to understand what was going on deep down in her heart. She looked up into his dear, concerned, serious face. How she wanted to want to marry him. But she couldn't give up every moment of every day for this man, seeking to please him, to be the woman he thought she was, the woman he wanted her to be. She had changed since Toby died. She was no longer the non-confrontational, pleasant, people-pleasing Jess she used to be. She tried, oh how she tried, but it was too hard. Making people happy was too hard. Impossible, in fact. And she couldn't marry Pierce just to make him happy.

'Think about it and pray about it?' Pierce asked.

She nodded, wishing she could bring herself to tell him what she already knew.

He turned and walked to his car, shoulders slumped. And she almost changed her mind. Guilt crashed through her heart. What was she doing?

God? What should I do?

No answer came.

CHAPTER SEVEN

Jess was tired of feeling troubled. She was just tired, full stop. It was hard to sleep when her mind tumbled over what she should say to Pierce. She couldn't talk to her parents about it because they would be so excited and presume marrying Pierce would be her dream come true. But nobody ever asked her these things. They presumed.

She shuffled through the clothes filed in her wardrobe. So much of the same. Smart work shirts and skirts all in winter colours. Today called for something different. Casual farm clothes weren't appropriate for work but surely she had a decent pair of jeans here somewhere?

Yes, there they were. She lifted them from the wardrobe shelf and something caught her eye. The shirt Toby had bought her as a joke. *Little Miss Bossy* it read, with the round, blue figure of Little Miss Bossy imprinted, her mouth wide open and a cheerful hat with a flower on her head.

She forced a bounce into her step as she walked into the office. She needed to add life to the place; needed to do something unpredictable. Lauren's early patient was already in the waiting room.

'Good morning Mr. Carey.'

He looked up with a smile, then chuckled as he read her shirt.

'Miss Bossy? You? No! You're the nicest person in town. Everybody knows it.'

What should she say to that? Thank you? No, it wasn't a compliment. Nice was so … bland. She was called to be a light. She wanted to love with such power it made a difference. Nice didn't cut it.

Lauren turned and saw her shirt. 'Are we safe here today, or should I go home while I can?'

Jess grinned. 'Only if you're scared.'

Mr. Carey stood, balancing on his walker. 'It's not you I'm scared of, Jess. It's Lauren. She makes me do exercises till I ache all over.'

Lauren chuckled. 'Sure do. Come on in, Mr. Carey, let's begin this torture.'

Jess smiled as the two made their way into the exercise room, Mr. Carey shuffling along and Lauren supporting him.

The smile was wiped from Jess's face as she glanced down her list of patients for the day. Tim Bateman was first. Was she ready to face him every day? She would do her best. After all, the more she saw him, the more she'd become de-sensitised to the memory of the train disaster.

He arrived looking as grumpy as ever, barked his name at Kelly who had only just arrived, then stared at Jess's shirt.

'What's this?' He waved his hand in the general direction of her clothing as though it were offensive.

'My uniform,' she told him with a cheerful smile.

He frowned, obviously not amused. 'Don't you know how to be a professional?' He wheeled himself into the consult room ahead of her. He still refused to let her push his chair.

She smiled wider. She would not be drawn into his dark mood.

'Being a professional is about training, skill, experience and character, not clothing. No one in Barrawi deems a certain standard of clothing appropriate for an occupational therapist. Especially when they've known the O.T. since the day she was born and know that she's a farmer's daughter through and through.'

Had she seen a spark of interest when she mentioned being a farmer's daughter? Just as quickly it was gone and he muttered into his lap.

'Speaking of yourself in third person? Sounds like you think of yourself as royalty even though you can't even dress properly.'

Jess bit her lip, refusing to be baited. Maybe she had been trying too hard to prove her academic prowess to Tim, but she needed him to respect and trust her if she was to help him. She sighed.

'I don't see some people as more professional than others. We all have different gifts to offer the world. None are better or of higher value than others.'

He grunted so she let it go and focused instead on his exercises.

'How have you been going with the exercises at home?'

He gave her a cold stare and she knew he hadn't been doing them.

'Have you found a support worker to help you with them?'

'I don't need help.'

She let that one go, handing him a sheet of paper. 'I printed this one out for you. It might be easier to do on your own if you prefer not to have a support worker.'

He studied it, then looked at her. 'Well? Are you going to demonstrate it for me first, Miss Professional Jessica?'

'Jess,' she corrected. 'Hardly anyone calls me Jessica.'

'Why not? Too professional?'

'No, it's just not me.'

Tim shook his head. 'That's ridiculous. People make a name. Names don't make people.'

'If that's true, then you'd be wrong suggesting Jessica is a professional name and Jess isn't.'

He glared at her, obviously put out because she had pointed out the flaw in his argument. She held out a stretch band.

He snatched it from her hand. 'What am I supposed to do with this, *Jessica*?'

He was being deliberately difficult. She lifted a brow. 'I don't know, *Timothy*. Maybe tie it around your mouth so you can stop snarling at me and focus on exercises.' She grinned, imagining herself grabbing it from his hands and forcing it around his mouth. It was a satisfying picture.

His mouth lifted in a sneer. 'You're not funny.'

She shrugged. 'Maybe you just don't have a sense of humour.'

'I do. I'm amused by people being clever or funny, not people trying to be.'

He really was a tough nut to crack. He watched as she demonstrated the exercises, then begrudgingly had a go himself.

She gave an approving nod. 'I think you're just about ready to move to the next stage.'

He fiddled with the edge of his chair and she saw the way the vinyl was coming off. His frustration was obvious but she couldn't blame him.

'So when can I go back to vet work?' he demanded. She opened her mouth to tell him it all depended on him, but he cut her off. 'And don't tell me you can't say. Just give me a bit of an idea. I promise I won't hold you to the date, hour and second.'

She studied him and for the first time saw hope in his eyes. Or was it desperation? 'I'll look into it and let you know tomorrow.' He narrowed his eyes and she narrowed hers back at him. 'I promise.'

He seemed satisfied with that, but she couldn't let it go. 'It all depends on you, though. You have to do the exercises I give you. I need you to be compliant if my estimation is going to be anywhere near accurate.'

'What? You're not a miracle worker? Why doesn't that surprise me?'

He was so good at that sarcastic voice. It bit down on her heart every time, no matter how hard she tried to put up walls.

He laughed again, a scornful, mocking sound as he wheeled himself out the door.

No, she wasn't a miracle worker. But she believed in the God who was.

MILLA GLANCED down the line of students beside her. She was the only girl in her age group who took the school cross country seriously. The whistle blew and the boys raced away. Under sixteen girls were called up. Milla moved into place. She stood poised at the starting line, tension gnawing at her stomach, heart pounding. She used to love this feeling but today it brought a sense of dread. What was wrong with her? Bodies tussled around her as classmates laughed and teased. She heard girls from her year group talking about their plan to walk the course and chat along the way. Not her. She would be right up there with Riley, making sure he didn't cross the line first. She loved that she could beat him even when his age group started five minutes before hers. Who cared if Jess said running was no good for the joints? It got you where you wanted to go fast and that's what mattered.

She looked across to see Kirra beside her. She stood quietly, relaxed, probably going to take it easy like the rest of the girls.

Mrs. Drewson called for their attention then blew the whistle. Milla charged forward. She couldn't wait to see the disgusted expression on Riley's face when she overtook him. Last year he'd put in an extra spurt of energy to get ahead but it hadn't lasted long.

She surged forward, wanting to round the first corner so she could at least see the runners in front. At the sound of footfalls behind, closing in she turned in surprise. Long, bare legs came into view. Kirra. Kirra passed with ease, picking up her pace and rounding the corner ahead of her. Dismay overwhelmed Milla. The rhythm of Kirra's legs was sure and steady. And in that moment she knew Kirra was unbeatable. She would have to be content with second in the cross country this year. She'd do anything to avoid coming third. Third didn't count.

But another girl passed her. And then came the biggest blow of all. As Kirra passed Riley he turned and ran backwards for a few steps, searching. When he spotted her, he gave her a triumphant wave. Humiliation made her chest tight but her legs refused to go any faster. Better to pretend not to be trying. She allowed herself to ease back, watching as runner after runner passed. The girls were walking. She couldn't quite bring herself to walk, so she kept jogging, slightly ahead of them.

By the time she crossed the finish line, no one was keeping track of places anymore. She drew in deep breaths, her heart as heavy as her legs. It had been like those nightmares where she wanted to run but couldn't make her legs move.

She refused to feel jealous as Kirra went up to receive her first place medal. It was a good thing to have another girl who shared her love of sport, wasn't it? Kirra could be a good ally. Once she caught her breath, she approached her.

'Congratulations.'

Kirra looked pleased. 'Thanks.'

'And I'm sorry if I embarrassed you at cadets the other day. I just hated the way those guys were carrying on.'

Kirra shrugged. 'It's fine. I'm used to it.'

'Maybe, but you shouldn't have to be.'

Kirra gave a shy smile. 'Well, thanks for standing up for me.'

Milla smiled and bit her lip. 'Actually, I wondered if you'd be interested in joining our soccer team? We have training straight after school today. There's only two girls so it'd be great to have another one. I wouldn't mind some support.'

Kirra smiled, her wide, perfect smile reminding Milla of Alan. Something tugged at her heart. She had a feeling Kirra might end up being a good friend. Most of the girls were more academic than sporty and she often felt like a misfit. It seemed that Kirra might be both.

'Thanks. I'd love to.'

THE COACH WAS DELIGHTED to have Kirra join the soccer team. Riley muttered under his breath that Milla needed Kirra, something about how slow Milla had been in the cross country. Milla tried to ignore him. He wasn't worth the effort and she was too tired. In fact, it took effort to focus. She caught a shimmer out the corner of her eyes and blinked, hoping she wasn't getting a migraine. If she could just get through training she'd head home and rest. She forced her legs to move.

'Pass, Milla,' the coach called. Milla waved to show she'd heard, but she didn't pass. She refocused on the goal.

'Mill!' She heard Zac calling, but she couldn't give up this opportunity to prove herself. To Riley. To herself.

Riley stood in front of the goal, moving back and forward, mimicking an ape and goading her. She blocked out the cheers and yells insisting she pass the ball. She couldn't. Not when Riley stood there, needing to be put in his place.

She turned her head to see who might be coming at her from the side. And saw double. What was that? The moment she hesitated, another player slid in from the side and stole the ball. Milla looked around, trying to get her bearings. Everything seemed to be moving. Or out of place. Dizziness overwhelmed her. She stumbled toward the sideline, her hand in her hands.

'Milla?' It was Zac's voice at her side.

'I can't see properly.'

'You can't see?' His face was a blur in front of her as he bent to look into her eyes. She could hear the concern in his tone. 'What's happening?'

'I don't know.'

'Coach! Over here!' Zac sounded worried. She wondered if he could see something she couldn't. Was she pale? Were her eyes not moving normally? Terror overwhelmed her at what this could mean.

'Milla, sit down.'

Someone lowered her to the ground. She blinked, trying to focus, then closed her eyes to shut out the truth. Something was terribly wrong.

Sarah, the only other girl on her team apart from Kirra, came in close. 'You okay, Milla?'

'I don't know.' Was she dying? Death was all too real and possible. She knew that from experience.

'Did you get a hit to the head?' That was coach's voice.

'No.'

'Open your eyes. Can you see my finger?'

She knew he'd be holding up a finger and just for a moment she thought she could see it. But then there were two. Or was it more? And why was it separate to his hand, kind of sitting in the air like that? 'Not really. It's all over the place.'

'I think we'd better call the ambulance just in case. Sarah, can you find her drink bottle? Give her a drink.'

Milla held herself together, but she wanted to scream. To escape. She knew there were people crowding around her, but she couldn't pick their faces. The voices were familiar but she was exposed and vulnerable in a way she never had been before. She was normally the strong, all-together one. Even when Toby was killed, she had continued being cheerful, bringing life and joy to all those around her. It was her job on this earth. To make people happy. Even Mum said that was her gift.

She held out a hand. 'Where's my phone? I'll call Jess.'

'I'll get it.'

A blur was held up in front of her. Or was it two? She reached for it and grasped empty air. Someone placed the phone in her hands. It felt real and solid, grounding her again, but how was she supposed to ring Jess? She couldn't see her phone screen. What was happening to her? *God, I need you.*

'I can't see it. You'll have to call for me.' She heard the tremor in her voice and hated it.

'What's Jess's number?' Sarah asked.

'I don't know it off by heart. She's in my contacts.'

'What's your password?' That was Riley.

As if she'd tell him. 'Don't worry about it. I'll wait.'

Zac knelt beside her. She knew his presence, his smell, even if it was of sweat. She'd played enough competitive sport with or against him to know. 'I'll call your parents.'

'No, they're too far out of town. They'll worry.'

'I'll get Jess's number from Pierce, then.' Grateful for Zac's quick thinking, she let out a sigh and sat on her hands, trying to stop them shaking. Her heart was pounding so fast it beat against her chest. Maybe she was having a heart attack. Surely not a panic attack? That would be plain embarrassing. But panic attacks didn't affect your eyesight, did they?

The ambulance arrived the same time Jess did.

'Milla, what's happening?' Jess's voice came at the same time a knee landed on the ground, against her leg.

Milla let out a nervous, almost hysterical giggle. 'Jess, did you just do a slide?'

'She did,' Zac said, and she heard the smile in his voice. 'It was a good one, too.'

'It's not funny,' Jess said. 'Milla. I'm worried. They said you can't see.'

'Not properly.'

The paramedics moved in, putting a blood pressure cuff around her arm, taking her temperature, shining a light in her eyes. She winced at the brightness of the light and the pain it caused behind her eyes.

To her embarrassment, she was loaded onto a stretcher and into the ambulance in front of all her soccer teammates. She closed her eyes to shut them out. Not that she could see them clearly or know what they were thinking, but that made it worse. This was humiliating in the worst way possible.

CHAPTER EIGHT

J ess prayed her heart out as they travelled to the hospital in the ambulance. Milla didn't look right. Her cheeks were flushed and the paramedic said she had a low grade fever. One of her eyelids drooped slightly and she kept closing her eyes.

Please God, I can't lose another sibling. Not Milla. She's all I have left.

And yet she knew God could choose to take her. God had done something she had never expected of him; never believed he could or would do, when he took Toby. He could do it again and there was nothing she could do to stop him. Except beg.

God, surely you wouldn't take Milla too. Please. I'm begging you. Don't do this.

She had basic medical knowledge and top of her list in guessing Milla's condition was brain tumour. Then stroke. The paramedics appeared to be treating it as stroke. From what she could tell, they'd given her Asprin, were checking oxygen levels and had a heart monitor already going. They had a cannula already in, ready to go. Milla hadn't complained. She never did. She was too tough for her own good, sometimes. But Jess could taste her fear. It consumed her, as well.

Milla reached out a hand and Jess took it, grasping it tight.

'It's going to be okay,' she whispered, more to reassure herself than anything.

'Have you called Mum and Dad?'

'Yes, Mum's calling Dad in from the paddock. They'll be here soon.'

At least if something happened to Milla, they could be here. She couldn't believe that God hadn't given them a chance to say goodbye to Toby. To tell him how much they loved him. It wasn't fair of God. It really wasn't.

Milla was raced into the Emergency Department and doctors converged on her, asking questions, looking in her eyes, checking her neural responses, prepping her for an MRI. And Milla looked at Jess with eyes begging for help; for reassurance. Her hand reached out, grasping the air, trying to find her. It broke Jess's heart.

'I'm here, Milly.' She took Milla's hand and held it firmly in her own.

Milla lay back in the bed and closed her eyes. 'Please pray for me.'

'I have been. Non-stop. God's got this.' Well, she hoped he did. Why was it that before Toby's death, life had been smooth and easy? No real death or loss. They still had all their grandparents! Not many people could claim that by her age. She looked back at Milla. She made an angelic picture lying there with her brown curls settled around her pixie face, eyes closed like sleeping beauty. She was so pretty. She supposed it was fair enough. God made her intelligent and he made Milla pretty. You couldn't have both.

Someone came around the corner. Zac. He was pale, still in his soccer boots and stinking of body odour. His eyes were fixed on Milla.

God, he loves her! Jess saw it for the first time. And why not? Their families had been close for years. And hadn't she been infatuated with Pierce for a time?

'Mill?'

Her eyes shot open at the sound of Zac's voice and she flushed. Her hands fluttered and smoothed down the hospital gown she wore, making sure she was modest. Jess almost smiled. Zac had rattled the unshakable Milla. That spoke volumes. But what if this was it for Milla? What if Zac never stood a chance, not because Milla was too busy running around living life to notice him, but because she was called home to heaven? She swallowed a lump in her throat, watching as Zac came closer to Milla's side.

'Do they know what's going on?'

Milla shook her head. 'No. They're doing some tests.'

'Oh. I told Buck. He's praying.'

'Thank you.'

'Can you see yet?'

She smiled. 'No. But I can smell you.'

He chuckled. 'I'll bet you can. You don't smell much better, though.'

'Thank you.'

'It's not a compliment.'

She grinned. 'I know.' She opened her eyes, and searched for his face before she closed them again with a sigh. 'What if I never see you again?'

He chuckled, the sound so much deeper than it had been even a month ago. He was growing up so fast. 'Then I guess you'll always remember me at this age. I'll never grow old.'

Jess swallowed the lump in her throat as she watched them. Close friends and something more. Why couldn't she feel the same about Pierce? She wanted to. It made sense to.

A doctor breezed in. 'We're ready for your MRI. A wardsman is on his way to take you.'

Milla's head jerked up. 'Jess, can you come?'

The doctor nodded at Jess, then faced Milla. 'She can come as far as the door. Once you are in the MRI room you'll be on your own. Are you claustrophobic?'

'I don't think so.' Milla drew in a deep breath, and Jess wanted to weep. Milla was the extrovert in the family. Always with people, always chatting, alive, drawing energy from her love of the human race and her natural connection with them. She might not be claustrophobic, but she wouldn't cope very well being alone.

MILLA DIDN'T KNOW what to think or feel. Her heart was pounding. She didn't need to look at the monitor attached to her to know that. As she was taken into the room for her MRI her mind raged. A nurse guided her to a hard, flat surface and helped her lie down.

Where are you, God? You're supposed to be here. You're supposed to give me peace. I can't feel you. I can't see you. You promised to be with me, always!

The nurse handed her some ear plugs.

'To cancel out some of the sound,' she said. Then she fixed Milla's head in a fitted brace and directed her to lie perfectly still. The machine moved her slowly into some kind of cylinder, her head held firm in place. It was not comfortable, lying completely flat on the hard surface. The noises, the whirring and hammering shook her. There was a picture above her for her to look at, they'd said. Well, she couldn't see it. Just a green fuzz like a rainforest and maybe a stream. The sound began again, like an off-tune guitar chord. Like when Zac was trying to learn the electric guitar.

She held in her smile, remembering the way she had teased him about it.

'It's not even music, Zac. It's just noise. Like the side of a tractor scraping along a barbed wire fence.'

He'd grimaced. 'Come on, that's a bit rough.'

'It's not. That's exactly what it sounds like.'

'And you know this, how? Did you have a go at driving the tractor and happen to run into a barbed wire fence?'

She'd giggled then. 'Maybe. But I'd never admit to it.'

He'd held the guitar out to her. 'See if you can do it better, then.'

'Nope. I'm not interested. Takes too long to learn and I'm hopeless at music. You've heard me sing. I've got better things to do with my life.'

He'd tilted his head at her with a smile. 'One day you might regret it, Mill. When I am standing on stage, the most loved member of an all boy band, you'll wish you'd asked to learn with me. You'll wish you'd valued my gift.'

'Gift? I value that noise as much as I value a dog throwing up all over my shoes.'

'Milla!'

She'd laughed at his horrified face. She loved making him react. He was just so calm and serious. He needed shaking up. Needed to be more passionate about life.

But now as she listened to the sounds of the MRI machine clanging in her ears, she was grateful for him. Grateful for the terrible noises he'd made with the electric guitar which were making her heart smile right now. Maybe her singing sounded terrible too, but what if God loved it the way she now loved the sounds Zac had made? Just because they reminded her of him. Just because she loved …? Yes, loved him as a close friend. Someone who knew her like her own family knew her. She allowed her mind to go back to her favourite camping trips with the Buckley family. Reliving the moments when they were still young, carefree and full of energy. Toby had been there too.

'All done. We're bringing you out now.'

Milla's eyes shot open. Had it been half an hour already? She tried to focus, but she still couldn't see. God hadn't healed her.

Mum and Dad met her on the other side of the door. Mum's arms came around her, warm and comforting. Dad rested a hand on her shoulder, silently adding his reassurance.

'The doctor said you'll need to be in overnight while we wait on scan results,' Dad said. 'Mum will stay with you. The whole church is praying.'

Grateful tears spilled down Milla's cheeks. God knew about this. He'd brought her comfort in the form of Zac, of her parents and sister and in memories.

MILLA AWOKE IN THE NIGHT, heart pounding. It was uncomfortable sleeping with monitors attached and a cannula in her arm. Every time she turned, something got caught on her hospital gown or cannula. Mum slept soundly beside her. She felt alone even with Mum there. Afraid of the future and what was happening to her body. Was this how Jesus felt when he was praying in the garden and the disciples fell asleep?

'Jesus!' She whispered his name and reached out her hands. She just needed to feel him. To touch the hem of his garment like the woman who had reached out when Jesus was on earth. All she'd needed was to touch the hem of his garment and she had been healed. 'Jesus, where are you?'

Had Toby felt alone in his last moments? The thought undid her and tears streamed down her face. She'd been so strong. She'd heard Mum telling people how well she'd coped. But had she really coped? Or had she just kept busy and distracted? Allowing herself to become absorbed in sport and people and activity so that she didn't need to face the reality of life and death. Now that she was here, alone, afraid, an emptiness threatened to swallow her whole. She couldn't stand the thought of leaving her family. Of going to be with Toby. Not yet. Not this way.

'Jesus, I need your peace. You said your Holy Spirit is with me. Where? I need him!'

She cried and wrestled with God until no more tears were left. She held out her arms, waiting desperately to receive his comfort and peace but she felt nothing.

CHAPTER NINE

Jess was drained. Tim grumped and growled like Mr. Callum's bull and was just as stubborn.

'Try this,' she said, guiding his knee to another position.

He slumped back against the wall. 'One stupid train ride,' he muttered, 'That's all it took … and this is what I've become. Not even allowed to move my own knee the way I want to.'

'Tim …' She hadn't meant her voice to come out pleading. 'Tim,' she said again, this time more firmly. 'I'm sorry for what happened that day. You can't begin to imagine how sorry I am. But I'm trying to help you.'

He snorted. 'Don't pretend you understand.'

She drew in a deep breath. She was tempted to tell him of her own loss. But she couldn't trust him with it, couldn't give him a chance to mock the wound still open and bleeding.

Clearly he was having trouble concentrating, but so was she. Concerns about Milla weighed heavily on her heart. She couldn't lose Milla too. She couldn't. She moved Tim's leg forward and back. Forward and back.

Tim had lost a foot, but she had lost a brother. She would give both feet to have Toby back. She shook her head at the thought. It was unprofessional to let her personal life distract her while treating a patient.

'What are you shaking your head about?'

Tim's clipped voice jarred her. She looked up at him. It was the first time he had taken an interest in her thoughts.

'Nothing you would want to know.'

He gave a harsh laugh. 'Oh, so you're an O.T. *and* a mind reader now, are you?'

She was tempted to ignore his question, but already knew that tactic didn't work. Tim was as persistent as he was hurtful. 'Not a mind reader, but I've learned a bit about the way you think.'

'I doubt that.'

Jess didn't bother to argue. She'd need to powerwalk an extra five kilometres this afternoon just to sort through a half hour session with this man. He was helping her get fit, that was for sure.

She stood up, turned to her desk and flipped through some papers. 'I've had a talk to the vets at the local clinic.' She paused, waiting for his reaction. She could never predict what it might be. He said nothing, so she continued. 'They are very keen to have you working in the local surgery. They have more than enough work on the farms to keep them busy ...'

His growl cut her off. His eyes had darkened to near black. 'If they think I'm willing to work on little household pets they're wrong!'

'Tim, this is the perfect opportunity for you to work until you can walk again.'

'There's no way I'm going to waste my time on domestic animals!' His hands fisted in his lap, knuckles going white. 'Cattle, horses, sheep, those animals all have a use. Even dogs do to some extent – but a spoiled poodle or Persian cat? Or some fluffy little bunny? No way! I'd prefer to study again to become an O.T. and actually put some use to my life.'

Jess frowned. 'I think an O.T. and a vet are similar occupations. The main objective of both is to heal. And you've no idea what great therapy an animal can be for an injured human. Someone has to keep those animals alive.'

Tim laughed. 'Don't waste your psychobabble on me, girl. You're an O.T., not a psychologist.'

Jess sat up straighter. 'Well actually, there's where you're wrong. I have a degree in occupational therapy, majoring in mental health. You'd be surprised how all of them are interlinked.'

Tim's eyes widened before they narrowed again. 'I'm surprised that someone smart enough to have so many qualifications would waste it on all that garbage.'

Jess gritted her teeth, then forced herself to relax her jaw. 'Perhaps if you didn't think of it as garbage you would lead a more fulfilled life.'

Tim's movement made Jess aware that if he could walk he would have marched out of there without another word. Instead, he sat back in defeat. 'I had a fulfilled life, once,' he said. 'I had everything I needed and wanted.'

Her heart softened. 'You thought you did. But there is so much more to life. Sometimes what we think we need and want is not what our soul is really thirsting for.'

He laughed, a scornful sound. 'You just say that because there are obvious things lacking in your life. Things you can do nothing about. You're just trying to comfort yourself.' He looked her up and down. 'There are some things we can't change because it's the way we were born.'

She didn't ask him what he meant. She knew. She wasn't pretty. Milla was the pretty one. Intelligence was all well and good, but it could never make up for unruly hair that couldn't decide if it wanted to be red or brown, a nose a little too large, a face marred by acne scars and murky green eyes. She had determined never to let Tim Bateman hurt her. God would be her shelter and her rock. But now, as he stared her up and down she felt ugly and exposed. As though she were back in high school being judged and picked on for her appearance. The years of nasty comments from classmates at school as they tried to pull her down weighed on her shoulders again. Being nice had helped. The more friends you had, the more people liked you, the more they stood up for you when the nasty ones snapped and tried to bite. Having a family who doted on you helped, and a smart and good-looking big brother the girls wanted to impress. But on her own she was nothing. Without Toby she was lost. How would she cope if she lost Milla too?

She felt herself withdrawing even as she put on her professional air and continued to work with Tim. But the moment he left her office, she sat at her desk and cried. Once she pulled herself together, she reached for her phone and called her parents to ask how Milla was going.

'Her MRI report is back,' Dad's cheerful voice said. 'It's all clear. No signs of stroke, tumour, or any of the nasties they were worried about. The neurologist thinks she may have nerve damage to her eyes. He has no idea what might have caused it, though. Maybe stress. Another possibility is an auto immune condition called myasthenia gravis. It would explain her muscle weakness, too. More tests are being carried out, but she can come home.'

'What about her eyesight?'

'It's an unknown. If it's nerve damage it may fix itself over time.'

'What kind of time?'

'Weeks. Possibly months.'

'And the other condition?'

'It's lifelong but there are treatments.'

With a sigh, Jess looked around her office, trying to find something to hold onto. Something solid and unchanging. So many unknowns. She was relieved the worst case scenarios hadn't played out, but it still wasn't good. How would the active, bubbly Milla cope without her eyesight? Truck driving was out of the question, now. Any kind of driving, for that matter. Milla had been so excited about going for her Learner's License next month when she turned sixteen. Just another loss drowned in the sea of uncertainty and grief. Who did she think she was, trying to offer Tim Bateman hope when she was struggling to find it herself?

MILLA SAT on the hospital bed, restless and bored.

Her heart quickened as footsteps approached. Zac? No, he'd still be in school. It was the neurologist who turned the corner.

He repeated all the neural function tests again, then held one hand over her eye.

'Does that help?'

She gasped. 'Yes!' She could focus. Her vision was still blurry, but the image stopped jumping around. The missing gaps returned and the dizziness left.

The neurologist nodded. 'If you do have Myasthenia, the condition I'm highly suspecting, it weakens your eye muscles as well, so your eyes can't focus together. I have written up a prescription for a medication that will strengthen your muscles and give you relief for a few hours at a time. In the meantime, you might find wearing an eye patch on one eye will help.'

Milla nodded, but she wasn't going to do that. She'd feel silly. She'd prefer to just close one eye and function that way.

However, as they travelled home, she quickly became weary of holding one eye shut. The pain behind it drove her to shut both. It wasn't going to work. The doctor had given her a medical certificate for extended time off school but she wanted to return to normal life. She needed school and cadets and soccer. But not with an eye patch. Not with a sign screaming at the world that something was wrong with her. That she was no longer the strong, carefree Milla Cardelle.

'God, please heal me!' She opened her eyes again, but the same dizziness and spurts of light and moving shapes overwhelmed her. How long? She wanted to scream, to escape her own body and be free again.

CHAPTER TEN

'Just put your chin down for me,' the hairdresser said, and Jess complied. She wished she hadn't agreed to be Naomi Stanwell's bridesmaid today. She was no stranger to the job – this was the fifth time. That's what happened when you had good social skills. When you were nice. She certainly hadn't been picked for her beauty, no matter how beautiful the dress was. Maybe the reason she was chosen so often was that she was no threat to the bride.

And yet, Pierce had asked her to marry him. Guilt tugged at her heart. She still hadn't confirmed her answer.

She glanced at her reflection in the mirror and sighed. She should be grateful people liked her enough to ignore her looks. Her wayward, wispy hair refused to be tamed. 'It's okay,' she told herself, swallowing hard. 'No one will be looking at you.'

She hoped not, anyway. If only Tim Bateman hadn't made that comment about the obvious things she was lacking. Why had he picked the one thing that could shake her confidence? Nobody knew how much it bothered her to be so plain. She made up for it in other ways. Being intelligent, fit, loveable. They were all things she could control. Her appearance was not.

The hairdresser twisted another curl into shape. Jess gave a sidelong glance at Naomi in the mirror. She was so pretty with her shiny blonde hair and appealing smile. Some might consider her a little plump, but it was shapeliness that Jess longed for. Being fit had helped her tone her muscles but hadn't given her the curves she envied in other girls.

'Do you have regrets?' Naomi asked, catching her eye.

'Regrets?'

'About Jock?'

Jess almost laughed, but managed not to. Naomi had tried to match her up with Jock in high school, but Jess had known he wouldn't be interested. Instead, she'd directed Jock's attention to Naomi. It hadn't been hard. Naomi remained as pretty as she'd been in kindergarten.

'I've got no regrets,' she assured Naomi. 'You and Jock are perfect for each other. He never could have loved me. It was always going to be you.'

Naomi gave her shy smile. 'You always know how to say the right thing, Jess.'

JESS HAD SPOKEN THE TRUTH. She watched as Naomi and Jock made their way through the congregation, now husband and wife, and she knew for certain that Jock was not for her. He liked living in this average town, being a mediocre Christian, having a job that merely got him by. Somewhere deep down, Jess had bigger dreams. Jock's lack of ambition would have frustrated her. Naomi, however, needed security and love. That's what Jock offered.

Naomi's mother came to stand beside Jess. 'Must be about

your turn, Jess,' she said as she looked in pride at her daughter standing beside her new husband.

'It will be her turn soon enough,' Dad said, coming to her defense.

Mrs. Stanwell shook her head. 'You can't stand around waiting for Mr. Perfect, you know. While you do, "Mr. Right For *You*" can pass you by.'

Jess laughed. 'I'm not waiting for Mr. Perfect. I know he doesn't exist.'

Dad grinned. 'Then again, maybe he does. Your mother thought the same thing, and then she found me …'

Jess rolled her eyes and held back her grin.

'Then what are you waiting for?' Mrs. Stanwell asked, studying Jess as though she were an interesting, new kind of bug.

Jess tried not to be offended. She bit her lip, knowing she needed to satisfy Mrs. Stanwell with her answer or she'd never let it go.

'I don't know. Maybe someone who can share my dreams. Someone who enjoys exercise and who'd want to walk with me, who enjoys the world and nature the way I do – someone to study the sunsets and enjoy not just their beauty, but their Creator.' Things that Pierce wouldn't do. He was a Christian, but he was also an indoor man. All neatness and order. She shrugged. 'That's not too being too picky, is it?'

Mrs. Stanwell smiled. 'A bit ironic, isn't it? You work all day with those who can't walk or exercise, but it's one of the things you value the most.'

'Exactly. I teach my patients to walk again.'

Except those who never could. She pitied them. Not Tim. He could walk again if he tried. He was just too stubborn for his own good. But she didn't want to be thinking about him. Not today.

She looked for an escape and saw Sasha. Standing alone.

'Excuse me,' she said, slipping away. 'There's someone I need to talk to.'

Poor Sasha. It must hurt to know this day could have been hers and Toby's. She must be feeling intense loss today. Sasha glanced her way at that moment, then elbowed her way into the group closest to her, cutting in on their conversation. What was that about? Sasha wasn't normally that forward or rude.

Just before Jess reached her, she slipped away into the Ladies' toilets. Jess waited. She desperately needed to speak with her, to acknowledge the pain and loss she must be feeling. Toby would want her to care for the woman he loved so deeply.

The moment Sasha came out from the Ladies', she headed the opposite direction, her high heeled shoes clipping across the floor at a dangerous pace. This was ridiculous. It looked like Sasha was deliberately avoiding her. Guilt niggled. Did Sasha somehow know the jealousy Jess had felt when Toby's affections and attention had become so consumed by her? She'd tried hard not to let it show; to abort the negative feelings.

Lord, I know she's hurting. Help me to be the friend Sasha needs.

She came outside just in time to see Sasha climbing into her car. Jess waved and hurried forward, ready to comfort Sasha and tell her she understood what she must be feeling. But even though she was sure Sasha saw her, she drove off without any kind of acknowledgement.

Throat tight, Jess watched her car disappear from the car park. Being a friend and support to people was something she prided herself in being good at. But two people in the world now didn't appear to like or want her friendship. Her friendliness and intelligence were no longer enough. Tim Bateman's dislike she could explain away, but Sasha's she could not. Heart constricting, she pasted on a smile and headed into the hall for the reception. Today of all days she needed to prove to people that everything was okay and reassure them she was overjoyed to see another friend married.

MILLA PUSHED her glasses up her nose, glad they could disguise her eye patch to some extent. Still, some people drew attention to it and made comments. Her medication was working, proving she did in fact have the condition the neurologist suspected. But by the evening it had worn off. She sat back, watching Jess as much as she was able. Her big sister moved around the room, putting people at ease. She was beautiful. She wasn't picture perfect, but her smile was so warm, her heart so big. She moved with an elegance and poise Milla hadn't noticed before. She'd been too involved in the action to sit back and watch.

'How's it going?'

She turned as Zac pulled a chair up beside her and leaned his elbows on the table. He looked awkward in his dress pants, button up shirt and dress shoes. He belonged in sports shirts and footy boots. She reached a hand to mess up his hair. 'Sorry, I had trouble recognising you. Just had to make sure it was you.'

He grinned, pushing her hand away and straightening his hair. 'You have no idea how long it took me to get it right this morning!'

She snorted. 'Yeah, right.'

He picked a rose out of the table decoration and began pulling it apart. 'So, still can't focus both eyes?'

'No.'

'I've been praying for you.' It was said quietly, but sincerely. It surprised her.

'Thank you. I really do want to see again.'

He bit his lip. 'I want you to as well. But even if God chooses not to heal, it will be okay. I know it's easy for me to say, here with two good eyes, but none of this changes who you are. Your value is in Christ, not what you can or can't do.'

She stared at him. Who was this boy-suddenly-become-man? It was as though he'd read her thoughts; as though he knew her identity had become wrapped up in her sporting prowess and physical abilities. 'Well, aren't you the deep thinker this evening?'

He chuckled. 'Not any more than usual.'

'What? You hardly ever say anything unless you're talking about the next soccer team we're facing.'

He gave her a questioning look, then smiled. 'Maybe that's because you don't give me a chance. You're usually so busy running around like a headless chook. It's weird to see you sitting here quietly watching the world instead of being the one making it go around.'

What was she supposed to make of that? Was he saying he preferred her this way? Because she didn't. This time to think was driving her crazy. So many thoughts swirled around her head she didn't know what to do with them. The lack of endorphins was leaving her depressed.

'Do you want to dance?'

Her good eye shot to his. Was he making fun of her? He knew she couldn't see properly. They'd danced plenty of bush dances together during their camping trips and holidays, but it was all action and fun. There was no way she could manage it now.

'I'll teach you to waltz. Then you just follow my lead.'

'You know how to waltz?'

He shrugged. 'You don't know everything about me, Milla Cardelle. But yes, I have a good enough idea how to waltz. So how about it?'

She bit her lip. 'Are you sure? I'll step on your toes. Embarrass you.'

'You'll never embarrass me.'

She swallowed, trying to work out what to make of this quiet, serious Zac. He was meeting her where she was at. She hadn't known he'd be so good at being a comforting friend. She'd enjoyed his teasing for years, his brotherly banter and fun. But maybe he'd been following her lead all this time. Maybe it was time for her to follow his. Still, she was unsure. 'People will see us.'

He laughed. 'When has that ever bothered you, Miss Extrovert?'

'Now.'

His smile faded. 'We can go out on the verandah. We can still hear the music from there.'

'Okay.'

He linked his arm through hers and she was surprised by the way her heart pounded at his touch. What was wrong with her? She had been sitting quietly all day but she felt as though she'd just played a full game of soccer. Zac led her out the door to a quiet place along the verandah. Fairy lights glittered across the railing and hung from the eves. Even with only one eye working, it was beautiful. She reached a hand to rub at the patch over her eye. It was itchy and annoying. She wanted to rip it off.

'Uncomfortable?' Zac asked.

She nodded.

'Take it off and just close your eyes. A good waltz is danced with your eyes closed.'

She glanced up at him. How did he know that? What was he doing, playing at grown-ups, as though they were romantically involved? But his tone told her he wasn't playing. She instinctively wanted to make a joke and dance away from him. Like she would have in the past. That's why she'd never seen him like this before. She'd never given him the chance, always making the world dance to the beat of her drum, never hearing the beat of another's heart or noticing their need.

She gritted her teeth as she ripped the patch off. Its sticky edges pulled at the skin around her eye. 'Have I got any eyebrow left?' she asked him with a grin. Then closed her eyes as his image blurred and jumped in front of her.

'You look fine,' he said and she heard the smile in his voice. She felt his hand as it reached for hers. 'Put your hand up on my shoulder like this.' He placed it there. 'Then take this hand. And then use all your senses – apart from sight, to work out where I'm going and what I'm doing. And just follow.'

Easy to say. Not so easy to do. She drew in a deep breath, trying to do as he instructed. She screwed up her nose. 'You don't smell like you.'

He laughed. 'That's because I haven't been running around so my deodorant is still working. But I don't like the way you're screwing up your nose. Anyone would think you prefer the smell of B.O.'

'Not likely.' She smiled, trying to work out his movements, to be aware of his presence. And to her surprise, her awareness of him was stronger than it had been for all those years she'd been seeing him. It was as confusing as it was overwhelming.

The fabric of his shirt as it brushed against her arm, the warmth of his skin beneath her hand, even the breeze that gently teased her hair, it all made her feel so alive.

He didn't speak and neither did she. And with the music and the hum of the reception inside, she felt a connection with him stronger than she'd had in all their years of playing sport together, of arguing and laughing and teasing.

She stumbled and he pulled her closer. 'You okay?'

Was she? Her brain felt foggy. It scared her the way she couldn't put into words what was going on. She was just tired. So tired. The neurologist was becoming more and more convinced she had myasthenia gravis, the auto immune condition which affected and weakened her muscles. He said the trauma of Toby's death had most likely triggered it.

'Do you want to sit down?'

Did she want to? No. But she needed to. 'I think I'd better.' He took her hand to lead her inside, but she hesitated. 'Zac?'

'Hmm?'

'Thank you.'

His hand squeezed hers. 'And thank you.' She heard the smile in his voice.

CHAPTER ELEVEN

Jess opened Sasha's front gate with a quick prayer for help and made her way to the front door. She needed to set things right with Sasha. God knew she had enough other things to worry about without worrying about why Sasha didn't like her. There was Milla. And Mum. Mum was having another sad day, remembering Toby. The wedding on Saturday had triggered that. And Tim had been more uncooperative than ever today. All things she couldn't fix. Hopefully, this she could …

She raised her hand and knocked.

Sasha opened her front door and stepped back. 'Hello Jess.' Jess held in a wince at the formal tone and the way Sasha eyed her so cautiously.

'Sasha! How are you?' She forced a relaxed, cheerfulness into her voice.

When Sasha remained silent, Jess ploughed ahead. 'I've been worried about you.'

Sasha shrugged. 'Don't be.'

It was such a closed response, but Jess couldn't leave it there. 'Can I come in?'

'Sure.' Sasha opened the door wider and led her down the hall. 'Do you want a drink? Something to eat?'

Jess shook her head, seating herself on the lounge. 'No thanks.'

Sasha stood there, looking at her. The awkward silence drove her crazy. She sat forward, deciding to be direct. Most people responded well to her warm, honest manner.

'Sasha, I've come because I feel like things haven't been the same between us since Toby died. I feel like you might be avoiding me. I just wanted to say that I'm really sorry if I've hurt or offended you somehow.'

Sasha didn't meet her eyes. 'What would you have done to offend me?'

Jess shrugged. 'I don't know. But things seem different between us. I miss our old friendship.'

Sasha laughed disbelievingly and looked at her, then. 'Jess, you have so many friends I don't know how you have time for them all. I've never been a bridesmaid once, let alone five times.'

So that was it? Sasha was feeling unwanted and unneeded. It was time Jess let Sasha know just how much she was valued. No more avoiding her just because she seemed a little aloof. She glanced at the photo on Sasha's buffet. Toby. It was the best photo she had seen of her brother. Her chest tightened. Sasha's eyes followed Jess's.

Jess bit her lip and cleared her throat. 'I miss him.'

To her surprise, Sasha stiffened and her chin came out. 'So do I, Jessica. In fact, I doubt there will ever be a day you come here and find that photo gone. He was my life, my joy, my future.'

Sasha had never used her full name before. She was clearly angry. But at who and what? Perhaps at pain and loss. Perhaps at her. Well, she'd tried. But had she tried enough?

'What can I do?' Jess pleaded. 'How can I make it easier for you?'

Sasha looked at the floor. 'Honestly?'

'Honestly.'

'Right now I just need to be alone.'

A cry caught in Jess's throat, but she pushed it back down. With all the appearance of calm and poise she could muster, she nodded and picked up her handbag. She was almost at the door when she turned back. 'Sasha, if you ever need anything …'

Sasha nodded looking somewhere over her shoulder. Jess didn't know what else to do but to walk out the door.

Oh God, I tried. What have I done wrong? Please show me.

JESS TRIED to focus on the physio exercises with Tim the following day. Her heart was in turmoil and it was hard to be professional when your patient was pushing your patience to its limits.

'Tim, you have to try,' she finally bit out in exasperation.

His glare was fierce. 'Why? So you can up your reputation as a good therapist?'

'No. So you can improve your quality of life.'

'Improve my life?' He waved his hand in her face. 'I'm not the one in need of improving. Look at you, kneeling there in front of some half man in a wheelchair as though you're his servant. Where's your self-respect?'

Jess stood. He'd worn down her politeness and tolerance a bit more every day. She'd had enough. 'I don't have to take this from you, you know. All these insults, the sarcasm, the anger. I think it takes a lot more strength to stay here kneeling in front of you than to walk away.'

Tim gave a searing laugh. 'If I could walk, believe me, I would have been the one to walk away by now.'

Jess sighed and moved to her desk. 'Tell me when you're ready to continue with the exercises, Tim.'

'What, I thought you like the personal talk. Isn't it all part of your job, Miss Psychologist?'

She didn't answer. He wheeled his chair closer. 'Come on Jessica, you know all about me. Why can't you reveal a bit about yourself?'

She looked at him. Took in his dark, closed features. 'I know very little about you, Timothy. You hide it all under a mask of anger and bitterness.'

His half smile was scornful. 'Come on Jess, tell me about yourself. For example, do you have a boyfriend? Why aren't you married? Are you scared of intimacy?' She jerked back and he let out a harsh laugh. 'I'm making you angry. Now you know how I feel all the time. All this prying, the questions ...'

'It's my job, Tim. I don't do it because I like making you uncomfortable.'

'But you must like working with me or you would have backed out by now. What is it about me? My one good foot? My dark, brooding, mysterious nature? Or the fact that you pity me and hope that one day I will be your success story?'

Jess rubbed her forehead. 'If you must know, Tim Bateman, I dread every session I have with you.' What was she saying? She couldn't say this to a patient. But the words kept coming. 'You are the only patient who has treated me with such disdain and disrespect. I feel sick every time I see your name on my appointment list, but I pull myself together and get on with my job.'

The surprise that passed through his eyes was so slight she almost missed it. He crossed his arms. 'Well, let me make this easy on you. You're fired.' He shot her a cold, dry smile. 'Or can't you *be* fired?'

'You can terminate your service agreement.' What had she done? Why couldn't she have bitten her tongue like she had hundreds of times before?

'Done.'

Jess hid her shaking hands, hoping he was fooled by the calm front she presented. 'Okay.'

'That's it?' Tim demanded. 'The psychologist accepts it when her disturbed, disabled patient refuses her help?'

Jess nodded again. She wouldn't be drawn into his bitterness. He wheeled himself out of the room. Guilt and relief warred within.

She let out a shuddery breath. Should she chase after him? Apologise? No, Tim had his own choices to make. If he wanted to come back, that was up to him.

JESS POPPED into the shops on the way home and glanced at her phone. What had Mum asked her to get? Bread, milk and cheese.

She pasted on a smile for the locals but strode toward the bread aisle. She didn't feel up to stopping to chat with everyone today. She turned the corner and stopped short. Sasha stood there, shopping basket over her arm. Jess couldn't handle more rejection today.

She moved to back away, but Sasha looked up. 'Hello.'

Jess nodded. 'Hey.'

Awkward.

Sasha filled in the silence. 'How's Milla going? I forgot to ask you yesterday.'

Jess didn't want to think about Milla any more than she wanted to think about Tim or Toby or Sasha. 'No improvement yet.'

'It must be so hard for her.' The intense sympathy and understanding in Sasha's tone was genuine.

'It is. She's been forced to give up everything she loves in life. Mum asked me to be her physio, but she doesn't want my help. Maybe she'll see Lauren.'

Jess bit her lip. What was up with her tongue today? She'd

never meant to reveal that to Sasha. It had stung when Milla refused her help.

Sasha frowned. 'But you're good at what you do.'

Jess drew in a deep breath. 'I don't know. I had a patient quit on me today.' There she went again. Blurting out something she'd never meant to tell anyone, let alone Sasha, especially not here in the middle of the supermarket.

Sasha shifted her shopping basket to the other arm. 'Why?'

Because she'd snapped. Been unprofessional. 'I didn't ask.'

'Perhaps you should have.'

Was that a bite in Sasha's tone? Jess felt her defenses rising. 'Maybe, but it's hard. He lost his foot in the train crash.'

Sasha flinched and Jess wished she hadn't mentioned the accident. How could she explain to Sasha what Tim was like? 'He lashes out for no reason and he's just so angry and bitter.'

'Sounds like he's hurting.'

Why was Sasha defending him? She didn't even know him. 'Yes, but he doesn't have to take it out on me. One thing I despise is sarcasm, and Tim is all sarcasm. It's not clever. It's cruel and selfish.'

Sasha reached for a loaf of bread and placed it in her basket. 'What about honesty and integrity? Aren't they just as important?'

'Probably more so.' What was Sasha getting at?

There was an awkward silence before Jess pasted on her warmest smile. 'I think you should be the one working with him, Sash. It sounds like you have more compassion for him than I have.'

Sasha's eyes narrowed. 'That would be romantic, wouldn't it? A woman who lost her fiancé in a train disaster goes and marries another man who only lost his foot.'

Jess's mouth rounded in surprise. 'No, Sash. I'd never want anyone I care for to have to put up with this man!'

'Not even someone who would find any available man to cling to?'

Jess felt her jaw drop. There was such hurt and accusation in Sasha's eyes. 'What are you saying?'

'What am *I* saying Jess? It's what *you* said. Remember at the funeral? I heard your comforting little chat with Pierce.'

Jess had no idea what she was talking about.

'About how I'd find another man soon enough?' Sasha prompted. 'How I couldn't possibly understand your grief because I'd only known Toby a couple of years?'

Jess's heart plummeted. 'I said that?' Surely not. And yet she had a vague, uncomfortable feeling that she had.

Sasha bit her lip and didn't answer.

'Oh Sash,' Jess's hands shook as she shifted the basket on her arm. What had she done? Sorry wasn't enough. An explanation or excuse wasn't enough. Was she truly that fickle? So insecure in herself that she had to bring others down to make herself feel better?

She swallowed painfully. She couldn't speak for the tears that filled her eyes then tracked down her cheeks. It didn't matter that she stood here in the middle of the supermarket aisle. Her sin had been exposed and she was broken.

'Don't cry,' Sasha said, voice tight. 'Sorry I mentioned it.'

Jess tried to talk, but all that came out was a sob. She dropped her basket, turned and raced out of the supermarket, to the safety of her car. She slumped into the driver's seat, pulled the door shut and cried.

Oh, God, I'm so sorry. I wanted so badly to be important, to be liked, to be noticed, that I did irreparable damage. The tongue is like a knife. Like fire. I've cut and burned Toby's fiancée in one jealous, thoughtless moment.

A knock came at her window. Sasha stood there, eyes troubled. Jess lowered the window. Sasha pointed to the passenger side seat. 'Can I hop in?'

Jess nodded, swiping at tears. Sasha opened the door, climbed in, then sat there, staring out the windscreen. Finally, Jess was able to speak. 'I wish there was something I could do to change what I said, Sasha. I hate the way I hurt you with words I didn't even mean. Sorry doesn't seem enough.'

Sasha reached into her bag and passed over a tissue. 'I forgive you, Jess.'

Jess cried harder. Then she looked over at Sasha sitting there with such a sincere, sweet expression, offering complete forgiveness. Unable to help herself, she threw her arms around her. When she pulled back, she saw the tears shining in Sasha's eyes, too. What could she do to make this right?

'Sash, we've missed you out at the farm. Mum is desperate for you to come for meals again. I know Toby was going to take you up Billy Can Hill one day. Can I take you and then you stay for dinner?'

Sasha's eyes lit up. 'Now?'

'If you want to. But first I need to get some bread, milk and cheese.'

Sasha reached over and touched Jess's face, red and puffy from crying. 'How about I go in and get them?'

Jess giggled, but it came out slightly hysterical. 'Might be a good idea. Can't have anyone thinking I'm less than all together, can we?'

Sasha smiled. 'Or maybe you should go in. I think I like you better when you're real. Makes you human like me.'

The words hit hard, but Jess knew she wasn't saying them to hurt. She was just stating the truth.

'You might be right. Still …'

Sasha laughed softly. 'I'll go in. See you shortly.'

Jess watched her and prayed. God had shown her the deceit of her own heart, today. Her envy, and jealousy and the pain it caused. For someone so intent on being 'nice' to everyone, it stung. She'd been stripped bare and yet in that had found reconciliation and forgiveness.

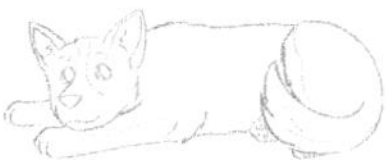

As Jess and Sasha climbed the hill on Cardelle's farm, they talked, really talked with each other for the first time. They spoke of Toby, of their pain and their heart's desires. There were many words shared and genuinely understood, but there was just one comment of Sasha's that ate deep into Jess's heart.

'I think you need to understand that you can disagree with someone without disliking them,' Sasha said. 'You can be a loving, warm, generous person without agreeing with everyone. If you try to please everyone you lose yourself.'

Jess knew she was right. It was the key to being real. True love wasn't afraid to be honest and real. It didn't deliberately hurt, but neither did it deceive or hide.

Toby had been right about Sasha's beautiful heart. A burden lifted from Jess as she forgave Toby for falling in love with Sasha.

CHAPTER TWELVE

Milla woke up and looked around the room. For just a moment she thought she could see. But very quickly the kaleidoscope that was her new normal returned. She let her eyes slide shut again.

'Please, God, I want to see.'

What would you like to see?

'Everything. I want to go back to playing sport. I want to go back to the way things were.'

Silence. Why did she feel like she was just starting to hear from God and then he disappeared again? What did he want from her?

'God, is this punishment? Is this because I did something wrong? Do you even care?'

What was she asking? Of course he cared. He gave his son Jesus for her, didn't he? She had accepted that and believed as a young girl in Kids Church. So why couldn't she feel him here and now? Had he taken away his blessing from her life because she had been charging down the wrong track, wanting to be a truck driver? 'God, what do you want from me?'

Silence again. She sighed and got up. She put the patch over her eye, then put on her glasses. She was going to youth group tomorrow and it terrified her. Riley came sometimes and he would have her at his mercy. She couldn't read body language anymore. She couldn't use her strength and wit to push back when he pushed someone. She didn't want to go but the youth minister had asked her to come so the group could pray for her. If felt wrong to refuse.

Mum and Jess were in the kitchen making pancakes. 'Want some?' Mum asked.

Milla nodded, plopping into a chair at the table. She would normally be helping but she'd already burned herself on the heater. It was hard to judge distances and she'd lost her depth perception. She had a tender spot on her shoulder where she'd bumped into the doorframe last night.

Mum prepared and cut the pancake for her. It was humiliating being treated like a toddler. The long morning stretched ahead of her. There was little she could do. She'd tried going for walks around the farm but she had to keep it slow. She couldn't see the dips in the uneven ground and had jarred her ankle. She wanted to run, to escape everything.

She heard the back door open. Dad slipped off his work boots as he came inside. 'What are your plans this morning, Milla?'

'No plans.'

'Want to come for a ride with me in the truck? I'm taking some cattle over to the sale yards.'

'I can't help you, Dad.'

He let out an uproarious laugh. 'Did I say I wanted help?'

She smiled. He had a point. As a small child she had often asked to come with him in the truck to 'help'. He had graciously let her, but she knew now that her three-year-old self had been more hindrance than help.

'I might slow you down.'

'And you might make my day a whole lot brighter. I haven't had your company for a long time.'

And so she went along with him. It was nice to sit beside him in the truck, hearing him chat about life and the farm. 'I'm still trying to get your mother to come in the truck with me again,' he said, a smile in his voice. 'When we were first married she came with me, but these days she's too caught up in housework and caring for everyone to want to spend a day in my company.'

He was smiling, but Milla could hear the wistfulness in his voice. She was glad she'd come, even with disturbed vision. Dad was an extrovert like her. He loved company. Mum was the opposite. And Zac … well, she wasn't sure exactly what he was. She was still finding out, but he was different with her these days. Almost as though he wanted more from their friendship.

'Dad, how old do I have to be to have a boyfriend?'

Dad changed gears on the truck before he answered, casting a glance her way. 'I don't know if that's the question you should be asking.'

'What should I be asking?'

'Maybe, how many times do you want your heart broken before you find the man you will spend the rest of your life with?'

'Oh.' She thought on that for a few minutes. Then, 'But is it inevitable my heart will be broken if it doesn't turn out?'

Dad took a hand off the steering wheel to rub his beard. 'Do you know of any relationships that have ended with both hearts intact?'

He had a point. She knew of girls in her class who'd been devastated by break-ups. And Sasha … well, that was different. Toby had died.

Dad gave her a cheeky grin. 'You got anyone in mind?'

She wasn't answering that. 'I just think I'm at the age where I might want to develop that kind of relationship with someone.'

'You mean an intentional, exclusive friendship? Or you mean having someone special you can hold hands with, show physical affection to? Because the way you are, I can't see you wanting to exclude other friends to develop a relationship with one person.

You're an extrovert, like me. And you're still young and finding your feet in life.'

Milla knew he was right. Only, things were changing. Now that she couldn't see properly, it was as though her eyes were being opened to the value of taking time to be still. To notice the depth and meaning of life, not just claim it for herself, for her own entertainment and pleasure.

Dad steered the truck onto a dirt road. 'You know that God wants us to be a relationship with him, first and foremost. He's the one who is always here. Who never leaves us. If we just open our eyes to him, we'll see him. But the plan he also has for most of us is to be married. To have that one person we are faithful to, who knows us intimately and who we can spend our lives loving, finding ways to give to them and bring them joy. But that's years away. I just don't want to see your heart broken between now and then.'

Milla stared out the windscreen. A cow scampered across the bumpy track in front of them. She could barely see the cow, but she could see what Dad was saying. And she knew that she had been looking at it all the wrong way. She'd been thinking how nice it would be to have someone love her and make her feel special. But she had to be ready and able to do the same in return. She had to stop and be still long enough to know what others needed and liked and wanted. She hadn't done that in her whole, effervescent, fast-paced, life.

ZAC WAS WAITING for her when she arrived at youth group. He came straight to her side. 'How are you doing?'

'Dreading this.'

'Why?'

'I just feel so silly wearing this eye patch. It looks like I'm missing an eye. It's freaky. And it gets so sweaty and itchy.'

'Have you tried one of those pirate patches?'

She sighed. 'That would be ten times worse. That's one sure way to draw attention to myself.'

He didn't answer, just touched her shoulder lightly before walking beside her into the church hall, a silent support. She'd never known this side of him before. But then, she'd never needed to.

'Woohoo, it's the pirate,' a year seven boy called out and Milla gave him a cheerful grin, but it was fake. Others laughed and it wasn't a nice feeling. They didn't understand what her patch meant; how much she had lost.

Kirra came over and Milla smiled at her. 'Riley still giving you a hard time?'

Kirra frowned. 'I wish you wouldn't do that.'

'Do what?'

'Try to be my protector. I don't need you to stand up for me, Milla. I know you do it with good intentions, but you don't really know me. You don't understand what it's like to be indigenous.'

Hurt filled Milla. 'I do. When I was little, we had this guy called Alan who worked for Dad. He told me what it's like …'

'No, Milla.'

Milla's defenses rose until she realised Kirra wasn't trying to hurt her. She was trying to make her understand. 'So tell me,' she said.

Kirra laughed. 'You think I can explain my life in one session? That you can get to know me just like that? Look, I know you were defending me because you have the right heart, but it comes across as though you think you're superior. I want to be your friend. As an equal. I don't want you to think you have to fight my battles for me.'

Kirra was right. Milla had taken it upon herself to fight

peoples' battles for them. To fight for mercy and justice without really knowing the people she was fighting for.

She thought back over her favourite verse, saying it in her mind,

He has shown you, O mortal, what is good. And what does the Lord require of you? To act justly and to love mercy and to walk humbly with your God.

God was the God of relationships. If she'd been walking humbly with him, she would have noticed people. Really noticed them. She would have seen them through God's eyes.

Oh God, help me see people. To really see people.

She reached a hand to Kirra. 'I want to be your friend. A real friend.'

Kirra smiled wide. 'Deal. But that means spending more time with me. Here. At school. At soccer.'

Milla grinned. She could handle that.

The youth pastor didn't get everyone to pray for her until the very end and by then Milla was exhausted. Her whole body sagged and she wondered how she'd manage school when it came time to go back. Thankfully she'd be seeing the neurologist again soon and he might have more answers.

'You coming to church tomorrow?' Zac asked as parents arrived to pick up their teenagers.

She shook her head. It was too exhausting. Processing all that was going on around her took too much effort.

'What about school on Monday?'

'I have an appointment with the neurologist.'

'Okay.'

She wished she could see him better; make out what he was thinking; what his body language was saying. There was so much more to him than she'd ever known, but now that she'd finally realised it, she couldn't fully appreciate it. She thought of her father's words about not having her heart broken and took a step back. 'See you later, Zac.' She couldn't afford to have her heart broken any more than it already was. It was a risk she wasn't willing to take.

But when he arrived at the farm with his dad on Monday afternoon with a gift for her, she thought she might just change her mind. 'Dad found them at the optometrist in Derby Street,' he said, as he passed her a small package. With a smile, she opened it to find discreet patches to place over one lens of her glasses.

'Thank you, Buck!' She threw her arms around Zac's dad, then stopped awkwardly, looking at Zac. He grinned. 'Do I get thanks, too?'

'You said your dad found them.'

He pulled her into a hug. 'Yeah, but I asked him to look for them.'

She laughed, her head resting on his shoulder before she pulled back. 'Then thank you.'

Buck grinned at her. 'We also found out that you can get opaque contact lenses the colour of your eyes. So, if you are wearing one it blocks out that eye, but you won't even look like anything's different.'

Milla was not the type to cry, but right now she felt a lump in her throat that refused to go down. The Buckleys were special. They knew her well and cared so much. Whatever happened between her and Zac, it would be okay. He didn't need to be exclusively hers. She just needed him to keep being Zac, just like she needed Pierce and Buck to keep being her special family friends.

She swiped at her eyes. 'Now look what you've done!' She was joking, but managed to sound annoyed at the same time.

'Ah, you're just a big softie under all that gruff exterior,' Zac said and Milla gave a mock growl.

Buck laughed. 'Careful, Zac. You'll get yourself into trouble.'

Milla laughed, too. 'No, not after he's given me a gift like this. No one has ever given me an eye patch before.'

Zac pulled a face. 'You make it sound like we gave you a

sparkling, jewel covered patch and presented it in a diamond studded box.'

She grinned. 'Now that would make me love you forever and I'd never speak another cross word to you in my life.'

'Promise?'

'Isaac!'

They all laughed and she felt more of her pain melt away. God was here. In the laughter of special friends, in family, in those who knew and loved her and provided her needs. God might not have healed her eyes, but he was healing her heart.

CHAPTER THIRTEEN

Jess packed up after work. It had been a good day. Mrs. Coban was walking with the use of a walker despite the specialists believing her third stroke would leave her bedbound. And Milla had been able to go without her eye patch for several hours with the new medication her neurologist was trialling. The lightness in her heart went deeper, though. She and Sasha were becoming friends. Real friends. They'd talked openly about Toby. They'd laughed and cried together, healing coming with every conversation shared.

'I thought you would come after me – try to convince me to come back.'

Jess jumped at the sound of Tim's deep, sharp voice in her doorway. She turned from the notes she was filing.

Her smile seemed to throw him. 'You don't dread seeing me today?'

She smiled wider. 'No, I didn't have to work myself up to it. Your appearance is a surprise.'

'You didn't come after me,' he repeated.

'No, but I hoped you'd choose to come back.'

He frowned. 'Do you have any idea how patronising that sounds?'

How could she safely respond to that? She had changed since that last day she spent with Tim. With God's help she was being real. Not offensive, but genuine, even if it meant disagreeing with someone. Not everyone on earth could like her – she had finally faced that fact and it was unexpectedly relieving. It was too big a burden to try to keep everyone happy.

'I don't mean to be patronising, but I have wondered how you're going.'

'Because you pity me?'

She shrugged. 'Maybe. But only because of the choices you've made. I don't pity you for losing your foot. Just your refusal to accept it and make the best of it.'

Tim looked as though he might disappear out the door again, but then he paused as though curiosity held him there, outweighing his indignation. 'I have to keep coming,' he said with a shrug. 'I found out I can't get any money from my employer if I don't.'

'Your employer?' Hope filled her. Had he decided to work as a local vet after all?

'Yeah, the government. They pay me to be handicapped. They steal from all the useful people in society and give it to me.'

Jess blinked. He was unbelievable. She shouldn't be amused, but she couldn't help the smile that peeked through.

'You find that funny?' he demanded and Jess covered her mouth.

'I do,' she confessed, lifting her chin. She braced herself for his continued raging, but instead, the hint of a smile played about his mouth. And those dark eyes softened. She was shocked speechless. Maybe there really was hope for this man. But how far could she push him? If he was going to live a fulfilled life, he needed to feel useful. She seized the moment.

'Would you reconsider working in the local vet clinic?'

Tim frowned, his eyes returning to their usual dark, shuttered state. 'I couldn't work the normal hours. I still have rehab and therapy to do.'

Jess tried to read below the surface. What was holding him back? Pride? Fear? The revulsion he felt at being a burden or a charity case? 'What if you worked voluntarily? When you can? I happen to know our local vets need all the help they can get. They're a husband and wife team and they're well known and respected in town, but they're getting older and their hands are full.'

Tim's narrowed eyes probed hers, as though searching for any kind of bending of the truth or manipulation. Finally, he sat back in his chair. 'I'll see.'

And she knew that was as good as she'd get for today, but it was a start.

JESS ARRIVED home to find a package shoved into their roadside mailbox. She screwed up her nose as she tried to pull it out. It must have been a struggle for the postie to get it in there. Surely they could have left a collection card? She would have happily picked up the parcel from the post office on the way home from work.

She glanced at the address. A knife stabbed her heart. The parcel was for Toby. Toby's mail had been re-directed to the lawyer in charge of his estate, so how had this one arrived here? She tried to read the postmark but couldn't. Flipping the parcel over, she saw that it had come from someone by the name of Rod Green in Kamira Creek.

Should she open it? Her heart wrestled with the idea, but finally curiosity won out. She took it into Toby's room and sat down on his bed. She missed him so deeply it hurt. Holding the package to her heart, she glanced around the walls and felt his presence here. There was a poster of the cross and the sun fading behind it with the words, 'He gave His life for me. I give mine to Him.'

Toby had lived those words. Jess had always expected God to use Toby in mighty ways. Sometimes she really couldn't understand God.

Sitting the parcel down, she worked her fingers under the seal, pulling, her heart beating harder as the parcel opened. She picked it up and buried her face in it, drinking in the smell of her brother.

'Oh, Toby.' Her tears soaked the jacket. 'I wish you were here.'

If only she could talk to him. She longed to tell him everything; so much had happened. What would he advise about Pierce's proposal? They'd been best friends after all. One thing she did know, he wouldn't be happy that she'd held off giving a definitive answer. She needed to talk to Pierce, to put an end to his hope. It felt cruel, but it was also cruel to leave him wondering.

She put the jacket down and reached into the packet for the slip of paper she saw there. Slowly she began to read.

Hey Tobes my man, I still have your jacket from that day you loaned it to me at the footy. Figured you should have it back, but I haven't been able to contact you. Have you changed your phone number and email address? I've also included the receipts from your last donations to the cause. Thanks so much! Rod.

Jess drew in a breath. Rod, whoever he was, clearly didn't know Toby had died. He mentioned the footy. This must be one of the friends Toby had made at Uni when he played football there. Toby had done a few years study before returning home to the farm.

She glanced at the receipts and her eyes widened. Toby had given a lot to 'the cause' as Rod had called it. And it appeared this cause was called 'Kamira Creek Project'.

What was that? She'd never heard of it. There was an email address and bank account details, but no information about this project Toby had been supporting. Taking out her phone, she searched the name.

Up came an image of a beautiful, country-style home and a farm. Below them was a photo of the accommodation quarters.

'A place to belong' was the caption. She read further.

'Kamira Creek project is a government funded venture which aims to provide a place of belonging and hope for young adults leaving the foster care system. Located on the Cairn family farm in the beautiful community of Kamira Creek, guests are given a place to develop skills, relationships and a sense of purpose before venturing into the adult world. We aim to provide the home and foundation these young adults have missed as children through no fault of their own.'

Jess's eyes widened. Wow. What a great initiative. But why had Toby chosen this one? She read on, caught by the image of a teen girl wearing a wistful, hopeful expression.

'My name is Courtney and this is my story. I never knew my father and my mother died of a drug overdose when I was a toddler. I never felt I belonged anywhere and I started shoplifting and getting into drugs and alcohol. When I came to Kamira Creek, I was angry and confused at first, but the people running the program really cared about me. They have a strong faith in God and I started to believe, too. Now I know that God loves me and I feel like I have a real family. I have always dreamed of being a teacher and I have just been accepted into Uni to study teaching. I wish every foster child could come to Kamira Creek.'

Now Jess understood. Toby's heart had always been for the suffering; for those who struggled or needed help.

She clicked on a tab at the top of the screen labelled 'Needs'.

Finances for the project were the main need. It appeared the project was expanding to a place by the name of 'Kangon Hill' where another home would be set up. It was near a large town and closer to the city for those who were interested in learning skills other than shearing and farming. This meant there was also need for new staff. She glanced down the list of employment opportunities. No Physio or O.T. listed, but 'social worker' was there. Her qualifications could cover that. Her heart pounded. Could she keep Toby alive by putting not just finances into this project, but her whole self?

No, she had enough work to do here. She couldn't let Lauren down.

In the meantime, she needed to write to Rod Green and let him know about Toby's passing. She sighed. Telling people was the worst job in the world. She'd do it later. But in the meantime, she would take up the cause where Toby left off. Donating to the Kamira Creek Project felt like such a noble cause and would honour Toby's heart.

She logged into her bank account. How much? Toby had given more than she felt able to give at this point, but once Toby's estate was cleared, she would have plenty to give. Maybe just a small amount to begin with.

She entered in the details and moved her finger over the 'confirm' button. Before she could, a notice flashed up on the screen.

Site maintenance in progress. We apologise for any inconvenience.

What? Now? With no warning? Frustration filled her, but there was nothing she could do. She logged out and rubbed her eyes.

The front door opened and with a sigh, Jess came to see who it was.

Pierce stood just inside the door, his eyes questioning. She still hadn't given him a definitive answer. It was cruel to leave him hanging this way, but now she knew for sure. She wanted to be free to pursue her dreams. To be free to make a choice to leave Lauren's practice one day. To give heart and soul to a ministry like the Kamira Creek project if she wanted to. Pierce was steady and loyal, but he would never understand her giving money away. He was all about saving. His father's recklessness had driven him to be the opposite. Tech support made a lot of money and Pierce invested it well.

'Jess?'

She came to him, sadness pulling her mouth down. She had to tell him; to get this over with.

'Pierce, you are so loyal, so dependable, such a good friend, but I can't marry you. I love you, but not that way. You deserve someone who will adore you; someone who needs you.'

Pierce blinked and his mouth twitched, but he didn't look surprised. He nodded.

'I understand.'

Hope surged. 'Do you? Really?'

'I do. You need time to heal. Toby's death hit all of us hard. Thinking about a wedding would be way too much right now.'

Hear heart sank. He didn't get it. 'Don't wait for me, Pierce,' she begged. 'I'm not the one for you.'

He came closer. 'It's time you did something for *you*, Jess. Stop looking out for other people and care about your own needs for a change.'

That was what she was doing, wasn't it? Did she need to be hurtful to get her message through? She couldn't do it. Wouldn't.

Her eyes slid shut. 'Pierce. Please. I'm not the one for you.'

His hand slid down her cheek and her eyes flew open. What was he doing? He wouldn't try to kiss her would he?

'Please don't touch me.' Her voice shook. 'I need space.'

As always, like the respectful, caring person he was, he stepped back with a nod. 'That's okay. I understand.'

But he didn't.

He walked out the door, then looked back. 'I'll be praying for you Jess. Always.'

Jess watched until he was out of sight, then sank into a chair at the table. 'Oh God, help Pierce understand. Please.'

CHAPTER FOURTEEN

Jess had not slept well and the day at work had been long. She couldn't stop thinking about the project at Kangon Hill. It would be nice to escape, to disappear for a while and find what her heart dreamed of. Was she really supposed to be a physiotherapist here in this town all her life? The thought alone made her feel trapped. She wanted to believe God had something bigger and more exciting for her to do.

She drove home in a daze, but her senses went into high alert as she came up the drive. An unfamiliar car was parked outside the house and someone sat on the front step. Who or what was he waiting for?

She studied the stranger as she approached, searching for anything that should make her wary. Instead she found herself looking into the face of a pleasant looking young man. His dark hair was neatly cut and his clothes were stylish. Salesman, was her first thought, but salespeople never came out to the farm. She guessed him to be close to her age.

'Hello,' he greeted her with an open, confident smile. 'No one was home so I thought I'd wait. I'm Tanner Elliott. I went to Uni with Toby. We were good mates, but then I moved overseas and lost touch. I'm hoping to catch up with him.'

Jess's heart plummeted and she looked out to the hills, searching for something to hold onto.

God?

Obviously another friend from Toby's past hadn't heard the news.

She licked dry lips, forcing herself to meet his direct gaze. 'He's not here. You didn't hear about the train accident?'

She'd learned how to do this. You didn't just blurt out that your brother was dead, especially not to friends or loved ones. You gently revealed the information, step by step.

'I know about it from the news, yes.'

'Toby was on that train.' She watched Tanner's expression carefully and saw the moment understanding came.

'He's ...'

'He died.'

Tanner's eyes widened and he drew in a sharp breath. His eyes slid shut and she watched him turn away in distress, heart breaking for him. 'Toby Cardelle? Are you sure?'

Jess nodded. 'He's my brother. I saw ... yes, I'm sure.'

Tanner lowered himself onto the step as though the news was too much for him to bear. 'Tell me what happened,' he said, voice catching.

Jess felt drawn to him. Here was a friend of Toby's who was also devastated by his loss. She had an immediate connection with him through his pain.

'He told us he had an appointment in the city that day. He didn't tell us what it was for. It was strange, really. He was a bit secretive about it and I've always wondered if it was a job interview. He seemed happy working with Dad on the farm, but ...' She shrugged. Why was she telling this stranger things she hadn't told anyone else?

'And he took the train?'

'He drove to the city, but must have taken the train to his appointment. Next thing, we get this phone call …' She cleared her throat. 'They needed one of us to identify him.'

Tanner shut his eyes and Jess stopped. No one should go through what she went through that day.

'And you're the one who went,' Tanner said, filling in the blanks.

'Yes. I'm the allied health professional in the family.'

'You offered to go?'

Jess bit her lip and found it trembling. 'I don't remember.'

'It was just presumed you would.'

She nodded. That's how it always was with her. People presumed. Of course they did, because they knew she would do whatever was needed. She was the level-headed one. The professional who was able to be calm and reasonable in all situations.

Only she hadn't been that day. She'd never told her parents how she'd sobbed over Toby's broken body, begged him to come back, begged God to bring the breath back into his lungs, even as she knew deep down in her heart that God wouldn't do it. He could, but he wouldn't.

And she'd never quite forgiven him for that.

'What about now?' Tanner asked quietly. 'I mean, are you all okay? Can I help financially or anything?'

Jess drew back. The young man rushed on. 'I know it might sound like a strange thing to say to you when you don't know me, but Toby and I were close, and well, he's the reason I'm in the secure financial position I am now. He helped me through Uni. He also encouraged me to love God by loving others and not claiming what I have as my own.'

She studied him guardedly. Who was this complete stranger who claimed to know Toby but whom Toby had never mentioned? But then, he'd never mentioned Rod Green and the Kamira Creek Project, either. As though hearing her thoughts, Tanner rushed on.

'He introduced me to a place by the name of Kamira Creek.

You might know it. Tobes and I have been giving money since the project began. I think it fitting that I withdraw my support there and help Toby's family after all the years of support Toby has given them. Besides, Kamira Creek is fully established now.'

Jess felt her guard falling away. This man shared Toby's heart and life in a way she hadn't been aware of. And it was telling that he still referred to Toby as though he were alive. It had taken her a while to speak of him in the past tense, too. And Sasha still slipped sometimes.

'I'm okay,' she said, 'All my family are.'

Tanner then held something out to her. 'I wanted to return this to Toby.'

What? Why were people returning Toby's things all of a sudden? She took the package from Tanner's hands and when she saw what was inside, she drew in a deep breath. Toby's sports watch. She'd given it to him for his 21st birthday.

'I borrowed it one night at footy training,' Tanner said. 'I was timing him with his single leg squats.' He shook his head. 'I've never seen anyone do them like Toby could.'

Jess studied Tanner. He was a lot slimmer than Toby had been. She couldn't imagine him playing football, but maybe he just went along for the friendship. It said a lot that he was the one timing the leg squats, not doing them.

'Thank you,' she managed, but it came out in a whisper.

'I can understand it's hard having this stuff of Toby's turn up,' Tanner said. 'I'm sorry if I've added to your pain.'

'No, no …' Jess drew in a deep breath. 'It's just … well, we haven't had access to a lot of Toby's things. It appears he didn't have a will but he'd pooled his assets with his fiancée. It's all a bit messy … and well, all the legal processes, it's been hard, that's all.'

'He had a fiancée?'

Tanner didn't know about Sasha? 'Yes. Sasha's well …' She hesitated. Why was she blurting out so much information to this guy? Yes, he was Toby's friend, but even then, it was as though a staying hand was touching her shoulder, reminding her to be careful of her words.

Tanner frowned. 'She doesn't like you?'

'No, no … It's more …' She stopped again.

And then Tanner reached his hand and touched her in that exact spot on her shoulder. 'Look, I understand. You don't know me, I didn't even know about Toby's death. But if you ever need to talk or ever need a friend, I'm here. And if Toby's fiancée needs to talk …'

She nodded, grateful. 'Thank you.' And then, before she could overthink it, she found herself blurting out, 'Sasha Leroy – Toby's fiancée – works at the local dry cleaners with her Aunt. You could get in contact with her there.'

Should she have said it? It wasn't like she'd given out Sasha's phone number or address, so it was okay, surely? And maybe it would help Sasha to see one of Toby's friends.

Tanner emanated confidence and empathy. She felt she could trust him. He studied her now as though he could read her every thought. It was unnerving in a way, but somehow reassuring, too.

'I'd like to meet the rest of your family,' he said, 'but I'm on my way through today and need to get going. I expect I'll be passing through again soon.'

'For work?'

'Yes. I work in IT in the city and was called out this way to set up a computer system for a company.'

He had? Why hadn't Pierce been called on? She supposed not all companies contracted locals.

Tanner's mouth turned down. 'I thought it was a great opportunity to spring a surprise visit on Toby. I should have guessed something was wrong when I couldn't get in touch with him.'

Jess felt his pain. 'I'm sorry.'

He nodded, looking away. Then he drew himself up and gave a half smile. 'Despite the sad circumstances, it's been good to meet you, Jessica.'

Jessica? She watched him walk toward his car, replaying the conversation in her mind. Had she told him her name? She must have, but she wouldn't have called herself Jessica. She tried to remember what she'd said about Sasha. Something niggled. What was it? Maybe she should call Sasha and let her know about Tanner. It was only fair. But right now she desperately needed some exercise.

And tomorrow was a very busy day. It might need to wait a couple of days.

MILLA CLIMBED out of the back of the car, a tight feeling in her chest. She was tired of not being able to see. Tired of feeling as though a major part of her was missing. The neurologist was pushing for her to see an OT. Seeing Jess as her own allied health professional was not something she'd ever dreamed would happen. To be one of those disabled people who sat in her big sister's waiting room, needing help with everyday life? How had it come to this? She wanted to weep, but held herself together.

Mum and Dad had been quiet the whole way home and she hated that they were feeling grief for her; at the loss of her eyesight and her strength.

Mum picked up a note from the table. 'Jess has gone for a walk.'

Dad glanced at the note, then kicked off his good shoes. 'I'm going to get changed and head out to check on that heifer who's ready to calve.'

Mum began clattering around in the kitchen, pulling out pots to cook dinner.

Milla's heart pounded. Her body ached but her mind was restless. She wanted to run. To visit Zac. To go out to check on the cow with Dad. Even to help Mum cook. But she couldn't. Her body had let her down. Instead, she fell onto the lounge. She was lonely and bored.

God, help me.

The door banged open and she smiled as a now deep, but familiar voice rang through the house. 'Mum? Milla? Anyone here?'

Zac.

Mum smiled. 'I'm here. Milla's on the lounge.'

'Thanks. Oh, and Buck is coming over for dinner too if that's okay? Pierce has a work dinner to go to.'

'Great.'

Milla could hear the smile in Mum's voice and found herself smiling too. Having Buck and Zac over for dinner would liven the place up a bit.

'Here you are.'

Zac plopped down beside her and she turned sideways to see him better out of her unpatched eye. 'Here I am.'

He studied her, looking concerned. 'You're a bit pale.'

She nodded. 'I guess that's what happens when you stay inside all the time because you can't run or be active or do all the stuff you used to love.'

He was quiet and she tried to read his expression. Suddenly he pulled her up.

'What you need is sunshine. Come on, we're going to sit out the back and chat like old times. It's not good for you to be inside, moping.'

'Old times?' He sounded like an old man. She chuckled and allowed him to pull her outside and guide her down the steps. It frustrated her that she had to move so slowly to judge the depth of each step and not miss her footing. Zac settled on the step beside her, his presence comforting.

'Remember when my mother first left and we stayed with your family for a while?'

Milla remembered. As a little girl so much younger than her

siblings, she'd loved having another child her age around. Buck needed someone to care for Zac while he was at work and Mum offered to have the whole family stay. For a lonely little girl, having Zac to play with was exciting.

He tapped her shoe with his own. 'Your mum kept sending you to sit out here on the step because you were too noisy and kept running in the house.'

Milla screwed up her nose. 'I remember. And then you got into trouble for running too, and they decided there must have been something in the biscuits we'd eaten. Funny how they believed I was just hyped and naughty, but not you. You were the angel child.'

His lips curved up in a smile as he looked away. That smile did something to her heart. She was so grateful for the medication that allowed her to see it. She poked him. 'Wasn't fair, was it?'

'It was fair.'

'But we were both affected by the food and it was only me who got in trouble.'

He turned sideways to face her and his knee rested against her thigh. 'It wasn't the food.'

Unsettled by his skin touching hers, she moved slightly. 'How would you know?' She studied his face intently, seeing the half smile that twisted his lips and the wry humour in his eyes.

'I tried to go and sit with you, but your mum said I couldn't because you were in trouble. So, I figured the only way I could be with you was to get in trouble, too. I even put some toy cars in my pockets for us to play with when I got sent out here. Then I ran through the house and even kicked the wall for good measure.'

'No way!'

'It's true.'

'They wouldn't have been stupid enough to send us both to the back step.'

'No, but it worked, didn't it? They decided it was the food and let you come back inside and play again.'

Milla shook her head, unable to stop her grin. 'I don't know how you get away with so much.'

'It's because, as you said, I'm an angel. And I'm quiet. And responsible. And thoughtful—'

She let out a snort, then frowned. 'I've never understood why being loud is an issue.'

He threw back his head and laughed.

She poked him in the side. 'What?'

He pushed her hand away, his eyes sparkling. 'It's not so much the being loud as being so strong-willed and untameable.'

'I'm not strong-willed.'

He reached down and pulled at the tongue of his shoes. 'Does the word 'snuck' mean anything to you?'

She didn't answer as the memories flooded in. It was in year three. Mrs. Hemford was standing, looking over Zac's shoulder while he wrote his story. Zac was visibly tense. She picked up Zac's work and looked around the room.

'Who can tell me what is wrong with this sentence?' The whole class looked up, eyes and ears trained on their teacher. 'I heard a noise in the dark, so I snuck out to see what was happening.'

Sarah's hand shot up.

'Yes, Sarah?'

'The word is sneaked.'

The self-satisfied look on Sarah's face riled Milla. 'No it's not. It's snuck.'

Sarah's face turned a blotchy red and Mrs. Hemford's glared at Milla. Milla glared back, eyes narrowed. Nobody was allowed to pick on her Zac.

'Okay, Milla,' Mrs. Hemford said. 'Go and collect the dictionary from the shelf and find the word 'snuck' in there.'

With a toss of her head, Milla went to the shelf. Zac sat with head down, shoulders slumped. It heightened her determination. She slid the dictionary from the shelf and flipped through. Her heart raced as she went through the alphabet in her head. Where was 'snuck'? It had to be there.

It wasn't.

'Show me,' Mrs. Hemford said, but Milla couldn't give up that easily. She flipped back a page and glanced through. 'Sneak, sneaking, sneak thief ...' No 'sneaked.' So Mrs. Hemford wasn't right, either. Her heart breathed a sigh of relief.

'Sneaked isn't in here, Mrs. Hemford,' she said loud enough for the class to hear.

Mrs. Hemford's brow wrinkled as she took the dictionary from Milla's fingers.

'Show me.'

Her frown deepened as she looked through. Then she turned to look at Milla. 'Snuck isn't in here either, but sneaked doesn't need to be in here,' she said, her voice hard, eyes unflinching. 'Grammatically, it is correct to add ed to a word to indicate past tense.'

Milla couldn't bring herself to back down. She knew she was right. She searched her mind for other examples, then let out a dramatic sigh, fell into her seat and said, 'Sorry, it must be because I *sleeped* very bad last night, Mrs. Hemford. I think it's because my room *stinked*.'

Mrs. Hemford's eyes narrowed. 'Sometimes I think you're just a bit too big for your boots, Miss Cardelle. You can join me on lunch duty today and pick up papers.'

It had been unjust, but Milla hadn't cared. She'd taken the attention away from Zac and made her point. Or at least she believed she had.

Zac poked her, jarring her out of the memories. 'Remember?'

She fluttered her eyelashes at him. 'Remember what?'

He laughed. 'It doesn't help to blink all innocently at me when you have a patch over one eye. I can't tell if you're blinking or winking.'

She crossed her arms, tilting her chin. 'I blinked and you know it.'

'No, you winked.'

She screwed up her nose. 'It's wunk, not winked.'

'Oh. Who would've thunk?'

Laughter bubbled up and Zac joined in as they sat on the back step, side by side, watching the sun sink over the hills, leaving streaks of colour that Milla could enjoy even with only one eye. He sat close, his skin brushing against hers and she tried to ignore the flutters in her heart. True, she wasn't able to run or keep active, but her mind felt more alive than it ever had before.

CHAPTER FIFTEEN

Jess hadn't told her family about Tanner's visit, but it played on her mind. Maybe she should have told them over dinner last night, but Milla's condition was foremost in everyone's minds and Tanner might not even return. But what if he did? And what if he went to see Sasha? It would be a shock. Maybe the right thing was to prepare Sasha first? She would go to see her this afternoon.

The first thing Jess noticed as she walked down the path to Sasha's front door after work was the open front door. Both the screen and wooden security doors were wide open. Strange. Jess hurried to the door and looked in. She gasped. The place was a mess! And there, sitting hunched on the floor, in the middle of it was Sasha.

'Sasha, what happened?'

Sasha looked up and in her eyes was an expression of such complete agony and defeat it shook Jess to the core. 'Someone went through and trashed the place.' Sasha's voice quavered. 'They took all my jewellery, the money I had in my room and my laptop.' She pointed to a place on the shelf and a sob broke free. 'They took the picture of Toby.'

Jess glanced to the shelf and frowned. Why would anyone take that picture except to hurt Sasha? She lowered herself to the floor beside Sasha and held her as she cried.

'I'm so sorry,' she whispered, and she meant it with all her heart.

'I've called the police,' Sasha said through tears. 'They said they'd be here soon.'

Jess stayed while the police asked questions and worked their way through Sasha's home. A back window was broken and the place was a mess but there was no real damage.

'Just a random break and enter,' the police suggested, but Jess wasn't so sure.

'What about the picture they took?'

'Probably just a coincidence, I don't think it's anything sinister,' the policeman said reassuringly. 'The thief may have grabbed it randomly, maybe thought it was valuable.'

Jess doubted it, but what other explanation was there? She and Sasha were left to clean up the glass from the broken back window.

'What now?' Jess tipped the final shards of glass into the bin. 'Do you want to come and stay with us?'

Sasha shook her head. 'I never thought I'd do it, Jess, but I think I'll go and live with Mum and Dad for a while. I just need some time. Some family.'

Jess nodded in understanding. Sasha's parents were in America which was why she came to live and work with her Aunt. She understood Sasha's need for family after all she'd been through.

'We'd miss you,' she told Sasha, giving her a hug. 'But if you go, I promise to keep in contact.' Suddenly she remembered why she'd come. But it wasn't even worth mentioning Tanner now, if Sasha would be moving.

Sasha rubbed a hand over her eyes. 'Jess, do you think you could send me the photos your family have of Toby? And the ones on his laptop, too?' Her chin quivered. 'I'm so scared of forgetting. Of waking up one day and not being able to picture his face. And now my laptop's gone … it had all my photos of him on it.'

Jess's heart went out to Sasha. 'Of course. I'll put them in a file for you.'

JESS STOOD at the entrance to Toby's room and drew in a deep breath. She was doing this for Sasha. She glanced at the pile of legal papers on Toby's desk and stifled a groan. His lack of a will made things so messy, especially when it became clear that Toby and Sasha had pooled all their assets in one account. And the house Sasha now lived in was in both their names too. Couldn't they have waited until they were married? Things would have been so much simpler. But no, neither of them had known this would happen any more than she had.

She pulled out the photobook Mum had put together for Toby when he'd left for Uni and opened it. Her heart jarred at the photo of them on a camping holiday with the Buckleys. Too many memories. She would scan them later. She'd gather the ones on Toby's laptop first.

Only his laptop wasn't there.

'Mum,' she called into the kitchen, 'have you seen Toby's laptop?'

Mum appeared at the door. 'There ...' she pointed to a spot on the desk, then stopped. 'That's where it usually is.'

Jess's heart hammered inside her. Who would take Toby's laptop? She rang her father on his mobile.

'Dad, have you got Toby's laptop?'

'No.' He was huffing. 'Hang on, I'll just put the phone down and close this gate.' She waited, then his heavy breathing came back on the phone. 'Isn't it on his desk?"

'No. And I can't see it anywhere in his room. I'll have a look around the house.'

'Okay, let me know how you go.'

'I will.' Jess hesitated. 'Dad, are you okay? You sound out of breath.'

He chuckled, but he sounded tired. 'Just getting old. I think it's time to get some more help around here.'

Jess's heart constricted. If only she could give up her job and help Dad on the farm like Toby had. 'Take it easy, Dad,' she said, then turned to her mother. 'Dad thought it was still on the shelf.'

'Let's look around the house.'

Milla tried to help in the search, but Jess could see her frustration. Poor Milla. Not being able to focus two eyes together made life so difficult.

Milla soon pulled out of the search, claiming dizziness. 'What do you think could have happened to it?' she asked.

Mum shook her head, her expression bewildered. 'I don't know what to think. First Sasha's laptop is stolen and now Toby's is missing. Maybe it's just coincidence.'

Jess doubted it but she didn't want to come across as being dramatic, so she kept quiet. Still, the suspicion there was a connection between the two computers going missing was unsettling. If they didn't come across Toby's laptop within the next few days, she would call the police.

Trying to put it out of her mind, she went to her laptop to sort through her own photos for Sasha.

By the time she had finished, her eyes streamed with tears. Memories were bittersweet. She'd had a good childhood. Loving Christian parents, a doting older brother and lovable little sister. Good family friends. If only change didn't have to come. If only the good moments could be held onto forever.

She went back into Toby's room to see if she could find any

printed photos she could scan for Sasha. She sifted through his filing cabinet and stopped at a photo envelope. She pulled it out. The first photo was of Toby with his football team. She flipped through, then stopped. There was a picture of someone wearing Toby's jacket. Rod Green? He had a goatee, a square jaw and a ring through one ear. Why did she feel as though this person in the photo was looking at her; as though he knew and understood her? Was it the fact that he wore Toby's jacket, or the fact that he'd been Toby's friend? He stared back at her, a wry smile twisting his lips and an air of confidence alluding to a strength she was drawn to. He looked like a rough diamond. The perfect person to manage the Kamira Creek Project.

CHAPTER SIXTEEN

Jess needed to forget about Toby and Sasha and concentrate on work. She tried to focus on the treatment plan she was writing up for Tim Bateman. He had agreed to sign a service agreement but would it be enough to motivate him? It was frustrating to watch a young, fit man throw away his chance of a normal life because of his pride. She needed to convince him to meet Ed Callum. If she could just get him to see the way Ed worked on his farm it would inspire him.

'Why would I want a fake foot?' Tim demanded when Jess tried to introduce the idea to him. 'The thought has always repulsed me, and nothing's changed now that I need one.'

'You're intelligent enough to see the advantages.' Jess worked to keep her voice calm and reasonable. 'I'm not going to spell them out for you.'

He gave her his leering smile. 'Do you think it might impress the girls if I walk again instead of sitting in this chair?'

'Is that what you live for? To impress girls?'

He chuckled. 'What do you think? Do I succeed?'

'With your sarcasm and wit? No.'

He studied her with his usual coldness. 'I can't say you have ever impressed me, either.'

'It's funny, I've never wanted to impress you.'

'Why? Because you know you could never meet my standards?'

She laughed without feeling. 'No. I don't want to meet your standards. I have no desire to be the kind of person who impresses you.'

He sat back, arms folded across his chest. 'And what kind of person is that?'

Jess averted her gaze. There was no reason to deliberately offend the man. She attempted to bring the conversation back. 'So, will you meet Ed Callum? I can call him now.'

Tim grunted but that wasn't a no. Jess picked up the phone. Tim didn't object even as she spoke to Ed and arranged a meeting. She'd take that as a win.

She put down the phone. 'Tuesday, ten a.m.' she told Tim. 'He wants to meet you at his farm. I will pick you up at—'

'I'll find my own way.' His dark eyes flashed.

'I'm happy to take you.'

'I said I'd find my own way. I'm not going to force the government to pay professional rates when all you'd be doing is driving me down country roads. As much as I'm sure you'd love to get paid for that, it's unethical. I'm surprised that a so-called professional like you would even suggest it.'

He tilted his head to study her and she shook her head and sighed.

'I'm happy for you to find your own way.' Maybe it was best that way. She wouldn't attend. Hopefully that would give Tim a chance to let his guard down and actually relate to the friendly Ed Callum.

TIM DESPISED the way his heart pounded as he wheeled himself toward the Callum's farmhouse. Having Bluey by his side was a comfort but still his hands were clammy. He hated that he couldn't drive himself and needed a taxi. There was no way he would have let Jess bring him. She would pick up on his emotion; the hope he hardly dared entertain.

A farmer came toward him, wearing an Akubra hat. It couldn't be Ed Callum. He walked with steady poise that could only belong to someone who was whole.

'I'm Tim Bateman here to see Ed Callum,' he said in a practiced dull, bored tone.

The man smiled, holding out his hand for Tim to shake. 'That's me. Pleased to meet you. Jess told me all about you.'

Tim was trying to think. This *was* Ed? His mistake made him defensive.

'I'm sure Jess told you all about me,' he muttered, sarcasm dripping from every word. 'She's the psychologist who knows everything.'

Ed raised one brow. 'Actually, she's extremely humble for who she is. She's about the brightest young woman I've ever met - and the nicest. She's got a special place in my heart, that Jess.'

He came behind Tim's chair and pushed it across the lawn without asking permission. 'Matter of fact, I think the whole town felt her pain when her brother was killed. I mean, we felt it for the whole family of course, but something about having our Jess suffer like that really got to us. Maybe that's why she cares so much about you - Toby being killed in that same train crash and all.'

Tim felt as though he'd received a punch to the stomach. Jess had a brother who had died in the train accident?

Ed didn't appear to notice Tim's shock. He kept up his chatter and pushed Tim toward the cattle yards.

Tim was still reeling when they stopped in front of a metal fence holding in several large bulls. He couldn't believe it. Jess had never let on about her brother. Maybe he should feel sympathy, but instead he felt anger. As though in not telling him she held power over him.

'Jess tells me you're a bright one yourself,' Ed said as they looked at the cows. 'I've heard being a vet takes a lot of study. You have to be smart and work hard to pass as a vet. I can understand you missing the farm animals. Never had time for the little household cats and dogs, myself. But I reckon you won't need to keep working with them. You might never tackle a bull and hold it down again, but you sure can run the paddocks and work on the quieter animals. I, myself, get the young lads to do the work that's above me. Reckon that's the secret, really. Knowing what you can and can't do. You'd be surprised how much people respect you for accepting your situation and making the best of what you have.'

Ed stopped at a gate and Tim watched as he steadily walked forward and opened it. Could he really walk again like this man some day? He listened and watched all morning as the friendly farmer revealed his life story and introduced Tim to his farm. For the first time, hope began to rise. He hated his missing foot, but he might not need to remain the helpless invalid he so despised.

Still, his heart and mind were in turmoil. Ed's revelations about Jess had rattled him. In fact, that she had a life apart from the one he imagined for her had never even occurred to him. He had put her in a box and suddenly she didn't fit anymore. Yet knowing her brother had been killed in the train disaster and she had never told him left him feeling betrayed and angry.

JESS'S HEART was heavy when she arrived at work the following day, but she managed to put that aside and force a bright smile as Tim came in the door. 'How did it go?'

He glowered and Jess's disappointment went deep. 'It was interesting. Quite a revelation,' was all he would say.

Jess tried to remain hopeful, but deep down she wondered if Tim would ever walk again; if he even wanted to.

As they worked through his exercises she became aware of the intense way he studied her. It was unsettling. She deliberately looked at his leg intently, working out how a prosthesis would fit.

'You'd probably need more surgery if you were to agree to —'

She stopped short at the way Tim's whole body jarred. 'What do you mean *more* surgery?' he spat. 'Is there nothing you didn't find out about me?'

Jess shook her head. 'Tim, anyone who has a limb missing has had surgery to clean up the stump. Don't you think I'd know that?'

Tim visibly relaxed, but Jess felt shaken. She would never understand this man.

'Is it such a bad thing for me to know about you?' she finally asked, her voice quiet.

It wasn't until the session was finished that Tim finally answered her question. Without thought she reached to push his chair out the door like she would any other patient, and he snapped.

'Don't help me! You know I need to develop my arm muscles.'

Jess stepped back, trying not to feel hurt. 'What's into you today, Tim?'

He spun his wheelchair around to face her. 'You are. You and your little secrets. You go on about me hiding things from you and all my stubborn pride, but you can't even happen to mention to me that you only feel sorry for me because your brother was killed in that same train crash.'

Jess drew back, swallowing painfully. How had he found out?

She managed to gain control of her emotions and answered calmly.

'Tim, that's a reason I *didn't* want to work with you – not the reason I *am*.'

'Then why are you, if it's not for your precious brother's memory?'

Jess stood taller, unfamiliar anger filling her. 'Don't talk to me about my brother, Tim. You didn't know him and I don't like your tone.'

Tim laughed scornfully. 'I can imagine he was like you. That he convinced himself in the goodness of a God who doesn't exist. That you imagine him up there now, flying with the angels, dancing on clouds or whatever it is people do in the afterlife.'

Jess stared at him, tears stinging her eyes and the back of her throat. Why was he saying these things?

'Let me tell you something, Jessica Cardelle, O.T., physio and psychologist. There is no God. There is no brother-dear waiting up there for you in heaven. I know, I know, you probably believe God needed him more than you do and so had to take him, but God doesn't need dead humans. God doesn't need you. God's as dead as your brother.'

The harsh, bitter crack of his voice left her head ringing, her heart horrified. Emotions raged as she processed his words.

Tim's eyes shot sparks and his face contorted in an ugly sneer.

Before she could think what she was doing, Jess's hand came out. She heard the resounding slap as it met the flesh of Tim's cheek. His head flew to the side under the force of it. Surprise and shock entered his eyes. She stared at him, trying to understand what had just happened. She felt the sting on the palm of her hand. Saw the white outline of her hand on his cheek before it turned into an angry red mark, displaying each finger outline on his face.

God, what have I done?

One tear slipped out, then another. She had never slapped anyone before in her life, let alone a patient.

She tried to speak, choked on the words, then tried again as he sat frozen, staring at her.

'I'll understand if you sue me,' she finally managed to whisper. She moved to her desk, not knowing what else to say, what to do. Confusion and disbelief swirled, making her nauseous. She slumped into her desk chair, head in her hands, waiting for him to say something.

He didn't. He wheeled his way out the door, without a word. She'd never see him again. Except maybe in court.

CHAPTER SEVENTEEN

'Mum, I've done something terrible.'

Mum looked up from the kitchen bench where she was preparing dinner. Jess burst into tears.

Mum raced over and led Jess to the table, pulling out a chair. 'I'm sure it's okay, Jess. Nothing is that bad.'

'Oh Mum ...' Why couldn't she speak? How would Mum react? Jess was the calm, loving, kind, patient good-girl of the family. She couldn't believe what she'd done. She could be charged with assault, could lose her job, and the whole town would know about it. Such a fall from grace would never be forgotten.

'Talk to me,' Mum pleaded gently. 'You're worrying me. It takes a lot to rattle my Jess like this.'

Jess managed to draw in a broken, shuddering breath and force the words from her mouth. 'I have a patient whose been really getting to me, and I ... I assaulted him.'

'You *what*?'

'He was talking about Toby. I slapped him ...'

Understanding filled Mum's eyes. 'Is this that bitter man who was in the train accident?'

Jess nodded. Her mother's arms came around her and held her tight.

'God will work it out, Jess. He is your shelter and your rock.'

Was he? Right now everything felt so overwhelming and out of control. What did God do when one of his children fell so drastically? When someone who should know better did something that would ruin any witness they'd ever had for God?

'Mum, I really believed God brought him to me so I could introduce him to Jesus. Instead …' she choked on another sob.

'Jess, Jess, …' Mum gently moved a strand of hair from Jess's wet cheek. 'What if it wasn't your job?'

Wasn't her job? Of course it was. God entrusted his people with being a witness for him in the world. And look what she'd done.

Mum sighed. 'Jess, I wonder, what would it look like to entrust Tim's salvation to the Lord?'

Jess looked at Mum through eyes blurred with tears. What would it look like? A huge burden would be let go. She would be free from responsibility. Free from the consequences of this terrible mistake. But did she deserve to be?

A knock came at the door and Jess drew in sharp breath. That was probably Tim's lawyers or the police now.

Mum opened the door and an unfamiliar, deep voice greeted her. Jess forced herself to wipe away her tears and look up. The man standing there was not a lawyer. Something about him was familiar. He appeared to be around her own age and had a square, determined jaw and an earring in one ear. He wore jeans and an uncollared shirt. Jess would have found his tough look intimidating were it not for the kindness in those eyes.

'Mrs. Cardelle?' He held out a hand for her to shake. 'I've come to see Toby.'

Mum's face paled and Jess wondered when it would stop happening. When would the world finally know about Toby Cardelle so their pain could ease?

'And you are?'

At Mum's tentative question, the stranger's face fell. 'It's true then? Is that why his support for our project stopped?'

That's when Jess knew. This was Rod Green. The man who ran the Kangon Hill home for teenagers.

'I'm afraid it's true,' Mum said, opening the door to allow him in. 'But I'd like to know who you are.'

A sheepish look came over his face. 'Oh, I'm so sorry. I'm Rod Green. I'm the manager of a government project run by a group of Christians. The Kamira Creek and Kangon Hill projects. We provide a home and rehabilitation for young people off the streets or out of detention centres. Toby used to support us financially.'

Mum took a deep breath then invited Rod in to sit down. Jess studied him carefully. There was something very appealing about him. In fact, she could imagine working with him some day.

'I didn't believe it at first,' Rod said, shaking his head as he sat down and rested his elbows on the table. 'But then I pieced things together. The way his support stopped, the way he suddenly disappeared from our lives. I kept trying to ring him but the phone was disconnected, so I thought I'd try his old address – here.'

Rod suddenly leaned forward in his chair. 'So do they know where he is? Has he been caught?'

Jess and Mum jarred at the same time and stared at Rod. What was he talking about?

Rod licked suddenly dry lips, seeming to sense some mistake had been made.

Jess took charge, putting her worries about Tim aside. 'Rod, I don't know what you're talking about, but Toby was killed in that train accident ...'

Rod's face paled and Jess felt sorry for him. Slowly he stood and paced the floor for a few minutes before turning back to them. Confused, Jess watched him. Nothing was making sense.

'I guess I owe you an explanation,' he said.

Mum smiled kindly at him. 'Sit down.'

Rod sat down and leaned forward.

'We had some money go missing from Kangon Hill.' He rubbed at the knees of his jeans, appearing uncomfortable. 'There were some witnesses who saw a couple of men leaving the property. One of them was described as ... well, I would have had no doubts it was Toby from the description, though I didn't think it made any sense. He was wearing Toby's sports jacket. Then a drug crop was found near our old property ...' he rolled his eyes. 'Not the first time. Anyway, this time a wallet was found, and in it was a bank card with Toby's name on it.'

Jess's throat tightened. Why would someone use Toby like that?

Rod gave a helpless shrug. 'The police told me they were looking into it and I just presumed ...'

Mum nodded. 'I can see why, but I can assure you Toby was not the one and if the police look into it properly they will soon work that out.'

Jess frowned. 'How could you have thought it was Toby? I thought you knew him. You were his friend.'

Rod flushed, his eyes darting away as though searching for an escape. 'I, well, it's just not the first time I've been fooled by someone pretending to be a Christian.'

'But Toby? If you really knew him ...'

Rod held up a hand. 'I know. I'm sorry. I don't know what I was thinking.' He cleared his throat and shook his head. 'And I am deeply sorry for your loss. Tobes was a great mate and a great supporter of our cause. I can't believe I've gone and put my foot in it like this.' He let out a shaky breath. 'I still can't quite believe he's dead. I'm relieved he isn't a con, but at the same time I'm devastated by his passing.'

Mum placed a hand on his shoulder. 'It's okay. It really is. Can I get you a cup of tea or something?'

Rod stood, glancing around and shaking his head again. 'If you don't mind, I think I need to go. I … my head is full.'

Jess understood. It was true Rod Green had made a terrible mistake in misjudging Toby, but he wasn't the only one who made terrible mistakes.

'Feel free to come back any time,' Mum said as Rod dazedly headed for the door. He nodded as he walked through and let it bang behind him.

'Wait!' Jess called after him. He stopped, his brows questioning. Jess bit her lip. 'You say the person was wearing Toby's sports jacket. But you sent it back to Toby.'

Rod looked puzzled. 'I did?' His face cleared. 'That's right. He loaned it to me and I was going to post it back.'

'It arrived last week.'

Rod frowned again. 'It wasn't me who posted it.'

Jess studied him, looking for any signs he wasn't telling the truth. 'It had a note from you.'

He nodded, looking directly into her eyes. 'Yeah, I wrote a note. Maybe someone else found it and posted it for me. Anyway, I'm glad you got it. Especially now.'

Jess believed him.

He got into the four wheel drive he'd parked out the front. The rugged farm vehicle appeared tough and strong. Like him. He revved the engine and sped out the gate, leaving a trail of dust behind him.

Jess and her mother were left staring at one another. 'I don't know what to say or think,' Mum admitted, before going back to preparing dinner. Jess would have smiled had her heart not been so heavy. At least Mum had an escape, doing what she did best. She loved cooking for people.

BUCK, Pierce and Zac came for dinner and the family table was full again.

Mum told them about the afternoon's visitor.

'How could someone think Toby was a con?' Buck demanded, jabbing his fork into the air. 'Especially someone who supposedly knew him?'

Jess was glad Rod wasn't here to be on the receiving end of that fork.

'Maybe he didn't know him that well,' Zac said, eyeing his dad's fork. 'If they were just footy mates, they probably didn't spend that much time together.

Buck harumphed and Jess watched with relief as the fork went back into his dinner. 'They knew each other well enough that Toby supported their program. Why would you support a program and then turn on them?'

Jess looked at Dad. He would normally join in the discussion but tonight his eyes looked sad. Mum noticed too, and Jess saw the way she rested her hand on his arm. Dad smiled gratefully at her and put his own hand over the top of hers. Jess's heart warmed. There was security in the way her parents loved one another. They didn't always agree, but they respected each other. She couldn't imagine them ever losing control and slapping someone. Heart in turmoil, she looked down.

'What do you think, Jess?'

She looked up at Pierce's question. He looked expectant, completely missing her distress. She couldn't expect him to be a mind reader, but she wished he could see that she wanted to be left alone.

'I don't know what to think,' she admitted. To her surprise, Milla reached for her hand under the table and gave it a quick, comforting squeeze. Grateful, she looked into her sister's one, good eye. There was such understanding and sympathy there that Jess wanted to weep. She and Milla always got along, but they hadn't connected like this before. Not at this deep level. Milla had always been too busy. She never sat still or stopped bouncing long enough to hear and see what Jess was going through.

'I think we should pray,' Milla said. 'And wait to see what God says.'

All eyes shot to hers. It wasn't as though Milla hadn't prayed out loud before, but she never instigated a prayer time.

Zac grinned at her, then around the table. 'I agree.'

Jess's heart pounded. She knew what she needed to do, but she hated to do it. 'Um, I need your prayers too.'

All eyes turned to her and she felt the shame and humiliation fill her again. 'I'm in trouble at work.'

Eyebrows raised, but Mum stepped in. 'No details need to be given right now, but let's just pray that God leads Jess, that his grace and forgiveness reign and that he turns what seems like a devastating situation around for good because Jess knows and loves him.'

Jess looked at Mum. Was she so ashamed of her daughter that she couldn't allow the truth to be told? No, she saw in Mum's eyes that she was protecting her. Thank God for Mum's wisdom.

As each person prayed, Jess tried to keep her mind focused. She was too weary and heart sick to pray aloud, and once more she felt Milla's hand on hers, warm and comforting. How had this happened? How had her younger sister who was now so sick, become the comforter; her strength and support? The world had turned upside down and she couldn't find her bearings.

MILLA LAY in bed trying to focus her eyes.

'Please God, please. I just want to see.' She squinted, trying to force the curtain rail back to its rightful position, but it stubbornly remained where it was. She looked to the cornices of her room. They criss-crossed, then jumped out of view. It appeared God wasn't performing a miracle for her tonight. She closed one eye and everything went back to its rightful position.

Something was very wrong with Jess. She'd seen it tonight. She'd seen the way Pierce studied her hopefully, waiting to catch her attention, but Jess had been completely unaware. She was not her usual, astute self. It was almost as though she weren't even there. It was unsettling. Jess was the together one in their family; the one they'd all depended on when Toby died. Milla bit her lip, remembering how Jess had left for the city, reassuring them all she'd be okay, that she'd identify Toby's body then come home again. That she'd help them organise the funeral, that she'd cover the costs from her savings. Dad had tried to object, but she'd insisted. Afterall, she'd said, she lived at home which meant she had been able to save. Who knew that God hadn't wanted her to save for such a time as this?

Milla smiled at Jess's reference to the story of Esther. Milla had always wanted to be an Esther. A beautiful, brave young woman chosen to be queen. Jess had been the beautiful brave young woman that day. She'd left for the unknown, her calm, logical reasoning setting them all at ease. Now, Milla bit her lip, trying to remember what Jess had said when she got home. Had she been upset? Did she tell them what she'd seen? She couldn't remember. She'd been too busy trying to keep her own mind active, to distract herself from the loss and pain. And Jess had let her. Everyone had. They'd smiled indulgently at her, allowing her the freedom to be young and carefree and not take on the burden of grief and sorrow they all shared.

How selfish she'd been. How blind.

'Oh Lord, I'm sorry. I didn't see Jess's pain. I've just always let her be the strong, in control one. I didn't see it. I'm so sorry.'

The irony hit her. Now that she had lost her vision, she saw what she'd been too distracted and blind to see for years. Her family did need her.

'Lord, open my spiritual eyes. Open the eyes of my heart. Let me see other people. Let me see you.'

CHAPTER EIGHTEEN

Jess called in to work sick. Normally she pushed through, but this wasn't a normal kind of sick. She was heart sick. She didn't trust herself. What if she lost control again?

Lauren was surprisingly understanding when Jess told her what had happened.

'There were extenuating circumstances, Jess. I will support you in whatever way I can. I just need you to write up a detailed account of what happened and send it to me. But in the meantime, take the break you need.'

Grateful for Lauren's support, she emailed a report to Lauren. But no matter how supportive Lauren was, the law might not see it the same way. No matter how much they provoked you and verbally abused you, you couldn't slap patients. It was as simple as that.

A police officer knocked on their door later that evening. Jess's heart pounded, waiting with dread. Could she be arrested for assault? She supposed she could. It would be just like Tim to wait all this time to report her and leave her stewing.

But the officer wanted to speak to the whole family. Dad

invited him in and they all sat at the kitchen table, tense and waiting.

'Someone has been trying to access Toby's trust account,' the police officer said. 'The bank called his lawyer as the funds haven't been released yet.'

Jess winced. It was taking so long. She hadn't realised the fact that Toby hadn't written a will would make it so difficult. And then pooling his accounts with Sasha's on top of that …

'There has also been the matter of someone using Toby's identity. A property was broken into and a credit card with Toby's name on it was found at the scene.'

Just like Rod Green had told them. Something was going on – something more significant than they'd realised. Did the police know about the laptops?

'I don't know if you're aware, but Toby's fiancée's house was broken into and the laptop was stolen. And Toby's laptop that we kept here also appears to be missing.'

The policeman frowned at her. 'You reported it?'

She shook her head, feeling guilty. She should have gone with her gut instinct. Or God's prompting or whatever it was. She should have informed the police as soon as they couldn't find Toby's laptop.

'We need to know these things,' the policeman said, his tone reprimanding. 'Even if you don't think it's unusual, let us know. We'll do the sifting through the information, working out what is important and what isn't. That's our job.'

Everyone nodded, and the police officer's eyes softened. 'We don't believe you are in danger, but keep your eyes and ears open. And if you're concerned about anything – *anything* – don't hesitate to call us.'

Jess watched Dad show him out the door and prayed for protection. She hated that so much had changed. This place no longer felt like home and her reputation at work was most likely destroyed.

What if … she shook her head, stopping the thought in its track, but it came back. What if she lost her job? Could she work at Kangon Hill and work for Rod Green instead? What if this was God's plan all along? Was he forcing her into a ministry that would be so much more fulfilling than her current job? A ministry that was more than she'd ever dreamed? She had the skills to help the foster kids. She could help find them jobs, help them live more fulfilled lives.

She remembered the photo of Rod Green wearing Toby's jacket and went back into his room to find it. She studied the photo, and something stirred deep inside. Toby had shared Rod's heart for those young people. Working for Rod would be a way she could feel connected to Toby again, a way of keeping Toby's heart and dreams alive.

'Lord, is this your plan for me?'

Jess drew in a deep breath, then got out her laptop. Time to email Rod Green. She'd only offer financial support at this stage, then see what happened at work. Her fingers tapped across the keyboard.

I can't begin to imagine what it must have been like to find out like that how Toby died. I'm sorry if we weren't as understanding as we should have been. Toby was special and we miss him.

Understatement. She sighed.

I still remember the day both he and I committed our lives completely to God. We were teenagers and we realised we'd been living for ourselves, depending on our parents' faith. We prayed together and that spiritual connection was deep and special.

I still feel that connection, even though he's in heaven. And I want to take up supporting your program where he left off. Can you please let me know what I need to do to begin making regular donations?

She wouldn't mention working for him yet. She'd wait until Tim reported or sued her and then she'd have the direction from God she was waiting for.

CHAPTER NINETEEN

Jess went back to work. What else could she do? Tim hadn't taken action against her, but she was sure it was coming.

'We've been worried about you,' Lauren said, giving her a warm hug. 'Your patients have all been asking after you, missing you.'

Jess forced a bright smile and glanced down the list of names on her clipboard. Tim's name hadn't been removed yet and her heart pounded, flashing back to the image of his cheek glowing red with the outline of her fingers.

'This letter came,' Kelly said, handing over an envelope. Jess took it and smiled at the crossed out and forwarded addresses on the front. It appeared the sender had tried to send it to her family's road mailbox address and gotten it totally wrong. The faithful postie had dropped it here for her instead. It was addressed to 'The Cardelle Family.' The writing looked familiar and it only took a moment to realise who it was from. Rod Green. Was this the answer from God she'd been waiting for? She glanced at the date and stamp. He'd sent it before she'd sent her email. She tucked it behind her clipboard and headed into her office.

Settling into the chair at her desk, she glanced at her phone. When would she hear from Tim Bateman's lawyers? Or the police? She unclenched her hands, straightening her fingers, remembering the dread she'd felt when the police arrived at the door. She'd expected to be handcuffed and taken away, not to be told someone had stolen Toby's identity.

She still hadn't told Sasha about that. Should she? Sasha was safely in America with her parents. It surprised her to realise she hadn't missed Sasha. She felt disconnected – from people, from the world, from all that was happening. Her mental health training niggled at her in warning, but she pushed it away. She was a Christian. She had God and she was okay. She had faced grief head on and she'd also faced her worst fears of failure. Nothing could affect her anymore and it was easier that way.

She studied the envelope from Rod Green then slowly, carefully opened it. Afterall, she was part of the Cardelle family. Toby would have torn it open. He loved mail and ripped it open like it would disappear if he took too long to read what was inside. She smiled at the memory, then pulled out the letter from Rod.

She read it slowly.

> To Toby's family,
>
> I just want to say how sorry I am for your loss. I feel bad that I could have thought badly of Toby and ask you to please forgive me. I, and all my team are praying for your family. Thanks to Toby and other donors like him, we now have all the money we need to complete the building here at Kangon Hill. I hope you can find comfort in knowing that what Toby gave will continue to make a difference in young lives for years to come.
>
> With sincere sympathy,
> Rod

Attached was another brochure about the project. Jess noted they still needed a social worker. Should she do it? She was over-qualified, if anything.

'Is this where you want me, Lord?'

If Tim reported her and she lost her job, that would be her answer. That's if Rod would employ someone who had lost it and slapped a patient. Although, Rod had been Toby's friend so he might understand the grief and hurt behind it.

She put the letter away. Whatever Tim decided to do, there were options.

Despite knowing everything was in God's hands, Jess couldn't help feeling nervous every time her work phone rang. Tim's name was last on her list so she might as well go home early. She had booked him in for a two hour assessment just before that career-ending slap.

'Help that man, Lord,' she prayed. 'Because clearly I'm not the one to help him!'

JESS HEARD Tim before she saw him. She'd packed up her desk, and collected her phone and car keys. His wheelchair made its familiar sound as it came across the threshold to the waiting room. She froze.

'Jess won't be long,' Kelly said. Jess tried to think. Was this the showdown she'd been waiting for?

Courage, Jess. She straightened her shoulders and stepped into the waiting room.

She met his dark eyes before her gaze flew to his cheek. She hadn't truly expected the mark to still be there, but it was a relief to see it gone.

'Would you like to speak to me here or in my office?' she asked.

He frowned. 'Do you usually work with your patients out here?'

What?

He gave an impatient huff. 'I'm here for my appointment.'

Jess gaped at him. She tried to speak, but all that came out was a nonsensical stutter. Tim wheeled himself past her and into the room.

When Jess finally managed to make her legs work, she felt his eyes following her every move. She lowered herself into her office chair, then opened her mouth to speak. Tim cut her off.

'Don't apologise. That would mean I should apologise too and a man with my pride hates apologising.'

She blinked, cleared her throat. 'Tim, the protocol of my work demands an apology. Even though I was upset, I should never have done that. Whether or not I give an apology, the truth is I am more sorry than I could ever express to you, anyway.'

Tim frowned. 'I told you not to do that. Do you like making things difficult for me?'

Despite his clipped tone, Jess was surprised to see a spark of … amusement? … in his eyes.

'Then again, perhaps you did it on purpose,' he said. 'Perhaps you wanted to see me grovel. Well, I know you enough to understand that wasn't the professional Jess. It was something way more personal and I shouldn't have pushed you.' He shrugged. 'Is that close enough to an apology?'

Jess cleared her throat, tried to gather her thoughts. 'I thought … I thought you would report me … that my career was over.'

He gave a disgusted snort. 'I would never dream of ruining your career.' He looked over her shoulder, out the window. 'You're bright, you're normally extremely patient and you're good at what you do.'

Well, that was unexpected. 'Um … Thank you.'

He scowled. 'I have a sister who wasted the opportunity to be a physiotherapist out of choice. There's no way I'd take it away from anyone who's making the most of it.'

That Tim even had a sister was a revelation.

'Go on,' Tim barked. 'Ask me more. I know you want to.'

Jess felt a laugh bubble up inside, but held it in. 'Why not just tell me so I don't have to ask?'

'Her name's Clare. She's younger than me and she was stupid enough to let herself be brainwashed into giving up physiotherapy. Now she's just a housewife and who knows, she might even have a kid by now.'

Just a housewife? She should leave that comment alone. She really should.

She couldn't. 'Clare may be living a life better than any physiotherapist you know. There are more ways of helping people than being a physio.' The fact that he didn't know how many children his sister had spoke volumes.

Tim's angry eyes bore into hers. 'Don't try to defend her. I'm paying you a compliment.'

She chuckled. 'Are you? Or are you raging at your sister for not being who you want her to be?'

Tim crossed his arms, jaw set, and Jess knew she should back out gracefully before she undid the fragile truce between them. He was here. That was miracle enough for today. She directed him through his exercises, trying to focus and praying that someday he would agree to more surgery so he could walk once more.

She had expected him to ruin her job. There was relief, but also a sense of disappointment at the anticlimax. Deep in her heart she had been hoping God was requiring more of her – something special. She sat back.

'Hey, focus!' Tim tapped her arm 'I'm right here in front of you.'

'Sorry.' Jess forced herself to pay attention.

'When can you get me in for surgery?' At her blank look, Tim glared. 'For a prosthesis, remember?'

'Oh. I thought you didn't—'

'It doesn't matter what you thought. I want surgery. So long as it means I can work with animals again. I mean real animals. On a farm.'

Jess stood. How to tell him he wasn't ready without offending him? 'We're working towards having you at optimum strength first.'

'I'm there. I'm ready *now.*'

She sighed. 'Tim, you have to learn your limits. And accept that you have some.'

Tim let out a harsh laugh. 'I never have before. I don't see why I should, now. I'm not going to let myself be a disabled victim.'

And yet his bitterness made him so. Perhaps if he was a bit gentler on himself he wouldn't be so stubborn and angry.

Jess shook her head. 'I think you need to wake up every morning and let yourself be human. None of us are perfect. We all have weaknesses, make mistakes.'

'Ha. Is that what you do?'

He had her there. Maybe she needed to listen to herself. Deep down she understood him; understood the need to be extraordinary, to strive for perfection.

Tim crossed his arms over his chest. 'Look, all I'm saying is, if you promise me I can work with cattle and horses again, I will get a prosthesis.'

'I don't know if I can.'

'Try.'

Jess bit back a smile.

He glared at her, but his lips twitched. 'Don't look at me like that!'

'Like what?'

'Like you think I'm being unreasonable.'

Jess did smile then. He looked down into his lap, but not before she saw the way he bit his lip to stop his own smile. He knew he was being difficult. But was there a way to give him what he wanted? Could Dad let him help with some things on the farm until she was sure he could manage? Dad had enough livestock to keep any vet busy. She would speak to him about it.

CHAPTER TWENTY

Milla squinted as she ran her finger down the recipe. She needed to do something to distract herself. The eye patch was driving her crazy and it was too quiet in the house. Mum was out shopping, getting some extra groceries she needed because the Buckleys were coming for dinner.

Milla was tired of feeling useless so she would make a cake. Cooking was normally Mum's thing, but it was worth a try. She tried to focus on the ingredients list. Two eggs. She carefully took them from the fridge, then reached for the flour container. Her hand closed around empty air and she tried again, pleased when her fingers hit the hard surface of the container. Things that had once been so easy took twice as long. She'd never take eyesight for granted again.

The specialist had recommended she try going back to school and it terrified her. She was on a surgery waiting list. The neurologist believed taking her thymus gland out might make a difference to her condition. She would end up with a big scar down her chest, but if it helped …

Feeling for the edge of the mixing bowl, she cracked the egg against it. Some ran down the side, but most of it went in. With a smile, Milla took the other egg. 'Please God, make this cake work.'

She could feel his presence as she worked. Strange how losing her physical sight made her spiritual sight so much clearer. Sometimes God's presence was so strong she almost felt she could physically see him with her, supporting her, helping her.

Milla mixed in all the ingredients, then searched through the cupboard for a cake tin. Her hand knocked a pile of trays and they clattered to the floor. Rather than become frustrated as she once would have, she picked them up and carefully put them back in the cupboard. Maybe she could help by sorting the cupboards tomorrow. It would take her twice as long as it would take Mum, but she had the time and Mum didn't.

Once she'd greased the pan, she closed her hands around the bowl of mixture. As she did, she felt her strength drain away. Her legs trembled and her hands shook. She'd overdone it.

'Oh, Lord,' she whispered. 'I so badly wanted to cook this cake for everyone. Please, please, just help me lift this bowl.'

She wrapped her arm around it. No, it was simply too heavy. Then her eye rested on the measuring cup she'd used. She could dip it into the bowl and tip cupful by cupful into the pan. But how would she then lift the heavy pan into the oven?

She pulled out another pan. She could make a two-layer cake. With only half the mixture in each pan they would be much lighter. She knew the idea had come from God. 'Thank you!'

Finally she had the tin full. Several drops of mixture smeared the kitchen bench, but she didn't mind. Her cake was ready to bake.

Carefully, aware she could easily burn herself, she lit the oven and slid the cakes inside. Then she watched. One cake was rising nicely, but the other appeared sloppy and …

Her heart sank. 'Please God, please lift your fingers under there. Please make it rise. I need your help here.'

She knew God could do it, and today she believed he would.

She watched as minute by minute the cake evened out, the bubbles dissolved and it rose to a perfect height. She couldn't stop smiling. God was good.

The timer went off and she reached in with a skewer. They were cooked perfectly. She reached for the pot mitt, then put a hand either side of the pan. It took only moments to realise she couldn't lift it.

'God, you helped me get them in there. Please help me get them out.'

She tried again, but the tin slipped from her fingers, throwing her hand onto the wire rack above. She yelped as the heat burnt into her skin. Leaving the door open, she raced to the tap and flipped it on.

'God?' What was she going to do?

The back door opened. 'Milla?'

'Zac! Can you turn the oven off for me and take out the cakes?'

Zac raced to do as asked and tears of relief filled her eyes. Zac came to her side and looked at her hand. He was still in his soccer gear.

'Is it bad?' he asked.

'I can't tell. I can't see it properly, but it hurts.'

'Show me.' He took her hand and turned it over to look, then put it back under the water. 'It might blister.' He put an arm around her, and then stood that way beside her as the water ran over her burn. His presence soothed her aching heart.

'It's a good-looking cake,' he finally said, and she rested her head on his shoulder. 'Smells good, too.'

'Better than you,' she said with a smile, but then sobered. 'Thank you, Zac. You're a gift from God.'

Jess came in from work to see Zac and Milla standing at the kitchen sink, side by side. Milla's head rested against Zac's now broad shoulder. When had Zac grown up, become a man? Her heart lurched and she blinked hard. They looked like Mum and Dad standing there like that. Cosy. So completely comfortable with each other despite the fact that Milla had obviously burned her hand. Jess blinked again and went straight into big-sister, health professional mode.

She marched over in auto pilot, ready to assess the damage and make sure her little sister was properly cared for. 'Show me your hand.'

'It's fine, Jess,' Milla said as Zac stepped back and the moment between them was broken.

'How long ago did it happen?' Jess turned Milla's hand over and inspected the burn. It had to hurt. It was blistering already.

'Um … I don't know.' Milla looked uncomfortable as she glanced at Zac.

He grinned. 'About 15 minutes, I'd say.'

'That long?' Milla looked dazed.

'Time flies when you're …' Zac winked at her, letting the sentence hang.

She screwed up her pretty nose. 'Did you just wink at me?'

He grinned wider. 'No, I wunk.'

'Funny, aren't you.'

Jess looked between them. She felt like an intruder watching their world from the outside. The connection between them was real, deep, and beautiful. Why had she never seen it before? What was clear, was that she was not a part of it. It was as though they didn't even see her.

It confirmed she couldn't marry Pierce. Not now, not ever. She desperately wanted what it was she saw between Zac and Milla. What she saw between Mum and Dad. Maybe she wasn't pretty like Milla, but neither was Zac good-looking, in her opinion. His mouth was too wide, his ears too big. It wasn't about matching good-looking people together and allowing the rejects to settle for one another. It was about spiritual connection and love.

Something she didn't have with Pierce.

DINNER WAS loud as usual with Buck and Dad stirring one another and letting out uproarious laughs in turn. Jess tried to catch Pierce's eye.

Finally she said his name out loud. 'Pierce.' He looked up and she nodded toward the back door. 'Can I have a word with you?'

He nodded. 'Sure.'

Once out on the back step, his eyes focused questioningly on hers, she forced herself to speak.

'Pierce, I've prayed about it and thought about it a lot, and I … don't believe we should marry. Not even in the future. You're more like a brother to me. I've prayed and wrestled over it, but I just can't feel peace about it. I'm not ready to get married. To anyone. But you are, so I will be praying for the right person to come along. You will make an excellent husband. For the right girl.'

Pierce didn't speak for a good few minutes, just searched her eyes as though seeing her for the first time. Really seeing her. Then his shoulders slumped.

'I hear what you're saying. I don't know if I agree, but I understand.'

She'd hurt him. She could see that. 'Pierce, I'm sorry.'

He shook his head. 'Don't be sorry. I want you to be honest.'

'So are we okay? The last thing I want to do is ruin our friendship. I need a brother,' her voice caught, 'now more than ever.'

He nodded again and to her surprise, drew her into an embrace. 'It's going to be okay, sister.'

Unwanted tears stung her throat but she held them back. 'Thank you,' she managed to whisper. 'I love you, Pierce.'

He stepped back and smiled. 'You too.'

And she knew everything was going to be okay. She was free.

Yet still her heart was heavy. Work didn't satisfy her anymore. Her family didn't need her. Not really. She longed for something more than the life she had now. Maybe she should move away and start somewhere completely fresh like Sasha had done.

Sasha. She missed her. She glanced at the clock, wondering what time it would be in the US right now. She sent a quick text.

Sash, would love to talk. When's a good time?

The phone rang and with a laugh, Jess answered. 'That was quick!'

Sasha chuckled. 'You've been on my heart. I've wanted to call but didn't know when would be a good time.'

Jess smiled at the sound of Sasha's voice. She'd missed her. 'How have you been?'

'Good. You?'

Jess told her about Pierce, about her longing to do more for God. About Rod Green and his project. 'I've been praying, waiting for God's direction but I just don't know.'

'Why don't you try pushing some doors?' Sasha suggested.

'Not wait for God?'

'Jess, don't you think God sometimes wants us to make the choice we believe is right without him pushing us all the way?'

She'd never thought of it like that before. 'I don't know ...'

Sasha's voice went quiet. 'You know what? I think you're scared. You're scared of making mistakes, of not being perfect, of not being the person everyone expects you to be. Who does God want you to be? He knows we're human. He made us that way. He knows we can't be perfect.'

That's exactly what she'd been trying to tell Tim. Still, Jess wasn't sure. No, God didn't expect perfection, but neither did he want his children to be reckless. Where was the balance? And had she been listening to God, or had she been listening to other people's expectations her whole life?

She couldn't stop thinking about it as she tried to settle for sleep. She pictured Milla and Zac standing together at the sink. She pictured Mum and Dad laughing together with Buck. She pictured Pierce's acceptance of her refusal to marry him. Maybe, deep down, part of her had wanted him to cling to her, to plead with her, to declare he couldn't live without her and loved her desperately. Passionately. But no, she wasn't needed here.

'Maybe it's time to make a choice,' she said quietly into the dark. 'Maybe I am copping out by waiting for God to force me. If God makes the choice, I can blame him if something goes wrong. Instead, I should be committing everything I have to him. Offering it.'

'Okay, Lord,' she prayed. 'I offer back to you the skills you have given - this life you have given. I am going to work for you full time. Stop me if this is not what you want.'

She got up and turned on her laptop. She typed an email to Rod, letting him know her skills and that she was available for the program if they could use her. Then she pressed send and fell back into bed. She felt free. She was doing this for God because she loved him and wanted to please him. She would see what God truly wanted of her when she received the reply. Now all she needed to do was wait.

Dad was only just getting up when Jess prepared for work the next morning. He was usually up before the sun, out on the farm.

'You okay, Dad?'

He shot her a smile. 'Yeah. Just tired.'

Jess put a slice of bread in the toaster and studied him. 'I have something to ask you. You can say no if it won't work – absolutely no obligation.'

Dad grinned. 'When have I ever said yes just because you wanted me to?'

'Good point.' Dad wasn't like her, living to please every person on earth. And yet he was loved, respected, accepted. Nobody looked past Dad as though he wasn't even there. She took a deep breath. 'You know my patient, Tim Bateman?'

'The one who realised he deserved your slap?'

She blinked, then cleared her throat. 'Um, yes. Well, he's desperate to work on a farm. I wondered if you could use his help. He's a trained vet, but he's not very mobile yet. He needs a bit of … well, love.'

Dad chuckled. 'And a good kick up the backside, I think.'

'Dad!'

'What?'

She shook her head, biting back her smile. 'As far as I can tell he doesn't connect with his family. He's bitter and alone.'

'Ah,' Dad's eyes became understanding. 'He needs a father's love. That I can do.'

'I think he could be a help to you, too.'

Dad grinned. 'I'll make sure of it. Yep, send him out. Tell him I need him. Got a heifer about to calve that I'm worried about.'

Jess laughed. 'I'm not sure how quickly I can get him out here and he'd be in a wheelchair to start with.'

'I can push a wheelchair.'

'Or get him to build up his own muscles and do it himself?'

Dad shrugged. 'Whatever's needed. Sounds like he needs a father and I need a son. It's a match made in heaven, wouldn't you say?'

Jess screwed up her nose. 'I wouldn't say that to him. He's a bit … anti Christian.'

'Ah.' Dad nodded in understanding. 'Well, I'm not going to

pretend not to be a Christian, but I won't make it my goal to preach at him every spare moment either.'

Jess grinned. 'Thanks Dad.' Her father might be just the person Tim needed.

She arrived at work feeling lighter and even able to look forward to her day's work. 'But is this really where I belong?' she asked God. She looked down her list of patients. No, this wasn't it. Deep in her heart there was still that restlessness that had been there ever since Toby's death. Life was short. She wanted to make the most of every moment.

Tim wheeled himself into her office and she studied him. His leg muscles were much more defined than when he'd first come to see her. He was making progress.

'I have something I need to ask you,' she said hesitantly.

Tim just raised an eyebrow.

'My Dad needs help with his animals on the farm. Would you be willing to help him out?'

Tim's dark eyes pierced hers, probably searching for any charity there. She didn't blink. 'You'd be helping him, Tim. He's been on his own since Toby died and I can see he's wearing out. Buck, our neighbour, helps sometimes but apart from that he's on his own.'

'I'm not a replacement for your brother.'

She smiled at his harsh tone. 'That's for sure.'

He almost returned her smile, but stopped it at the last minute, making it more like a grimace.

'Please, Tim.'

'Alright. But I'll need to be out of this chair. When did you say I can be fitted for the prosthesis?'

Jess couldn't hold in her smile of joy. She'd once thought this man would be sitting in a wheelchair his whole life.

'I'm onto it. I'll send off a report today and get you booked in. But Dad also has a cow he's worried about. She's about to calve.

Would you mind if I took you out there to check her over with him?'

Tim shrugged. 'Can't hurt.'

CHAPTER TWENTY-ONE

Milla wanted to cry. She looked around the classroom, realising how much she'd missed when she had been able to see. The sounds, the smells, even the meaningful looks passing between other students, their body language and their tone. People didn't always mean what they said.

Most of her classmates were now cautious around her, unsure what to expect. She didn't know what to expect, either. She hated that some of them saw her as disabled. Maybe she was, but it was awful to know people were seeing her as a lesser person. Only Zac and Kirra treated her the same as they always had.

'I've been missing you at soccer,' Kirra told her. 'Riley is still being a … Riley.'

Milla smiled, knowing what Kirra had been going to say. 'That about sums him up.'

Kirra nodded. 'Want some help catching up on this work?'

Milla looked down at the page. Her mind was fuzzy, but she needed to do well academically. After all, she didn't have her physical prowess anymore. She needed to get good marks. If that were possible.

By the time the lunch bell rang, Milla couldn't keep going. It hurt her pride, but she turned to Zac who had sat beside her for history.

'Zac, I can't climb any more stairs today. My legs are too weak. And my arms …'

He looked at the way they shook and touched a hand to her arm. Then he packed up her pens and books, put her backpack over his shoulder and walked beside her to the office. He helped her sit down in the waiting area, then asked the admin staff to call her parents.

He sat down beside her to wait.

'I'm sorry, Zac,' she muttered, embarrassed.

He turned so she could look him full in the face. 'I'm not sorry, Mill. I hate that you have to go through this, but I love that I can finally do something for you.'

She swallowed, fighting tears. He meant it. And for the first time she realised that giving wasn't always better than receiving. Because in receiving, she was giving Zac a chance to give and allow him to be blessed the way she had been in all her years of giving. With a grateful smile, she let her head fall to his shoulder. He was strong, steady and reliable. And she loved him.

MUM ARRIVED to take her home.

'Dad's got a new helper,' she told Milla as they travelled. 'He's one of Jess's patients and he's a vet. He's in a wheelchair. It made me wonder, would a wheelchair help you?'

Milla couldn't help the little cry that escaped. How had it come to this?

God, please …!

'Just until your surgery,' Mum said, sensing her distress. 'Dr Treen is convinced the surgery will help you get back some semblance of your old life.'

She sighed. Dr Treen had also said that after surgery she would probably need monthly infusions of protein. She'd still need days in hospital and she'd never be able to fully see.

As they pulled up at the farm, Milla saw Dad and Jess standing beside a man in a wheelchair. Jess held out some crutches to him. He looked young. Maybe in his mid- twenties. When he stood and took the crutches, he towered over Jess. Milla could see that he was missing a foot.

She felt for the man. She knew how it felt to be disabled. Knew the frustration.

Dad smiled and waved them over as they got out of the car. 'Milla. Lydia. This is Tim Bateman. Tim, my wife and daughter.'

Tim looked over and gave a brief nod, curiosity lighting his dark eyes when he saw Milla with her eye patch.

'Milla has a condition called myasthenia gravis,' Jess explained. 'It causes muscle weakness and her eyes can't focus together.'

Tim's dark eyes met Milla's and she felt a brief connection. He understood.

'Take a seat if you like,' he said, indicating his wheelchair. 'I won't need it for a while.' He set the crutches under his arms and moved away.

Everything in Milla wanted to scream that no, she didn't need a wheelchair, but her legs trembled beneath her.

She fell into the wheelchair with a groan. 'I hate this!'

'I'm hearing you.'

She looked up. Tim's mouth was set in a grim line but there it was again. That connection.

'Where are you going?' she asked Dad.

'To that cow who's having trouble calving.'

Milla wanted to cry. She had once helped Dad with those kinds of things. She had been so involved. But here was this wheelchair. Maybe …

'Can I come?' She heard the desperate hope in her own voice. 'In the chair?'

Jess looked unsure. 'Well, I'm officially at work and–'

'Just push her,' Tim cut her off. 'I don't need you breathing down my neck every second. What's she going to do? Do wheelies in the paddock and scare the cows?'

Milla held her breath, but Jess's eyes sparkled and her lips twitched as she met Milla's gaze. 'Looks like I'm pushing you, Mill.'

What was that about? Jess was calm and logical, but she was also sensitive. So why did this man's aggression seem to amuse her? There was a kind of … fondness? … in her expression.

Milla enjoyed the trip to the paddocks. She hated that she couldn't run anymore, but Tim's slow pace on his crutches gave them time to talk.

Tim had been in the train accident, she learned. The same one Toby had been in. He clearly wasn't a Christian. She saw the dark looks he gave Dad whenever he talked about God and his creation. Dad wasn't deliberately adding them into his conversation. That was just Dad. God was so much a part of his everyday life that he wouldn't be Dad if he didn't talk about God.

Tim inspected the cow. He was confident and clearly in his element.

'The calf needs to come out now,' he told Dad. 'I can instruct you, but you'll need extra muscle power.'

'I'll help,' Jess said.

Tim gave her a skeptical glance that made Milla defensive. 'Jess is good at this! She's good at everything.'

Tim gave her a sideways look, one corner of his mouth tipping. 'Fine.'

He directed them through until a calf lay on the ground. Lifeless.

Milla hated this part. The stillness. The waiting. She held her own breath.

'Just give her a moment,' Tim said.

The mother sniffed her calf. Tim looked over at Dad. 'Help me kneel next to her.'

Dad helped lower him to the ground and Tim cleared the calf's mouth and nose. Then he picked up a stalk of grass and tickled the inside of the calf's nose. The calf let out a sneeze, made a coughing noise and began to breathe. Tim smiled in triumph and even Milla felt the impact of that smile. It lit his whole face and brought it to life the way he'd brought the calf to life.

Dad helped him up from the ground and Jess handed him his crutches.

'Thank you,' Dad said, his words heartfelt.

'You're welcome.'

Tim wanted to see more of the farm animals, but Jess suggested he wait for another day. He glared at her but didn't argue.

'So, any hope your condition will improve?' Tim asked Milla as they headed back to the house.

She sighed. 'No.'

'We're praying for a miracle, though,' Dad said.

Tim's head jerked to look at Dad and Milla saw that he wanted to make a biting remark. Whether it was politeness or something else, he held back.

'Do you see Jess too?' he asked Milla instead.

'I will. Once I have surgery, Jess will help me manage my days. I have to learn to pace my energy and be ready for relapses or crashes.'

'Ah, the helper and saviour of all,' Tim said, looking at Jess, but his tone held a barb. What was that about?

'What about you?' she asked.

He frowned. 'What do you mean? I can't grow back a foot.' At her shocked expression, his tone softened. 'I'll be going for surgery and getting a prosthetic.'

'Oh.' Milla studied him. She didn't know what to make of him. He spoke like he had class and he was nice-looking, but his words and expressions were harsh. There was a darkness to his eyes and he had such a closed expression that she wondered if even Dad could get through to him.

God, please help Tim Bateman. And don't let him hurt Jess.

He turned those dark eyes on her. 'I have a dog. Blue. He's a pet but he's more like a support dog. I'm needing a pet sitter while I'm in hospital. Would you be up to it? He's used to having someone with him most of the day - '

Jess frowned. 'An inside dog?'

Tim glared at Jess. 'He is.' He turned back to Milla. 'What do you think *Milla*?'

He said her name forcefully and she knew he was telling Jess to keep out of it. She smiled. She liked the thought of having a dog around. Company and entertainment. She looked at Dad.

He smiled. 'It's up to you.'

'I'd love to look after him.'

Tim chuckled, a dry, mirthless sound. 'He's more likely to look after you, but I think he'll like you.'

Wow. That was almost a compliment. Milla shot a wry smile at Jess whose mouth tilted in return. Poor Jess. Tim Bateman was clearly a difficult man to work with.

JESS ENJOYED HAVING Blue in the house as much as Milla did. He lay stretched out on the bed beside her as she flipped through her Bible. He pushed his nose into her hand and she laughed, stroking his silky ears.

'Pushy, aren't you?'

He grinned at her, tongue lolling. Tim must be missing him.

'Please let Tim walk again,' she prayed as she had done over and over since he'd left for hospital last week.

'God can easily do it, you know,' Sasha had reminded her on the phone earlier that evening. 'Remember all those miracles in the Bible? Several of them were healing lame men.'

So now Jess flipped through her Bible, searching for the stories. The first she came across was the man whose friends lowered him through the roof to get him to Jesus. Even if Tim had any friends willing to do that for him, he probably wouldn't let them. She pictured him yelling at them to put his stretcher down and smiled.

She read on. First Jesus forgave the man's sin, then as a sign of his forgiven sins, told him to get up and walk.

Jesus forgave the man's sin first. The truth hit Jess. Only Jesus could bring Tim to that point. She could help his physical restoration, but walking was temporary. God was the only one who could offer eternal, spiritual healing.

'Lord Jesus,' she prayed. 'You know what's most important. Help me see it too. Please heal Tim's heart and show him your love. And if you want to use me, I'm available.'

Yes, even if it meant she wasn't meant to work for Rod Green. Even if she was meant to stay here in Barrawi. She hadn't heard back from Rod, so maybe this was what God wanted her to do.

She thought of Tim in hospital. She needed to visit him – to show she cared for him as a person, not just as a patient. She would be the friend who brought him to Jesus, the real Saviour. It was worth a trip to the city where Toby had lost his life. She would avoid the trains – she wasn't ready to see the place of the crash. But with God's help, she would brave the hospital.

JESS WALKED through the hospital corridors, feeling sick inside. This was where Toby had first been brought – along with all the other victims. And yet it wasn't Toby. Just his body. Toby was in heaven.

She approached a nurse at the nurse's station. 'I'm looking for Tim Bateman.'

The nurse shuffled some papers. 'I'm sorry, but Tim doesn't want visitors.'

Jess's heart sank. She'd come all this way. She needed to see him. She changed tack.

'I'm his physiotherapist from back home. Jessica Cardelle.'

'Oh, sorry. I didn't realise.' The nurse looked up his file, then gave her directions to his room. A man with a food tray was leaving Tim's room as Jess arrived.

'Good luck,' he said, rolling his eyes.

Jess shook her head, smiling bemusedly. She could imagine what the poor staff were going through.

Tim glanced at Jess as she came through his door, then sat bolt upright.

'What do you think you're doing here?'

Jess should have expected his anger, but she realised now that she had hoped for at least a little bit of a welcome. She'd been dreaming.

'I wanted to see how you're doing.'

'You could have rung the hospital to find that out.' His normally neat hair was ruffled and he looked pale and tired.

She shrugged. 'Well, perhaps I missed you a bit, too. Though, now I don't know why.'

Her response seemed to shock him. She saw the anger drain from him as he lay back against the pillows. 'So this isn't a professional visit?'

'No, not really.'

'But you used that to get you in, didn't you.'

It wasn't a question. He was perceptive. 'What's so wrong with me coming to visit?'

He glared down at his bandaged leg, then at the cannula in his arm. Suddenly Jess understood. Tim despised his weakness. He hated anyone to see him vulnerable. That's why he'd cut off his family.

'Do your family know you're here?'

His eyes narrowed. 'No. And they don't need to know.'

'But would they want to know?'

'That's not your business.'

She sighed. 'It is in a way. As your O.T. I'm supposed to be helping you live a fulfilled life. Family connections are part of that.'

'Look, I can't afford to be a burden on my family, okay. They're fine. I'm fine.'

'Why do you think they'd see you as a burden?'

It seemed for a while that he wouldn't answer, then he sighed and ran a hand through his hair, ruffling it further.

'My father died when I was eight. I had siblings who needed caring for - a mother who was devastated. Someone needed to care for the family. I had to become a man from a very young age.' He shrugged. 'And now I'm the age when I should be a man and I'm only half of one. But they need to feel as though I'm still strong, still capable. I can't let them see me like this. When I can walk again, I might re-connect. But not yet.'

Jess wanted to remind him a foot wasn't half his body, but remained quiet. Tim had finally been vulnerable with her and she wasn't going to do anything to make him regret it. She spoke quietly, gently.

'I don't believe it's physical strength or ability that makes a man.'

His mouth tipped up on one side. 'But I don't have the things that you think make a man, either, do I?' He rubbed his eyes, lines creasing his forehead. 'Though why I should care what you think is driving me crazy. You come in here and I'm all embarrassed because I'm at my worst and for some reason I don't even understand, I want to impress you.'

Jess stared at him. Had he meant to say that out loud?

'I can't even impress myself,' he ground out in frustration, fists clenched. 'When I was a child I fought to be the man my family needed. Nothing I did was enough, but I was only a boy. Now I'm a man and it's still not enough. I couldn't even get my trapped leg from under that train seat. I need to be more. My family deserve more. But now I'm even less than I was back then.' He shrugged in defeat and turned to look out the window. Jess didn't know what to say.

He turned back to her and she saw the conflict written in his eyes. He cleared his throat. 'Go home, Jess. Please.'

Her heart broke, but she understood. He was drained and vulnerable. He needed his dignity. Slowly she stood. On impulse, she lifted his hand from where it lay on the crisp, white hospital sheet. Like she'd done to Toby's cold, lifeless hand after the accident. But Tim's hand was warm. Life still flowed through his veins. She traced the veins with her finger, realised what she was doing and froze. He stared at her.

'I'll see you soon, Tim.'

He grasped her hand with strength that surprised her. 'Back home,' he said.

She nodded. She would grant him the privacy he desired. But all the way home she prayed for him, pleaded with God to soften his heart and claim him as his child. He was hurting and she was only just beginning to catch a glimpse of all he'd been through.

CHAPTER TWENTY-TWO

Tim was grateful to be home in Barrawi after two months away. The time in the city for the fittings and trials of his new prosthesis and his rehabilitation had felt like years. Now he was home in the fresh country air, walking on two legs, and almost feeling alive again. His NDIS support worker took him out to collect Blue from the Cardelle's. He could hear Blue's excited barking before he even reached the front door of the farmhouse. Milla opened the door and Blue flew out, a streak of blue-grey. Tim braced himself as the dog launched at him.

'Bluey!' Milla yelled, racing out after him. She gasped, brow drawn with worry as Blue jumped high enough to lick Tim's face. 'You alright, Tim? I thought he was going to knock you over!'

Tim grinned, bending to hold off Blue's enthusiastic tongue. 'I'm fine.'

With a relieved laugh, Milla came to study him. 'Look at you standing all tall and strong. Wow! Welcome home.'

He couldn't help his pleased smile. 'Anyone else home?'

'No, sorry. Dad had to go and help Buck today. He'll be so glad to have you back, though. He's missed you.'

Likewise, but he'd never admit it. The truth was, he desperately wanted to see Charlie. He liked the man, although he'd been determined not to. He couldn't remember much of his own father, but Charlie was exactly as he imagined his father would be had he lived beyond his early thirties. His father had loved nature and Charlie's love of the land and animals were in the glow of his eyes as he talked about them.

He had to admit he'd missed Jess, too. His next big challenge would be seeing her for physio this afternoon. It could be awkward. She'd been different in the hospital. There'd been a vulnerability that made her more approachable. Less the professional merely doing her job and more someone who really cared. He hadn't meant to pour his heart out to her like that; was still surprised he had. He appreciated that she'd respected his request not to visit in hospital, but how would she react when he walked into her office?

Jess called Tim into her office as though he'd never been away. He didn't know whether to be annoyed or relieved at the anticlimax. He stood and walked in for the first time and she didn't even comment. Maybe he'd expected her to react with excitement and admiration the way Milla had. But this was Jess. Calm and composed.

He could handle that, but he had at least expected to feel some of the connection they'd had in the hospital. Instead, she was back to the woman with the professional composure that irritated him. She was warm and friendly, but there was that wall she put up. The one that said she was superior and that he was merely another patient. Something had happened in his heart when she'd held his hand in hospital. He hadn't realised how much he craved that kind of care and connection. But today she had emotionally cut him off. It felt as though she'd slapped him again.

'You're doing well,' she told him after inspecting his prosthesis and working through some movement exercises. 'Dad wondered if you would be up to coming out to see that calf you helped deliver. I think you're probably up to it.'

'Of course, I am,' he growled, put out with her.

She nodded, ignoring his tone. 'Let's do it then.'

CHARLIE'S FACE lit up with a huge smile when Tim stepped out of Jess's car at the farm.

'So good to see you, mate.' Charlie slapped him on the back. 'Want to come and see how the young calf is doing? Try out your new foot?'

Tim looked down at his new prosthetic. 'Sure.'

Bluey kept his nose to Tim's leg as they made their way across the paddocks, slow enough to allow for Tim's stilted walk.

The fresh air made Tim feel alive again.

'I'll never give up this land,' Charlie said, looking out at the hills. 'Unless God requires it of me, of course.'

Tim's body jarred. He bent subconsciously to rub at it his prosthesis. Why did Charlie always have to bring God into everything? Couldn't he respect that Tim didn't share his faith and never would? It was just another barrier that cut him off, disconnected him from people he so desperately wanted to connect with.

He scowled. 'God can't take it from you unless you let him.'

Charlie turned to study him. His eyes softened. 'Not only would I let him – I would offer it to him if I thought he wanted it.'

'Why?'

'Because he gave everything for me and there's nothing I wouldn't do for him.'

Tim grunted. He'd heard the whole cross story before. About God giving his only son to die for the sins of the people on earth. But it was overly dramatic and unnecessary. He, and most people, had never done anything drastic enough to cause the crucifixion of God. There had been occasional mistakes and wrong-doing of course, but all Tim's life he had strived to do good. To be a leader in his family, to help them be all they could be, to live his life as best he could and achieve as much as he possibly could. He had been a good example to his siblings and he was a vet. And yet, it hadn't worked out. Belief in God had taken away any real ambition his siblings had, and now he - well, he didn't even have a foot, let alone a position as a vet.

'Jess loves this spot,' Charlie said as they made their way slowly up a hill. He smiled at Tim. 'It's worth the view if you can manage it.'

Tim gritted his teeth. 'I can manage.' There was no way he would admit how much he was hurting.

Charlie studied him as though he knew and slowed his pace. When they reached the top of the hill, Tim looked around and drew in a deep breath. He knew why Jess loved coming here. The Cardelle's farmland spread out before them, divided into paddocks of livestock and crops. Canola stood out in a hi-lighter yellow against the green hills and purple Paterson's Curse interspersed with Capeweed. Even the weeds were beautiful. The land appeared vast, open and free.

'Jess usually goes for a walk up here after work. She says it's a good place to sort through the day and just talk to God.'

Tim said nothing, but familiar rage built up inside. He'd bet she did. She probably prayed for him. For magical healing. She probably thought he was now walking because of her prayers. Well, he was walking because he chose to. He'd made the choice, suffered the surgery, put in the hard work. She probably prayed she'd be able to convert him, too, would be patting herself on the back for making him share what he did in the hospital; probably thanked God that she was getting somewhere with poor, helpless Tim.

He could bet his sisters were praying for him, too. Why couldn't they see he had no need for some god up in the sky who did what he wanted when he wanted? Who cared nothing for children who needed their fathers, for young men who needed their limbs?

He would never believe in God any more than he believed in pink, fluffy unicorns and angels in the clouds.

JESS COULD TELL Tim was angry from the moment she spotted him coming back down the hill with her father. His dark, glowering expression, clenched fists and hunched shoulders made him look like a storm cloud ready to burst.

'Things okay?' she ventured as she drove him home.

He grunted.

'Things go okay with Dad?'

He shuffled in the seat. 'Quite revealing.'

What was that supposed to mean? Should she push him further? 'In what way?'

Tim spun to face her. 'Your dad's a Christian and lives this Jesus thing like it's the very air he breathes. And you believe exactly the same and you've never told me.'

She screwed up her nose. What was his issue? 'You knew. That's why you made it so clear you don't believe. And I'm not supposed to infiltrate my work with my personal beliefs. I don't proselytise.' They pulled up outside his flat and she turned to study him.

He glared, his intense eyes drilling into her. 'I bet you've made me your little salvation project. I bet that's why you put up with me. You think it pleases God and that you can brainwash me into believing what you do. All this good you do is not because you really care, Jessica Cardelle. It's because you're a try-hard like every other Christian who likes to think they know more than everyone else and that they can know God himself. It's pure arrogance and I don't need it – or you.'

Jess reeled back. The hatred in his eyes cut to her heart. 'Why are you being like this?'

'Because it's true, isn't it? Tell me I'm not right.'

She swallowed. She had hoped to help him believe, but she hadn't treated him like a project, had she? It was true that when he'd turned up for therapy this morning she'd been determined to put what had happened in hospital out of her mind. She needed to be professional. She had to put walls up; be composed, didn't she? That was her job.

'What? No defense? Nothing to say?'

She shook her head and looked way. Why was he being like this? One step forward, two steps back.

Oh God, I thought we were getting somewhere! But Lord, I entrust Tim's salvation to you. Completely. He's yours.

It was so hard to keep holding onto her professional façade when deep down her heart was involved. Whether it was because of Toby, or God, what she felt for Tim was personal.

'Well, I'm done,' Tim said, getting out of the car. Jess watched him, mind and heart in turmoil. What else was there to say?

Tim slammed his front door closed behind him and Jess drew in a deep breath. 'Oh God, it hurts too much. I don't know what to do.'

She drove home, tears falling unchecked down her cheeks. She'd tried so hard to be professional and genuinely caring at the same time. Clearly she'd failed.

CHAPTER TWENTY-THREE

J ess stopped at the mailbox on her way in the drive. She wiped her eyes. Maybe today there would be a letter from Rod Green. If not, maybe she should try contacting him again. She could at least ask if he received her previous email. Or maybe she should just up and go ...

She sat back in her car and shuffled through the letters. She stopped at one with a hospital logo. The hospital where she'd last seen Toby. Where Tim had just had surgery. With shaking hands, she opened it.

Jess read and re-read the letter. She had known Toby wanted to be an organ donor. They all had. That's why they had agreed with the doctors wishes to donate any of his organs if they were needed. It seemed they had been. This anonymous letter was from one of the recipients. Jess began reading parts of the letter aloud, trying to grasp the reality of it.

I'm sorry it's taken me so long to write to you. For a while I was too unwell. A kidney transplant is quite a

major operation. Then I just didn't feel able. Please under-
stand that I am grateful, but I struggle to accept that
such a big sacrifice was made for me.

Jess shook her head at the recipient's open confession.

I wonder why I'm here and others aren't - especially
your son, your brother, your husband or lover. I don't even
know what his life was like. I just know I still have mine,
but that often I wish I didn't. I've seen some awful things
and felt emotions I never knew I could feel. I wish I could
shut it all out, but something is eating at me, pushing me,
driving me to contact you. My injuries have changed my
life, but most of all, knowing I could have died has changed
me. I don't know if I'm making sense. I've been a strong
person all my life. Capable and independent and perhaps
even a little hard, but always in control. Now I just feel
helpless and angry. I don't want to hurt or offend you, but
sometimes I wonder if your lost loved one has the better
deal. I feel such huge pressure to live a life he would be
proud of, and yet, with my injuries both emotional and
physical, I don't know that I can live up to the mark. Some
days I wish there was someone here to tell me to keep
going when I so badly want to give up.

Tim's face came to Jess's mind. Tim had also given up after the
train accident. Did he need someone to tell him to keep going?
Should she really abandon him this way?

'Why now, Lord?' she asked God. She had been ready to move
on. To escape and find a new life and job. And then this letter.

There was no name - nothing to suggest who this person was. Just a letter from the hospital, sent through the organ donor organisation. This person obviously wanted to remain anonymous, and she could see why if they needed to bare their heart this way.

Jess let her head fall into her hands and prayed. She prayed for this person whose body now held Toby's kidney. She prayed for the person's soul, longing that they would come to a place where they were as spiritually safe and free as Toby had been. She also prayed for the stranger she'd dreamed of; the one with Toby's heart beating inside them. And she prayed for Tim and for wisdom and tolerance.

Then, with a prayerful and burdened heart she turned the car around and went back into town. Tim's eyes widened in surprise when he saw her at the door. Then he almost smirked.

'Come to apologise? I was right after all?'

She took a deep breath. He wasn't making this easy. 'In some ways, yes.'

The smirk grew.

She sighed. 'Look Tim, I find it hard being your therapist. I probably blurred the lines between personal and professional and for that I'm sorry. I do care. I really do. But I have this wrestle going on inside me. Every time I work with you I remember Toby. I try to shut myself off to the memories and maybe I do come across as arrogant, but really I'm just trying to find my bearings. I don't know, maybe it is better for you to work with Lauren, but if you're willing, I'm willing to give it another go. I'll try to be more ... open. And I'll be open about my faith if that's what you want.'

He barked out a laugh. 'No, it's not what I want. Keep your faith to yourself.'

Jess studied him. 'So, I'll see you in my office tomorrow?'

'If that's what you want.'

Was it? She didn't answer.

He watched her, silent, waiting. His silence wasn't going to draw her out this time. The silent combat raged, neither giving in. Finally, he crossed his arms, letting out a grunt.

'You don't even know what you really want, do you?'

She knew. She wanted to escape the office. To work on the land, in the wind, feeling alive, watching the miracle of growth, depending on God for the rain and the sunshine at the right time. Just like Tim wanted to be outdoors, rather than cooped up in a small veterinary office. But it was no good wishing for what you couldn't have. It appeared God wanted her here.

'I believe we can work together,' she finally said. 'I think we should give it another go.'

He gave a curt nod and shut the door in her face. Jess laughed quietly to herself. It was better than crying.

JESS WAS RELIEVED every time Tim turned up for therapy. Her apology had helped. She felt more free to be real and clearly he did, too.

Dad was delighted to have Tim working with him on the farm, too.

'He struggles with balance sometimes, but he never gives up,' Dad reported to Jess. 'He takes pride in every new achievement.'

Jess smiled at the pride she saw in Dad's eyes. She loved that he shared every triumph with as much enthusiasm as Tim. The connection between them was growing, and Tim seemed more tolerant of Dad's talk about God.

'He's been opening up more,' Dad said. 'And he's getting less angry and frustrated.'

'He doesn't look so dark and intimidating,' Milla added. 'His face is relaxing and he even has smile lines around his eyes now.'

Jess looked at her little sister in surprise. Milla was observant despite her vision issues. Her surgery date was coming up and the neurologist was going to trial her on a new medication. Jess was setting up a program for after the surgery, but she wondered if she would be around to take her little sister through it.

She still hadn't heard back from Rod Green, but she hoped God had a place for her at Kangon Hill. God could provide another Physio and O.T. for Barrawi. For Tim and her little sister. Although, she had to admit she'd like to see Tim's therapy through. He was much easier to work with now. More co-operative with less venom dripping from his tongue. In fact, Jess began to feel she could actually like the man. She felt she understood him. They had received another letter from the recipient of Toby's kidney. It revealed a little more of the person's heart. There was a lot of fear and helplessness there, but a slow acceptance of the situation. It helped her better understand and connect with Tim. He was going through the same thing as he came to terms with the loss of his foot and the need to use a prosthesis.

However, she had noticed a change in Tim these last few days. He had slowed down and was constantly rubbing the area of his stump. It was time to broach the subject with him. And she might as well come straight out with it. Tim seemed to appreciate direct.

'Tim, I think you're in pain but you haven't told me,' she said as he took a seat in her office.

He stared at her unblinkingly.

'I've looked at your stump and although I've tried to adjust the prosthesis for you, it's just not working.'

Tim's shoulders slumped. 'It's not as comfortable as it seemed at first,' he admitted.

'I think you need more surgery.'

To her surprise Tim shrugged. 'Okay.'

Jess smiled wide. She would begin the arrangements straight away. Tim would walk like an able-bodied man again soon. Now she just needed to keep praying for his spiritual walk. In that area he was still crippled and determined to remain so.

CHAPTER TWENTY-FOUR

It was the second anniversary of Toby's death and Milla hated the sombre mood in the house. During the first months after Toby's death, people remembered and brought comfort in any way they could. The house had been full of people, of meals, of flowers. But now everyone else had moved on. Lucky them. For her family, the pain never went away. Toby's room was still empty and his chair at the dinner table was still empty. She missed his voice, his presence. At least when he'd been away at Uni she could still talk to him on the phone, know he would come home again.

Feeling restless and lost, she closed her eyes and lay back on the lounge. It would be a quiet, painful Saturday morning. Dad was out in the paddocks and Jess was talking to Sasha on the phone. The family had sent Sasha flowers, knowing she'd be struggling today, too. Mum was in the kitchen baking a batch of biscuits and muttering to herself as she tried to decide whether to cook double quantity.

A knock came at the door. Milla sat up, and Mum dropped a cooking tray.

'Sash, I'd better go,' Jess said, and went to the door. She always did that, Milla realised. Always stepped in when others didn't feel able. Always sacrificed her own comfort for others.

'Tanner!' Jess said as though she recognised the person. Milla tried to see. Who was this guy? He stood there with a huge bunch of flowers in his hands. He handed them to Jess and stepped inside. 'I just knew how you'd be feeling today,' he said quietly. 'Because I'm feeling it, too.'

Mum left her cooking, eyes questioning, and Milla stood.

Jess looked around at them. 'Mum, Milla, this is Tanner. He was a friend of Toby's at Uni.'

Mum reached for the flowers, her eyes sheening with tears. 'Thank you, Tanner. Come in. I'll just find a vase.'

Tanner looked hesitant, then nodded. Jess led him into the lounge room. 'So you're Milla,' he said.

She nodded. He was nice looking. He studied her eye patch and she self-consciously reached up to touch it. 'I have a condition where my eyes can't focus together.'

'Sorry to hear,' he said as though he meant it. Then he looked to Jess. 'Sorry I haven't been in contact. Work took me the other direction for a while and I've only just now had a chance to come back.'

'Tanner works with an IT company,' Jess explained to the family. He dropped in about six months back.'

Milla studied Tanner. Why hadn't Jess told them? Tanner was good-looking, but there was something else about him. A kind of knowing intelligence. He looked at her now and she felt as though he knew what she was thinking. It was comforting but disconcerting, too. She watched him carefully and noticed that despite his friendly ease, he was observing, too. He seemed aware of every movement they made, studied every corner of the room, heard every ting of their phones as messages arrived. He appeared to have an extra depth perception that put her on edge.

And yet, Tanner was good company that afternoon. He seemed

to know that although Toby was being thought of, the family didn't really want to talk about him in detail. He was lively, but not too lively as he teased Jess about her social life.

'I would have thought a young woman like you would be out on the town every weekend,' he ribbed her gently.

'Young woman?' she laughed at him. 'I'm old now.'

'And what does that say about me?'

She tilted her head at him. 'I can't see you out on the town.'

'Not this weekend,' he agreed with a smile, 'but if I lived around here, I'd take you out every weekend.'

Milla wondered at the way her usually controlled sister blushed at the compliment. 'No you wouldn't. You'd find much more exciting, attractive young women to spend your time with.'

Tanner eyed her carefully. 'I think you're way too good at running yourself down, Jessica Cardelle. You and I both know you're a lot more interesting than most women out there.'

Milla shook her head, wondering what kind of conversation this was to be having on a day like this. But at least it was distracting them all from their sadness.

Tanner and Jess were still bantering when Buck, Pierce and Zac arrived. Milla saw the way they all shot looks at Tanner.

'This is Tanner,' Jess said. 'He was a friend of Toby's at Uni.'

'Really?' Pierce's gaze pinned Tanner. 'Toby didn't mention you.'

Tanner gazed steadily back. 'And you are?'

'Pierce. His best mate.'

Tanner frowned. 'He didn't mention you, either.'

Pierce narrowed his gaze and Milla glanced at Zac. What was going on here? Some kind of male testosterone battle?

'I don't talk a lot about my friendship with Toby,' Tanner said, looking around at the family, his intelligent eyes resting on Jess. 'And he was protecting me by not talking about me. He was helping me through a gambling addiction.' He looked down at his feet. 'It can be hard opening up a vulnerable part of yourself like that. Toby said he understood when I asked him to keep my situation confidential. I'm sorry if that made him keep something from you.'

Jess nodded as though she understood, but Milla wasn't sure she did. Was Tanner ashamed of his connection with Toby or was he hiding something more than a past gambling addiction?

What was Zac thinking? She turned her head so she could see him. He raised his eyebrows, then came to sit beside her.

'How are you doing?'

'Better than I expected,' she admitted. 'Having company helps.'

'Him?' He nodded his head toward Tanner.

She grinned and spoke quietly. 'Maybe for Jess, but I prefer you.'

His eyebrows shot higher. 'He's not right for Jess,' he mouthed into her ear. 'And what about Pierce?'

'What about him?'

Zac tugged at her hand. 'Let's talk outside.'

She allowed him to lead her to the back step, then carefully sat down.

'Who is that Tanner guy?' Zac asked the moment they shut the back door behind them. 'And why did he come here? Really?'

'I don't know. He's very … observant.'

'As in creepy? A perve?'

No, that wasn't it. But what? 'I don't know. He just sees and notices everything. Not in a creepy way.' She shrugged. 'I don't know. It's just a feeling I get.'

'You sure he hasn't got the hots for you? Or Jess?'

Milla laughed. 'I'm sure. He did flirt a bit with Jess, but …' She shrugged.

Zac bit his lip. 'If you ever feel uncomfortable with him, tell me?'

She smiled, appreciating his concern. 'I will. Then you can come riding over on your white steed and rescue me.'

He leaned an elbow on his knee and rested his chin in his hand, studying her. 'You know, I kind of like that idea.'

She screwed up her nose. 'I've needed rescuing a bit, lately. No more independent, capable Milla.'

'No, just brave, strong Milla who never gives up but who is smart enough to let others help when she knows she needs it.'

She blinked at him. 'You think that about me?'

He nodded and reached a hand to settle one of her curls behind her ear. His touch was gentle, his eyes tender. 'I do.'

She threw her arms around him. 'I love you, Zac.'

'I love you, too.' His arms came around her and she settled her cheek against his chest. She felt the beat of his heart against her ear. Tenderness filled her and a strange fluttering settled in her stomach. What would happen if she lifted her face? Would he kiss her? What was the right time for that kind of relationship? She didn't want to ruin this; didn't want to have her heart broken. Zac would never hurt her on purpose, but what if something came between them?

'Should we go back in?' Zac asked.

She nodded. 'And see if you can see what I mean about Tanner.'

'I will.'

He helped her up from the step and they came back into the loungeroom where Buck was setting up a game of cards.

'You two playing?' he asked.

Zac looked at her. 'You up to it?'

At her nod, they both sat down and joined the game. Milla was aware of Zac's watchful eyes on Tanner. She watched, too.

Dad and Buck started up a theological discussion about healing part way through. Typical.

'Jesus always healed when he was on earth,' Buck said. 'Anyone who came to him was healed. Jesus was so full of compassion it's like he couldn't help himself.'

'But what about the man at the pool in Bethesda?' Dad asked.

'It doesn't say Jesus healed everyone there. He singled out that one guy.'

'But what if the others had asked?'

'They probably did.'

Dad and Buck argued back and forth with Mum, Jess and Pierce throwing in their two cents worth every now and then.

'It doesn't say that.'

'Neither does it say he didn't.'

'He would have if they'd asked.'

'I've asked Jesus to heal me,' Milla inserted quietly. 'And he hasn't.'

All eyes turned to her, soft with compassion.

Jess reached over to touch her hand. 'I still believe he will.'

'I'm not so sure. I've learned a lot being like this. It's like my spiritual eyes are open now my physical eyes can't focus. Sometimes I almost feel like I can see Jesus right here with me.'

Dad's eyes widened and Milla saw the glisten of tears. She knew it was all he'd ever wanted for his children; for them to have a personal walk with God and understand the depth of his love for them.

'I want you to be healed too,' he said, his voice catching slightly. 'I pray for it often. But I also want God's will above our own.'

The table was quiet, then Tanner stood, clearing his throat and setting down his cards. 'Well guys, I'd better get going. Thanks for having me.'

Mum, Dad and Buck beamed at him and Dad shook his hand. 'It's been great having you. Come any time. Lydia loves visitors, don't you Lydie? There's always room at our table and enough food.'

Tanner tilted his chin. 'Thank you. I might take you up on that.'

Or he might not, Milla thought. He was clearly uncomfortable with the God-talk.

JESS SAT at the kitchen table re-reading the latest letter from the person they now referred to as 'Toby's friend.' The donor recipient's letters were becoming more revealing. As though the person felt they had nothing to lose. They claimed their social worker had encouraged them to write the letters. Jess supposed it must be easier to pour out your heart to people in a letter, but part of her began to worry about why they were doing it. Was the person dying?

> My family are the main reason I had the transplant,

she read.

> My brother was willing to give me his own kidney but there was no way I could let him go through that for me. It was my mother who convinced me to have the transplant. She reminded me that my siblings have already been through enough loss. And my youngest sister was only just recovering from depression, anxiety and an eating disorder. Mum even cried as she begged me to accept the transplant. She never cries. To this day I still don't know if she was manipulating me.

Jess needed air. She laced up her walking shoes and marched out the door. She needed to think and spend some time with God. She powerwalked her way to her favourite place on the hill, her mind clearing a little more each step she took. The kangaroos had made the hill their resting place, too, and eyed her suspiciously as she approached. Most hopped away, apart from one rather large male who stood to his full height and snorted.

Jess shook her head at him. 'I'm not scared of you. This is my place, so go away.'

The kangaroo made a growling sound in his chest, but moved down the hill toward the rest of the mob.

Jess walked on, her mind far away. This place was home and she loved it, but she still believed deep down that God had something more for her. She was almost at the bottom of the hill when her eye caught movement. That large male kangaroo again. It had reached its full height once more, chest puffed out, staring a challenge into her eyes. Jess chuckled and broke eye contact with it. She needed to get past, but perhaps if she didn't look at it, it wouldn't consider her a threat. She sensed, rather than saw it take a huge bound toward her.

She backed up, eyeing it warily. 'What are you doing?'

She realised too late. It came at her, its large powerful legs pounded her in the chest and knocked her to the ground. She tried to draw breath. Felt its large claws slice her forehead. Instinct took over and she rolled herself into a ball, gasping for breath. She had heard of kangaroos attacking before but never had it happened on her farm. She'd never dreamed it would happen to her.

She lay perfectly still, trying to breathe, knowing the kangaroo was still there, just watching and waiting, making occasional coughing, snorting sounds. Pain tore through her chest at every breath and her head felt as though an axe had sliced through it, but she was too scared to move.

She heard the thump of the kangaroo's powerful legs as it came at her again. She'd seen male kangaroos fight to the death. Seen the damage they could do to one another.

God, help me!

Her head was pounded into the ground and she moaned. Then came a bark and the sound of man yelling. The kangaroo bounded away and Jess dared look up.

Bluey was chasing the kangaroos, scattering them across the hill. And Tim was charging toward her, his face etched with worry. Relief filled her at the sight of him. From where she lay on the ground, he looked tall and strong despite his limp. The kangaroo buck obviously thought so too and disappeared over the hill. Jess tried to move but it hurt and a groan filled her throat. Tim fell to his knees beside her.

'It just came at me,' Jess said, trembling.

Tim nodded and reached for her forehead. Instinctively she moved back and he frowned.

'I need to stop the bleeding,' he said, reaching for her again, his every move business-like but gentle. He held his hand to her forehead and she winced.

'Sorry.' Gently, he turned her face to study the wound. 'You have a scratch down your cheek too, but it's not open like the forehead wound.'

Her head pounded and her eyes slid shut. 'Is it bad?'

'It will need stitches, but you'll be okay. Head wounds tend to bleed a lot.'

His low, confident tone and gentleness set her at ease. She opened her eyes to study him. His forehead crinkled in concentration, but he looked friendly. Competent and in control. In his element, even.

'Is this how you used to be?' she mumbled. 'When you were doctoring animals? Before you got so angry and frustrated?'

He almost smiled. 'It's how I still am, somewhere deep inside.' He picked up her left hand and moved it to her forehead. 'Hold your hand here. Put pressure on.'

She did so, watching as he used both arms to lift up his shirt and pull it over his head. Jess found her eyes fixed on his lithe, defined chest and she drew in a deep breath.

'Sorry, but I need it for the wound.' Tim explained, almost smiling as he went about ripping the shirt into strips.

But Jess's eyes were fixed on the scar that spanned one side of

Tim's bare abdomen and extended to his back. Tim had obviously forgotten about it as he focused on caring for her. She didn't know what to think; couldn't quite put it all together as she fought the pounding of her head and throbbing pain in her chest. Tim looked as though he had had a kidney transplant.

'How many brothers and sisters do you have?' she found herself asking in a voice not quite her own.

He chuckled. 'What kind of question is that at a time like this?' When she didn't respond, he shrugged. 'Two younger sisters and a younger brother.'

'What?' he asked with a friendly grin, catching her staring at his chest in a daze. 'Too spellbinding?'

Jess drew her eyes away. 'Yes,' she whispered. 'I mean, no ... I ...'

Chuckling again, he gently pulled her to her feet. 'Must've been a worse bump to the head than I thought,' he teased. 'No other woman has ever looked at me that way.'

Who was this man? This warm, confident, caring man? Jess groaned as a sharp pain knifed her ribs. Her hand flew to her side.

'It kicked you?' Tim asked, eyes shadowed with concern.

She nodded. 'I think so. Something has, anyway.'

'Here. Hold this for a minute.' He guided her hand until she held the strip of his shirt against the wound on her forehead. He heaved himself up from the ground and held out his hand to help her up.

She tried to hold herself up. Tried so hard. But her head was spinning and the pain in her ribs shot through her whole left side. She bit her lip to keep from crying out and managed to hold onto his arm.

'Looks like it's my turn to help you,' he said, his voice sounding far off. 'I'll carry you down the hill 'til I can get a signal on my phone.'

Jess's head jarred as she looked up at him in shock, trying to focus. 'I can walk.'

'You can't even get up without gasping in pain.'

'Then just leave me here and find a place with phone signal.'

He shook his head. 'Not with that rogue kangaroo still out here.'

She bit her lip. If she was honest, she didn't want to stay there alone with that kangaroo nearby. However, she had also seen the marks on Tim's stump where the prosthesis had rubbed away at his skin. She didn't like to think of the pain it would cause him to carry her.

She managed to shoot him a wry smile. 'I'm all sweaty and I've never let a man carry me before in my life. I'm not about to start now.'

He looked as though he might just swoop down and lift her, and Jess found her heart pounding for a reason she couldn't explain except that she wasn't used to a bare-chested man coming to her rescue and offering to carry her in his arms. She spoke fast.

'How about if you stay here with me and Dad will come soon enough. He knows where I am.'

Tim searched her face, then nodded, helping lower her to the ground. 'Okay. But if he's not here within an hour, I'm carrying you.'

She nodded. 'At least I'll have stopped sweating by then.'

He smiled at her, and she looked away. What was wrong with her? She felt strange. She couldn't think straight when he smiled at her like that. It must be the cut to the head.

She said very little as Tim sat beside her, keeping a close eye on her condition. He held his shirt to her head and she found herself leaning against his shoulder. It reminded her of the day she'd come in and found Zac and Milla standing together at the kitchen sink. Hadn't she longed for this? But not from Tim Bateman. Not from someone who could never love her, let alone treat her with common decency. Although, right now … she shut her eyes, breathing in the smell of him, feeling his closeness and feeling comforted.

Bluey finished chasing kangaroos and came to sit beside Tim, tongue lolling. Tim pointed toward the farmhouse. 'Home, Bluey. Go and find Charlie.'

Bluey's ears pricked up, but he didn't move.

Tim shrugged and shot her a wry smile. 'Thought it was worth a try.'

It wasn't more than twenty minutes before Dad came in search of Tim, rather than her.

'I knew you were working on the calves,' he said to Tim as he lifted Jess into his arms. 'I was imagining all kinds of dramas. Never dreamed it was Jess and that she'd be attacked by one of those kangaroos.' He glowered. 'So much for not culling them. I've a good mind to go and shoot them all.'

Jess managed a chuckle that made her head hurt. 'No, Dad. It's okay.'

'It's not okay. Your Dad's right.'

Jess twisted her head to look at Tim. His fierce scowl made her smile. 'Who invited you in on the conversation? Siding with my Dad is not allowed.'

To her surprise, Tim grinned. 'You're in no state to argue, Miss Cardelle. I'd quietly lie back and accept defeat if I were you.'

He was right. She was in no state to argue right now, but when she was patched up and feeling better she would take him on.

Jess was put into hospital under observation overnight. X-rays revealed a fractured rib but no other internal damage. Her forehead was stitched and reporters came to get her story.

Jess tossed and turned that night with the constant beeping and the footsteps outside her door. She replayed the incident over and over in her mind. Tim's smile kept coming back to her. She couldn't get his face out of her mind. It was an expressive, likeable face. It was almost as though it had been another man who had tended to her wounds so gently and proficiently. A man she could fall for.

CHAPTER TWENTY-FIVE

Jess sat on the lounge, trying to get comfortable despite her bruises and broken rib. She shuffled, then looked up as Dad came into the room. He was holding a letter.

'Another letter from Toby's organ recipient.' He sounded serious and Jess saw something more in his look. She reached for the letter with the hospital logo, heart pounding. She hadn't told Dad about Tim's scar, but he had to have seen it, too. Had Tim Bateman received Toby's kidney? Was he the one writing these letters?

'Show me, Lord,' she prayed as she began to read. Her heart constricted as this man revealed his heart.

I keep thinking back over that day. It seemed like such an ordinary day. I was going to my brother's graduation ceremony. I was sitting there thinking he ought to have dressed better, thinking through how else I could help him grow into a better man. Then there was a scraping kind of noise. Those trains are noisy anyway, so I thought nothing of it until it came again and the carriage rocked violently. Then there was a loud crash and the carriage tipped. People screamed and I felt a horrible weight come down on my foot, crushing and tearing it. At the same time I felt my whole body jar and the breath was squeezed from my lungs as something else fell on me. I've never felt such pain before in my life, but I think the thing that gets me most is that I was petrified. All my life I've managed to be strong, but in that moment I thought I was going to die I was completely helpless. I couldn't move and people were rushing over me to get to the door. Except my brother. He wouldn't leave me even when the carriage caught fire. I'm ashamed to say, I didn't want him to leave me to save his own life. I was scared to be alone.

And then, my brother wanted to give me his kidney. I couldn't accept it. I wouldn't be able to live with myself if the brother I've always been responsible for and cared for, gave up a body organ for me.

But then, you selflessly allowed the loss of your family member to save my life. I hate that it took the death of your loved one. I hate that someone had to die so I can live. It kills me somewhere inside every single day.

I don't want to be a burden on my family, but I haven't let them be in contact with me for months. I can't help thinking I don't really deserve to be alive. I'm a hard man. Ungrateful and thankless. I don't know how to change. Maybe that's why I'm still here – because I need to learn to change.

Jess put down the letter, heart pounding. There was no doubt in her mind. It was Tim. Tim Bateman had received Toby's kidney. She wanted to cry. Tim guarded his heart so carefully and she had felt the barriers were too high to ever get through. But without knowing it, he had revealed himself to her completely; cut open his heart and bled all over her the way she'd bled all over him yesterday.

She looked up. Dad stood in the doorway, watching her.

'It's Tim,' she said.

He nodded. 'I know. I saw his scar.' Slowly, he lowered himself onto the lounge beside her. 'It's not a coincidence. I believe God brought him into our lives for a reason.'

Jess agreed. 'Only God could have orchestrated this.'

'How's the rib?' Tim asked as he came into her office for his weekly appointment.

Jess's hand went to her side. 'A lot less painful now. I just thank God he brought you when he did or that kangaroo would have had me.'

Tim laughed scornfully. 'I brought me when I did, Jess. You can't try to bring God into the equation.'

'I'm not trying. He was a part of it whether you like to think so or not.'

Tim shook his head. 'I got restless standing still on my leg, that's all. It was me. All me.'

She smiled. Tim might seem like a hopeless case, but she knew better. God had brought him here and she wasn't ready to give up on him.

Tim studied her. 'I can't understand why a sensible, professional woman would believe all that garbage,' he said. 'Come on, Jess, be straight with me here. We both know it's not true. Jesus is just another one of those religious leaders people want to follow because they can't think for themselves. Me, well I'm strong enough to be independent.' He glanced down at his leg. 'Of mind, anyway.'

Jess tried not to feel hurt. Having her saviour made out to be mere human put her on the defensive. 'Jesus is not just like all the other religious leaders, Tim. He did all kinds of miracles to prove he was actually God.'

'So why hasn't he healed your sister?'

Good question. 'Maybe because he can use her condition in her life. Because he can turn it around for good.'

Tim grunted, then crossed his arms. 'What about Muhammad? He was supposed to do miracles, too, wasn't he? What's so different about him and your Jesus?'

She wished she had an answer. When she didn't respond, Tim chuckled and pointed to the papers on her desk. 'Come on, let's get on with the real reason I'm here.'

As he was leaving, he gave her a pitying look. 'There's so much you can't prove about your belief, Jess. No one of sound mind can truly believe it.'

She sighed, fighting back the sting of tears. He seemed to sense her struggle and took advantage of it.

'Why are there so many religions that believe they are right?' he demanded. 'Why are you going to heaven and I'm not? And if God made everyone - their personalities and minds, then what's so special about you that you were chosen to believe and understand?'

He limped out her door, and Jess was consumed by crippling guilt. She didn't have the answers for Tim. She was supposed to be ready with an answer for the hope within her in season and out of season. She had none.

She leaned her head on her desk. 'I've let you down, Lord. I don't know why there are so many religions that believe they are right. I don't know why you are the only way to heaven. I don't know why you've chosen me and not others.'

She shook her head. She was supposed to be an intellectual and yet reason defied her faith. She didn't know enough. She needed to learn more. She needed to study the Bible more.

And so Jess went to work. She asked her father, she asked her mother, her church minister, Sasha, anyone who might have answers. She bought Christian books and studied them. She read her Bible, asking God for insight. In it all, she found her own faith increasing, and yet still she had questions of her own. There was so much she couldn't answer.

'We're not meant to understand everything, Jess,' Dad said, his eyes concerned. 'Otherwise we'd be God.'

But she wasn't satisfied. She needed the answers for Tim.

CHAPTER TWENTY-SIX

Jess studied Tim as he sat down on a stump of wood, taking a break from inspecting the leg of an injured cow. He seemed … content, but she still prayed for him constantly. She'd rehearsed answers to all the questions he'd asked that day in her office, and to all those he could potentially ask as well. Then, she prayed for opportunities to introduce them naturally into conversation. The more she waited for him to ask, the more frustrated she became. Maybe she should give up. Maybe she should up and leave. Turn up at Kangon Hill and tell Rod Green that God had sent her.

She smiled, picturing Tim's reaction should she choose to do that.

'What are you smiling at?' he asked, rubbing absently at his leg. Jess sat down beside him. His operation was only a week away and she was glad. She hated seeing him in pain.

'Nothing.'

He raised a brow, but didn't push. A wattle bird with a deep blue patch around its eye came and landed on a nearby bush. Seeing it for the welcome distraction it was, Jess exclaimed with delight. 'Did you see that bird? It's so pretty. I've never seen a wattle bird like that before!'

Tim looked to where she pointed, then shook his head. 'You're a funny mixture. One minute you're all professional and the next you're like an excited little kid. I can't work you out.'

She screwed up her nose like she'd seen Milla so often do, then stopped herself. She wasn't a teenager. And neither was Tim.

Tim kept looking at her and she couldn't look away. His eyes were becoming less dark and sorrowful and she knew her father had something to do with that. His legs which had become thin with lack of use were now solid and strong. His fitness had returned to him quickly as had his hope to be a practicing vet again someday.

'Your faith is also something I still can't work out,' he added, setting Jess's senses on high alert. Here it was, the opportunity she'd been waiting for. 'I guess that's part of the childish side of you,' Tim mused. 'The side that needs to hope in someone else and believe in a world of fantasy. It adds an exciting dimension of the supernatural to your world.'

Jess smiled, answers ready, adrenaline surging through her veins. 'Jesus is no fairy tale, Tim. In fact, I found the answers to those questions you were asking me.'

He bent down to rub his leg again. Jess pushed on.

'Jesus is not like all the other spiritual leaders. He is the only one who claimed to be the Son of God and who proved it by rising from the dead.'

He looked up with a smirk. 'Says who? Your Bible? How do you know your Bible's right?'

Jess smiled. She had the answer to that, too. 'Because there are so many prophecies fulfilled. And they were written hundreds of years before they were fulfilled. And because —'

Tim cut her off with a wave of his hand. 'You're wasting your time on me, Jess. I don't believe and that's that.'

Jess drew back, disappointed. But he was right. Faith wasn't about reason. It was the complete opposite. True faith came from the heart, not the mind. Faith was about trusting when you didn't have the answers – when you didn't understand.

Lord, I believe in you and I believe you really want Tim to as well. I don't understand, but I trust you and believe.

Peace filled her despite the burden she felt for Tim. When would he stop fighting against God? She could give him all the logical reasons in the world to believe, but as long as his heart was hard, he would never believe. All she could do was continue to pray for him. Only God could change him.

'Come on, let's get this cow's leg splinted,' Tim said, standing and reaching a hand to lift Jess to her feet. She wondered at how gentle and proficient he was with the animals. Dad said he was the best vet he'd come across. But he would always need an assistant. Today Jess's rib was healed enough that she could do the physical work that required someone steady on their feet. Tim was extremely capable with the rest. She enjoyed working with him. He was patient, clear in his requests and grateful for a job well done.

Maybe all along he'd just needed to be needed. It was clear he was a man whose identity was wrapped up in work and achievements.

But then, wasn't she the same? She felt better when she was needed, too. It scared her to think she might not be important. That she might become invisible and unnoticed. She was desperate to have some kind of valuable impact on the world. That's why she wanted to work with Rod Green and his team at Kangon Hill. She was used to being extraordinary and the thought of being ordinary didn't sit well.

'Hang on, she's trying to move,' Tim said, bringing Jess's attention back to the work at hand. 'I've got her leg, you just keep her steady. That's it. That's great.'

Jess smiled at his approval. It would be a lot easier if she didn't enjoy it so much.

CHAPTER TWENTY-SEVEN

Tim lay in hospital, restlessness making it hard to lie still. The surgery had gone well, but he hated being here. This place, the confining walls, the inability to walk steadily on his own two legs, drove him crazy. Having a nurse shower him was the height of humiliation. He felt trapped. He wanted a hamburger. Some chips. He stared at the clock, watching each second tick away. He hated having nothing to do but think. It drove him crazy.

Milla Cardelle's surgery was coming up. He would go and see her in hospital, despite hating the place so much. He genuinely liked the girl. She was bubbly despite her disability and her one good eye always looked at him with respect, appreciation and understanding. She saw him for who he was, not for what he couldn't do. Now there was a girl of faith. Blind, useless faith, but a faith he admired all the same. She reminded him of his sister, Clare. Clare had always been full of life and fun. A bit too mischievous and reckless for her own good at times, but he'd loved her just the same. Still loved her. A pang hit his heart, surprising him.

He missed her. How much must his donor's family miss their loved one? He continued to write to them, baring his heart, and with each letter the weight on his shoulders lifted a bit more. They'd become important to him, even though he'd never met them. Maybe he should.

A rap came at his door. 'Tim?'

He looked up to see Erin, his social worker enter the room. He nodded at her.

'How are you doing?' she asked him.

'Fine.'

She smiled. 'You mean you're desperate to get out of here. You're like a caged bull.'

He managed a tight-lipped smile in return. She was intuitive. Like Jess Cardelle. Only more motherly. Not like his own mother. Veronica Bateman was classy. And as cold and hard as … well, as he was. But his social worker was warm and friendly. A bit on the overweight side, but beautiful in her own, unique way. A family woman. How he imagined his donor's mother to be.

'I've been lying here thinking that maybe I should meet my donor's family in person,' he said.

Erin's eyes widened. 'You took my challenge, didn't you. You've written to them.'

'I have.'

'What about if they write back to you first? Introduce themselves? That's if they're amenable to the idea. Then we can take it from there.'

Tim nodded. 'Sounds like a plan.'

Erin smiled. 'I'll contact them today and let you know how it goes.'

What had he done? Tim shut his eyes, suddenly wishing he could back out. Would the family reject him? Or even worse, cry all over him and expect him to take the place of their lost loved one?

He knew how much the Cardelles missed Toby. He saw it and felt it in their words, their eyes. He thought of Jess. She puzzled him. She was clearly intelligent and yet at times she lacked confidence. Probably because she was so unexceptional to look at. She had a fit, toned figure but nothing about her face stood out. She did have some things going for her, though. She was friendly, professional, and had a sharp mind. When she relaxed, a spark of life would come to her eyes that suggested there was so much more to her. But mostly she was a professional doing the job expected of her. Unfortunately that job required her to analyse his every move, his every thought. It was irritating and threatening. He wasn't going to let his guard down for her. His heart and his hurts were his own. He refused to give in and join the ranks of weak, needy people in her world.

Jess answered the phone. Shock reverberated through her as the social worker explained that Toby's donor would like to meet them.

'There is absolutely no pressure,' she said. 'I understand the emotional turmoil it could create for you and your family.'

Jess tried to put her thoughts together. 'But … but would it help? I mean, would you advise it?'

There was a pause. 'We don't usually recommend it unless both parties have a desire to meet. It can be especially hard for the donor's family.'

Jess cleared her throat. It was Tim who would find it hard if he found out who his donor's family was. She drew in a breath. 'Can I talk to my family and get back to you?'

'Of course. Call the hospital number and ask them to page Erin in the social work department. They'll put you straight through to me.'

Jess hung up feeling stunned.

'Who was it?' Milla asked.

Jess looked around at her family. 'A social worker. Tim wants to meet his donor's family.'

Mum's mouth dropped open. Dad rubbed the back of his neck and Milla shook her head in disbelief.

Dad spoke first. 'We need to pray.'

And so they all prayed, begging God for wisdom. Then they opened their eyes and stared at one another.

'I guess it's good that he feels ready to meet the donor's family.' Mum ventured.

Jess felt sick. They couldn't let Tim know it was them. Not yet. But then, what would it do to him if they refused to have contact with him?

'Can we say we do want to connect with him but are unable to at this stage? Can we say we'll contact him as soon as it's possible?'

Dad nodded. 'That's a good idea. And it gives us time to gauge his reaction to the news. If he comes back more troubled we can rethink our decision and timing.'

Jess called Erin back to let her know their decision.

TIM LISTENED to Erin with some confusion as she relayed the message back to him. What could possibly make them unable to meet him? Had he been too revealing in his letters? Had he freaked them out with his honesty? It had taken so much to come to a place where he felt ready to meet them, and now it seemed that they weren't ready. He shrugged. He supposed he should be relieved. It would have been hard to see them in person. He'd seen the way Charlie Cardelle grieved over his son. The way he missed him. There were times Charlie would stop and look out into the distance, unspeaking. And Tim would know he was thinking of Toby. What would it be like for Charlie to meet someone who actually had a part of his loved son's body in him? His donor's family would no doubt feel the same. The last thing he wanted was to cause the family more pain. Maybe this was for the best.

CHAPTER TWENTY-EIGHT

Milla, we have a surgery date,' the neurosurgeon said, smiling. 'Two weeks.'

So this was it. Milla drew in a deep breath. Soon she might be able to see better, at least for a time. And then the infusions would begin. It seemed God had decided to heal through medicine. Partially. She'd never be the same as she was before, never have that same level of energy, but God had brought her this far and she trusted him.

She thought of the dreams she'd had to give up. Soccer and cadets. Truck driving. Helping Dad with his work around the farm. Chopping up dead wood and selling it. So much good she could have done. But was it what really mattered? Suddenly she pictured herself standing beside Zac in the kitchen. And at their feet were children. Their children. On her finger was her wedding ring and Zac was looking at her lovingly. But Zac was doing all the work. She was unable to help him. Sure, he loved her, but she wanted to help. Wanted to work as a team. Surely God didn't want this? Surely her being permanently disabled wasn't his best plan?

Is it, God?

She believed it wasn't. 'Dr Treen,' she said hesitantly, 'what would happen if I went off all my medication?'

His brows shot up. 'Why?'

She glanced at Mum and Dad. They looked just as puzzled.

She bit her lip. 'I don't know. I might be in denial, but I just can't quite believe I really have myasthenia. It didn't show up in my bloods, did it?'

Dr Treen leaned forward, his expression sympathetic. 'No, but I explained that to you.' His tone was patient, as though speaking to a slow child. 'Often it doesn't. All your symptoms show you have it.'

'What if I were to go off all my medications for a few days? Just as a trial?'

He chuckled indulgently. 'You can if you like. All that will happen is your eyes will get very bad again and your muscles will weaken. You'll be back at square one.'

'But it won't do any damage?'

'No, we'll just start again when you're ready. You're welcome to try it.'

Milla beamed. 'Thank you.' Now God would have time and space to heal her. And deep inside, she believed he would. If he didn't, that was okay, but she wanted to trust him to do this. To give him the chance.

Mum and Dad were silent as Milla bounced out to the car. She grinned at them.

'Now we start praying, and get everyone else in the church praying, too.'

Mum and Dad looked at one another, then back at her. 'You believe you'll be healed?' Dad asked.

'I do.'

Dad smiled. 'Then I believe it, too. Let's call the Buckley's over to our place and we'll all pray.'

TANNER WAS DRAWN to the Cardelle's house that night like a moth to a flame. He'd visited his dad and Joel in jail again. The love the Cardelles had for one another made him long for the same thing. But his family would never be like theirs.

'Don't make the mistakes I did, Tanner,' his dad had said.

Tanner knew what he really meant. Don't get caught. And yet being in jail stopped his dad from defrauding others. It made life fairer and brought justice to many. Dad had brought his fall on himself. He'd become too greedy. Careless. But Joel hadn't. Joel's capture had been a fate no one could have predicted. It was almost as though a higher being orchestrated the connections to bring Joel down. No human could have planned the link between the Batemans, the Lesters, and the policewoman Joel had bribed to work with him. It still did his head in. He knew the Cardelles would claim it was God's doing.

Lydia Cardelle welcomed him with a hug that warmed him to his soul.

'Of course you're welcome for dinner,' she said. 'The Buckley's are coming too and they'll be staying to pray with us for healing for Milla. You're very welcome to stay for that, too.'

Curiosity made him stay. The fact that they would be praying for healing for the disabled Milla and expecting it to happen, fascinated him.

After dinner, they gathered in the lounge room, each resting a hand on Milla's shoulder. He really should go. He didn't belong here. But his legs took him to the lounge room almost of their own accord, as though a supernatural force compelled him. He watched the way Mr. and Mrs. Cardelle kept glancing at one another, hope and love shining in their eyes. He saw the way Zac and Milla shared a connection deeper than romance. And Jess sat there quietly, concern written all over her face. Maybe she, like him, didn't expect a miracle. Knew it was an impossibility. Poor Jess.

The big man named Buck was the one who prayed first. The man was guileless. He was loud, almost demanding. Tanner winced. If God was real, surely he'd strike Buck dead? Who had the right to demand anything of God? But maybe God also forgave lack of intelligence, for if God existed and he created everyone, then it also followed that God was the one who made Buck so simple.

But then Buck's language changed. Tanner frowned, trying to work out exactly what language the man was using. He'd never heard it before. Maybe Dutch? Spanish? No, none of them fit. Then he jarred at a name he heard. Joel. No, it was just the intonation Buck used in whatever language this was. Buck's face lifted to the light from the ceiling and Tanner saw the moisture around his eyes. Buck was a strange man.

Charlie Cardelle then spoke to the group. 'Buck prayed for Milla's spiritual eyesight to always be as clear as it is now. And he prayed for someone by the name of Joel. He asked that God would set the captives free from the prisons of their own making. That their hearts would be changed and renewed. And that Joel would find his true identity in God.'

Tanner darted a look around the room, heart pounding. What was this? He knew every sleight of hand, every trick of the mind, every deception under the sun. So what was going on? How did they know about Joel? That he was trying to find a way to break him out of prison? Everything in him wanted to run, to escape whatever this was, but his feet wouldn't move. It appeared he was the only one freaked out here, and no one had guessed his true identity or purpose in being here. Still, he couldn't relax.

Charlie Cardelle prayed next. He prayed in English and he was quieter. Just as firm in his conviction that God could and would heal his daughter, but more respectful. Then came Lydia, Milla's mother. She wept for her daughter, her mother's heart clearly tearing in two over Milla's plight. Jess didn't pray out loud, but he saw her mouth moving. Then Zac prayed, his voice quiet but full of strength and confidence in God. Milla shifted under their hands that rested heavily on her shoulders. Didn't they remember the weakness myasthenia left her with?

She cleared her throat. Then she talked to God like he was in the room.

'Lord Jesus, you've heard our prayers. I don't know why, but I just have this feeling that you don't want me to have this condition. I know you can heal. I believe you want to. I am reaching out, touching the hem of your garment.'

Tanner watched in fascination as she physically reached out her hand in to the air, then lowered it, settling as though Jesus was right there in front of her and she was grabbing his robe.

'No matter what you choose to do, Lord Jesus, I trust you. I see you. I choose to follow you all the days of my life. Able bodied or not, I am your child and I know you know what's best for me.'

Tanner watched, spellbound, unable to take his eyes from Milla's face. It was shining. With hope. With joy. With trust. He looked up. She must be reflecting the light above them.

Milla opened her eyes, then took off her eye patch. Her eyes were beautiful, Tanner realised. A hazel colour, sparkling and alive.

She smiled. Could she fully see? Surely not? And yet right now, if she'd told him she could see again, he'd believe her.

She shook her head, but still smiled. 'Let's see what happens tomorrow.'

'Tomorrow,' Zac said, taking her hand and squeezing it. And Tanner felt as though he'd just been part of something out of this world. Something he couldn't understand. Something he wanted to be a part of but that scared him speechless.

Tonight he really should be working out a way to get Joel out of prison. He was supposed to be hacking into more computers, stealing more identities. Growing his money and power. He'd used Toby's legal documentation and identity to get into the bank and he would soon be ready to empty Toby and Sasha's account.

But being here tonight shone a light on the futility of it all. He wanted what he felt here. The joy. The peace. The faith. The family. The love.

He no longer wanted to take from this family who gave so much. Of themselves, of the love of God.

And the supernatural power he'd witnessed tonight was too strong, too real to fight against.

He was on the wrong side. Was it too late to change?

MILLA OPENED her eyes and blinked into the morning sunlight. She looked to the left. The right. Up into the far left where her eyes had given her the most trouble. Images weren't jumping about. Everything was steady. But then, it was early morning. Since having stronger medication, she did sometimes have a few hours a day where she could see okay.

Was that what was happening now? She wasn't sure, but she felt as though she was seeing perfectly. Maybe she was tricking her own mind. She was tempted to jump out of bed, but stayed herself.

'Lord? Thank you. Thank you that I can see well this morning. Thank you for being here with me. Help me remember you throughout the day. I want to walk with you.'

She felt the warmth of his smile in the sunshine that filtered through the blinds and rested on her cheeks. She felt his delight in the colours that surrounded her, in the roof over her head and the cool sheets against her skin. She felt whole. God loved her.

She went out to the kitchen. Jess was getting ready for work and smiled at her.

'How's the vision?'

'Good at the moment.'

Jess nodded. 'We'll see how you are this afternoon.' Then she grinned. 'You know you didn't have to go this far to avoid having to see me.'

Milla scrunched up her forehead. 'Huh?'

'Well, you'd prefer a miracle than to have me as your O.T. and physio.'

Milla laughed. 'Yeah. Funny that.' She sobered. She didn't want to take Jess for granted ever again. 'Thanks for all you've done for me, Jess.'

Jess turned from where she'd been putting a slice of bread in the toaster and her eyes showed her surprise.

'For all the times you picked me up from cadets or soccer. For all the times you babysat me while Mum and Dad were out or played games with me because I was restless and bored.'

Jess smiled, her eyes full of tenderness. 'It wasn't work, Milla. You're a delight. From the moment you were born you've been a delight. No one can help loving you …' She shoved Milla's shoulder gently. 'Except for when you drive us crazy with your non-stop talking, or borrow clothes from my wardrobe without asking, of course.'

Milla's heart warmed, but she also knew how much she'd taken others for granted. She'd basked in their love, bouncing through life without a care in the world. Until Toby's death.

'What do you think he was doing in the city that day?'

'Pardon?' Jess turned around.

'The day Toby died. What do you think he was doing? Do you think that whatever it was, it has something to do with his laptop being stolen? With someone trying to steal his trust money?'

Jess's eyes widened. 'I hadn't thought of that. I thought he might have a job interview, to be honest.'

Milla thought about it. It was possible. But Toby had seemed happy on the farm. And he'd been so in love with Sasha. Had he planned to move back to the city with Sasha when they married?

'Sasha might know.'

Jess shook her head. 'I asked her. She said she didn't know why he went.'

Milla sighed. 'Sometimes I imagine what life would be like if he was still here. I miss him.'

'Me too.' Jess bit her lip. 'Toby was … a blessing. He always made me feel noticed. He saw me.'

Milla swallowed, a lump filling her throat. 'I see you now too, Jess. And God always saw you.'

She saw the way Jess froze. Tried to pull herself together. Forced a cheerful smile.

'Well,' she said, 'I'd really better get ready for work.' And she left her toast in the toaster and rushed off to her room. When the toast popped, Milla took it from the toaster and buttered it just the way she knew Jess liked it. Then she left it at Jess's place at the table and went to prepare her own breakfast.

JESS WONDERED at the way her heart pounded this morning. Tim had come home from hospital. He had an appointment with her mid-morning. She hoped and prayed he was okay and that he wasn't upset about his donor's family not wanting to see him.

She heard his voice as he greeted Kelly, then watched him come into her office. She tried to be professional and focus on his walk – which had a decidedly stronger gait and no sign of a limp – but she couldn't help being distracted by the half smile he gave her and the way her heart warmed under his look.

'When do you reckon I can start with your dad again?' he asked once she'd assessed him.

'Well, all the work seems to have been done by rehab and the guys who fitted your prosthesis. I have no problem with you starting tomorrow. I know Dad's been missing you.'

Tim's smile was full and heart-stopping. Jess forced herself not to stare. She marvelled at the change in him. He was a different person from the glowering, bitter young man who had first entered her waiting room in a wheelchair. And the changes were not just physical.

It was with a joyful heart that she arrived home and changed into her exercise clothes. She headed to her favourite place. Dad had destroyed the large male kangaroo that had attacked her and although more cautious of the creatures, she felt ease going out on her own again.

Mum was out shopping with Milla and Dad was negotiating a cattle sale with some new buyers. She didn't bother locking the house. No one did when you lived this far out of town. In fact, she left the front door wide open.

TIM WAS lonely and restless in his little flat. Bluey was great, but even he would love to visit Charlie. There was something warm and caring yet so masculine about the man. Tim wished he was his father. As the taxi dropped him off and disappeared back down the road, Tim walked in the open front door.

'Jess? Mrs. Cardelle?'

No response. Perhaps they were in the back room or on the verandah. He looked on the table. Maybe they'd left a note. No, only a pile of mail sat there. Tim glanced around the room, but his eyes came back to the pile of mail. He recognised one of those envelopes. He'd received similar ones from the hospital. He frowned, pulling it from the pile and turning it over. Had one of the Cardelles been in the same hospital? Was Milla going to have her surgery in the city too? He shrugged. It was none of his business.

But then he saw it. Over on the sideboard was a letter. One end was partly folded, but he recognised the paper before his own writing. His leg felt wooden as he forced his way over to it. The paper felt like fire in his hands. He unfolded it and began to read. It was his last letter to his donor's family. His heart raced, his mind tumbling over. What was going on? Why did they have his letter? Why couldn't he think?

Suddenly it all fell into place. Toby. Toby Cardelle had been an organ donor. *His* organ donor. And they knew. A feeling of betrayal worked its way from his head to his heart and he tried to breathe. He felt exposed, violated. He had begun to trust these people ...

The side door banged and Tim stood perfectly still.

JESS WAS SHOCKED to see Tim standing alone in the open plan living room. But then, she had left everything open as she always did. Her face broke into a wide smile until she glanced and saw the letter on the table. Oops. She needed to move that before Tim saw it. He was so close. Almost touching it. She'd been careful to clear away his mail in the past, but she hadn't expected him today.

'How are you?' she asked, forcing herself to remain cheerful. 'Looking for Dad?'

He didn't answer and she gestured to a chair. 'Have a seat. I'll just tidy up.' She reached for the letter, but he snatched it up. She felt the blood drain from her face.

'You're about ten minutes too late,' he said, and his voice shook with fury.

Jess stared at the letter that shook in his hand, his handwriting visible on the pages.

'You and your Christian morals,' he spat. 'Thought it was smart to deceive me, did you? To find out all you can about me so you have more in your Christian arsenal to fire at me? To convert me?'

'Tim,' she began, tears threatening, but he held up his hand.

'Don't bother. I don't want to hear it.'

'But you have to hear it, Tim.' She was pleading with him now, but his expression remained hard and closed.

'Hear what? That you're sorry and will never do such a thing again?'

'No. That I was about to give up on you, but then your first letter arrived. It gave me hope. And in every letter I started to understand you a bit more. Your letters show your human side. The side I like and relate to.'

Tim's laugh was dry and cold. 'Really? Well, I don't want to be liked for my weakness.'

He pulled his phone from his pocket and Jess listened as he called a taxi.

Please God, she prayed. *Let Mum and Dad get home. I don't know how to handle this.*

'Now I know why my donor's family couldn't see me yet,' Tim said, disgust seeping from every syllable. 'They needed to keep having the upper hand. They already knew who I was. It was me who was in the dark.'

'Upper hand?' Jess tried to swallow back her tears. What did he mean? She wasn't game to ask as she watched him angrily pace the floor, then go out into the yard to wait for his taxi, slamming the door behind him.

Jess didn't know how long she cried and prayed, but she felt as though her heart was breaking. She heard Dad's vehicle crunch the gravel before he took his boots off. She couldn't hold in her rasping sobs.

Dad raced to her side. 'Jess! What's wrong?'

'Tim,' she managed, 'He found the letter.'

It only took Dad a moment to work out what had happened. With a sigh, he pulled out a chair and sat beside her.

'Oh Jess. We may have made a big mistake. Maybe we should have told Tim as soon as we knew.'

Jess nodded. 'He was so hurt. So angry.'

Dad bowed his head, hands clasped in front of him. 'Lord, you know our mistakes and this one was devastating.' He drew in a shaky breath. 'Please don't let it cost a man his soul. Guide us to mend our relationship with Tim Bateman. Let it grow stronger than it ever was before and keep softening his heart.'

CHAPTER TWENTY-NINE

Mum and Milla arrived home full of smiles.

'I can still see!' Milla said, bouncing over. Then her steps slowed. 'Jess? Dad?'

Jess filled them in, hating the way Milla's joy faded into concern.

Dad gave Milla a hug. 'Sorry Milla. I want to stay and celebrate with you right now, but I have to go and see Tim.' He grabbed his wallet and car keys and headed out the door.

Milla shook her head. 'All we can do is pray.' Then she smiled. 'Rephrase that. The best thing we can do is pray. God is the God of miracles.'

Was he? Was Milla really healed? And would Tim ever forgive them?

Please God … Jess prayed, not even able to finish the prayer, too scared to hope for the miracle they were longing for.

TIM EXPECTED, even hoped Charlie Cardelle would come to see him. When the farmer arrived at his door, he let him in. Charlie settled himself into Tim's lounge before saying what he had to say.

'I know you're angry, Tim,' he said and the complete understanding in the man's tone did something to Tim's heart. 'I know, because I've been where you are.'

He had? That was a surprise. Charlie was the most calm, easy-going man Tim had ever known. Even Milla's disability hadn't seemed to rattle him.

'I expressed it differently, though,' he said. 'When Toby died, I didn't express my pain in anger. It was through inaction. I stopped trying to keep the farm going. I didn't try to comfort my wife and daughters in their grief. And I stopped trying to live. Don't get me wrong, I didn't attempt suicide or anything, but when we first heard about Toby I just didn't bother looking after myself or anyone else. Then one day out on the farm I hit a log on the quad and I didn't try to save myself. I wasn't wearing a helmet. I let myself fall under that bike. I think I kind of hoped God's time for me was up.'

Charlie cleared his throat. 'But when I opened my eyes, that bike wasn't on top of me. And I was fine. I stared up at the sky and I yelled at God. I told him I'd had enough. Told him he needed to put my heart back together because it was broken and I was broken.'

Tim listened, but said nothing. This man didn't understand. He had everything to live for. Yes, he'd lost his son, but he was whole. He had his farm, a career. His God.

Charlie shuffled before looking directly into Tim's eyes. 'You opened your heart to us, Tim, and it meant the world to me. I want to do the same for you. You've been good for me. You've taken some of the emptiness I felt when my son died. Each day I've let you into my heart just a bit more, and frankly, I can't stand the thought of losing you, now. I've started to live again because of you. God knows I need you.'

Still Tim said nothing, but something in his heart stirred. Perhaps it was the longing for a father that reached him so deeply. He wasn't sure, but he knew he couldn't let his own anger leave this man in pain. He saw it now. It was fear of losing him that had caused Charlie to deceive him. Fear of losing another … son. And how Tim wanted to be a son to this man. His heart hurt at the mere thought of losing Charlie's fatherly care. He craved it more desperately than food and water.

Charlie stood. 'I just wanted to let you know.'

Tim nodded, watching him head for the door. It was not until he was outside that Tim gave him a brief wave.

'See you tomorrow,' he said.

Charlie beamed. 'Tomorrow.'

JESS WAITED in her office for Tim, hoping, praying he would come.

He didn't.

She picked up her handbag. 'Kelly, I'm going to Tim Bateman's house to see him. He hasn't turned up.'

Kelly nodded. 'No worries. Will you be back before your next patient gets here?'

Jess nodded. 'Of course.' But her heart wasn't in the clinic anymore. If Tim didn't come back …

It seemed forgiving her father didn't automatically mean Tim had forgiven her as well.

Blue's bark alerted Tim to her presence before she had a chance to knock. Tim came to the door.

His lip curled. 'What are you doing here?' Then he stared at her shirt. She'd chosen an orange and pink shirt with slashes of lightning down it. 'You're not working today?'

She forced a smile. 'I am. I came to see where you were.'

'You wore *that* to work?' His nose wrinkled in disgust.

'I did.' It had been her way of celebrating Milla's returned eyesight.

He sneered. 'You look like you're trying to be artistic but instead proving you're colour blind.'

It seemed they were back to the insults. But at least he was talking to her. She sighed. 'You'd prefer I wore black every day? You think everyone should look as dark and miserable as you feel?'

She bit her lip. That was one sure way to destroy an already fragile relationship. But it hurt that he would forgive her father and not her.

'I don't think you have any right to stand there criticising me, Christian Jess.' He glared at her. 'You claim to have the Christian faith but you have an awful lot of trouble carrying out its principles. Does truth and honesty mean anything to you at all?'

'Look, I'm sorry Tim—'

'Sorry? Well, *I'm* sorry, but sorry doesn't cut it, Jess. For months now you've been stealing my privacy. And deceiving me about it. You're more than a disloyal friend. You're a thief.'

He had considered her a friend? Well that was clearly over now. He despised her. She could see it in the twist of his mouth, the revulsion in his eyes.

She cleared her throat, trying to be professional Jess again. 'I'm hearing you. But I don't want your progress to suffer because of me. Are you still willing to see me?'

'As my allied health professional? You don't get it, do you? You have violated my trust. You should have told me as soon as you knew. Because the truth is, you are the last person I would have willingly opened my heart up to like that.'

His words cut to the heart. 'What's so wrong with letting me see into your heart?' Jess finally asked, her voice catching. 'What's so wrong with understanding you?'

He turned away, tapping his fingers on the doorframe in a

heavy, tense beat. When he turned back, she was stunned by what she saw. Tim's eyes were filled with tears just as hers were.

'I'm a mess,' he said, shaking his head. 'I'm full of pain and bitterness and there's nothing anyone – not even you – can do about it. Somewhere inside it's so dark it's black.'

'Then let the sunshine in!'

Silence stretched between them and she swiped at her tears.

'Little Miss Sunshine,' Tim said, grinding out the words through clenched teeth. 'You're light and I'm dark. That's the way it is.' He waved a hand at her shirt. 'Look at you. All happiness and positivity. I'm not going to contaminate your world. I'll help your dad because he needs it, but I don't need you and the last thing you need is me.'

Jess stepped toward him, but he moved out of reach.

'Tim,' she pleaded. 'Haven't you seen the way light works? Light overcomes darkness. Darkness never overcomes light. That's why we have lightbulbs to turn on and off – never darkness bulbs. Light is so much more powerful than darkness.'

'You finished?'

How dare he dismiss her as though she were making no sense? 'No. No, I haven't—'

He shut the door in her face. And Jess turned and walked away. How could an already broken heart break all over again?

CHAPTER THIRTY

Milla looked around, squinted, looked around again. She could see. She really could. It was two weeks since she'd stopped all medication and she hadn't worn the eye patch since. She was slower now, but it would take a while to rebuild her strength. And she wasn't sure she wanted to go back to that fast-paced, busy life she had had. The life where she'd had no time to see God's hand, no time to see people – to really see them and connect.

Milla looked out across the paddocks and smiled. She would be able to drive. She'd be able to help Dad.

She came into the shed where Dad had been working. Tim was there. He looked up with a grim smile. Milla knew Jess was no longer Tim's physio. Dad said his ability to work was lapsing without therapy.

'How's it going?' Milla asked him.

He gave a jerky nod, his expression wary. Clearly he didn't trust her anymore, either.

Then he frowned. 'Where's your eye patch?'

She laughed. 'Haven't you heard? I can see.'

'You had the surgery?'

How to explain? She knew he wouldn't believe. She struggled to believe it herself. 'No, I'm off all medication. I know you won't believe it because I can hardly believe it myself, but everyone was praying and … I'm better.'

'Just your eyes? Or everything?'

'Everything. I have complete vision and I'm growing stronger every day. We saw the optometrist and the neurosurgeon yesterday. I thought it might be all in my mind, but it's not. They tested me. I can see.'

One eyebrow lifted. 'What does the neurologist think?'

She laughed again. 'He was as skeptical as you. He said to come back when the symptoms return and we'll go ahead with surgery then.'

'And if they don't return?'

'He didn't seem to think that was a possibility.'

'Hmph.' Tim went back to his work, and Milla knew he needed time to process. Everyone searched for a logical explanation first. She understood that. She had, too. She'd been over and over it in her mind. Could it have been stress related? Could her brain have forced her eyes and body to stop working because she was missing Toby? Could the doctors have missed something?

But no, the fact was, they had prayed, she had stopped all medication, and now a condition that was getting worse and worse over time had gone. Overnight.

WITH A SIGH, Jess wandered the house, feeling lost. Saturday mornings were once her chance to enjoy working with Dad on the farm, but Tim was here again. Milla was out there with them, making the most of her return of sight and energy. It was a miracle. But God hadn't performed a miracle on Tim's heart. It continued to be dark. She occasionally bumped into him as he worked around the farm with Dad. It was clear he loved being a vet but he couldn't accept being an amputee. If he didn't look after himself and learn how to use his muscles properly he would always have a limp and never walk the same again. It burdened her, but there was nothing more she could do. She had already overstepped the mark with Tim Bateman and now she had to leave him to make his own choices. He had stopped insulting her whenever they ran into each other, but he was always so stiff and formal – too polite. She was tired of the hope followed by disappointment.

A knock came at the door. Tanner stood there. She hadn't seen him since the prayer meeting for Milla. She suspected they'd scared him off.

'Came to see how Milla's doing,' he said as Jess let him in.

She felt the smile fill her cheeks.

He drew back. 'No.'

'Yes. She can see, Tanner. Completely. The neurologist and opthalmologist can't explain it. She doesn't need surgery. She has full, complete vision without an eye patch. Without medication.' She watched the blood drain from Tanner's face. 'Are you okay? Here, have a seat.'

Looking dazed, he fell into the chair she pulled out for him. 'So all that stuff … the prayer, it works?'

'Obviously we can't force God to do anything, but he hears our prayers and answers. In his timing, in his way.'

He frowned. 'And when Buck was speaking in another language …?'

'It's called tongues. Some say it's a heavenly language. It's what happens when Buck prays in the Spirit of Jesus.'

'And what your dad said?'

'He interpreted.'

'How?'

'He just knew what Buck was saying. The Holy Spirit showed him.'

Tanner looked confused and Jess didn't blame him. It was impossible to explain things of the Spirit to those who didn't have the Holy Spirit.

He rubbed his hand across a pattern on the tablecloth, then shrugged. 'They could have made it up.'

True. She'd thought that herself at times, but then one day when Buck had spoken in tongues, she's just somehow known what he was saying. And she saw in Tanner's eyes that he didn't really think that. He was normally so confident and in control, but today he looked rattled.

'Do you want to see Milla?'

He shook his head. 'No. Well, yes, but first there's something I need to tell you.'

He looked so serious. Her heart beat harder and she tried to remain calm as her mind raced through all kinds of scenarios.

'Toby had a heart condition.'

She hadn't expected that. 'What? No, he was healthy. He was the fittest of all of us.'

Tanner's mouth tilted in a sympathetic line. 'Maybe, but still, he had a heart problem. That day … in the city … he was seeing a specialist. A cardiologist.'

No. Surely not. He would have told them. She frowned at Tanner. 'And you know this, how?'

He looked away, avoiding her eyes.

'How?' she demanded. 'Where are you getting this from? Why are you saying this?'

He cleared his throat, still avoiding her eyes. 'It's hereditary. You should get tested. All of you. Make your dad go, too. I'd just … I'd hate for something to happen to him.'

Jess stared at him. It was true Dad was slowing down, that he'd become more breathless lately. That he was so tired. But … but she was an allied health professional. If anything was wrong she would have picked up on it. Except that she'd been so busy. So absorbed with Tim, with Milla, with her own pain.

'So what *is* this supposed heart condition, Tanner? If you know so much about my brother's medical history, what is it?'

She knew she wasn't being fair, but it hurt that this stranger knew more about Toby than she did. That Toby told him something so important without telling *her*.

'I don't know. And I'm sorry, Jess. Sorry for so many things.'

Jess bit her lip, trying to sort through everything Tanner was saying. It was all too much. She shoved herself out of the chair and headed to the door.

'I'm going for a walk. Dad and Milla are in the shed if you want to see them.'

On autopilot she headed for Billy Can Hill. She understood the betrayal Tim felt, now. Really understood it. Keeping truth from someone, important truth, showed a lack of respect and love for that person. Toby hadn't told her about his heart condition. She hadn't told Tim who his donor was; that she was so irrevocably connected with him.

'Oh God,' she cried out, gazing out at the hills, trying to make sense of her heart, of the world, of God.

It was Dad who eventually came to find her. He didn't say a word, just settled down beside her and followed her gaze out to the hills. A gentle breeze blew a wisp of hair across her cheek, tickling her skin. It annoyed her, but she couldn't bring herself to move. How could she feel so alive and yet so empty at the same time?

'Tanner told me,' Dad finally said. 'About Toby's heart condition.'

Jess sighed, then stared down at her shoes. 'He could be making it up, you know.'

'He's not.'

Her head whipped up. 'How do you know?'

'I have it, too.'

'What? Dad, what are you talking about?'

'It's called Familial Hypertrophic Cardiomyopathy. It's where the heart muscle thickens—'

'I know what it is, Dad. One of my patients died from it.' Jess was crying, now. 'Why did you never tell me this before?'

Dad sighed. 'Any of us can die at any time, Jess. I didn't want to worry you. God keeps every one of us here on earth for as long as he wants us here. Every day is written in his book. I only told Toby because he was getting married. I thought it was only fair that he and Sasha went into marriage with their eyes wide open. According to Tanner, Toby was seeing a heart specialist on the day of his accident. The local GP must have found something and referred him to my specialist.'

Toby knew he had a heart condition? And he didn't tell her? She had thought they were close. Maybe she was invisible. Maybe she didn't matter at all. Maybe there never would be anyone for her; that someone she dreamed of whose body held Toby's heart.

And then it hit her. Toby's heart wasn't in someone else. Toby's heart had been faulty. It couldn't have been donated, it would have had to be discarded. Like she was. Like her dreams were. The depth of her devastation couldn't be expressed. Toby's heart had stopped beating for good the day he was killed. And her dream was over. That special someone who understood her didn't exist. Cold, cruel reality hit.

Dad put his arm around her, but Jess needed more than he could offer. She shivered. Tears dripped down her cheeks and off her chin. Dad would not always be there for her. No-one would.

TIM WATCHED in concern as Charlie Cardelle came back into the shed. He looked broken, as though a heavy bale of hay had landed on him. His shoulders were hunched, his eyes red-rimmed.

'We've had some bad news, Tim,' Charlie said and the despondency in his tone scared Tim. 'I think my Jess is going to need you.'

Jess? He would have laughed if Charlie hadn't so obviously meant it. Jessica Cardelle needed nothing and no one, especially not him.

'What's going on?' Tim hated how Charlie was drawing this – whatever this was – out for so long. If Charlie had something to say, he should just say it.

'I have a heart condition that could take my life any day.' Charlie gnawed on his lower lip, then looked up, meeting Tim's eyes. 'Toby had it too. Only he never told us.'

Tim turned to look out the window, needing privacy. He didn't care about Toby Cardelle. He was dead. But Charlie … well, why did he feel as though he'd just been told his father was dead all over again? And why would Charlie say Jess needed him? He'd felt the weight of caring for the grieving before and he didn't want to go through it again. He'd made a complete mess of it with his siblings. Why would Charlie want him to care for his own daughter? He was less of a man now than he'd been back then, back when he'd tried to keep a tight rein on Clare, Dan and Beth. He'd messed it up and they'd resented him. He'd failed his own father enough without failing Charlie, too.

JESS DIDN'T COME HOME until the sun had set. She had cried and prayed and cried some more. She needed to talk with Sasha. Needed to understand. Taking out her phone, she went to Toby's room, needing to feel as though he was near, that he understood.

Then she stopped. Toby's laptop was there, sitting on his desk. What was going on?

'Mum? Dad? Who found Toby's laptop?'

Mum, Dad and Milla came running. They stopped and stared in confusion at the laptop sitting on his desk. There was also a letter on top, already opened, but with a city hospital logo. It had Toby's name on it but was addressed to a PO Box.

Mum pulled out the letter, then her eyes filled with tears as she passed it to Jess. Jess skimmed the medical language, but she knew exactly what it was saying. This was Toby's diagnosis letter, confirming he had Familial Hypertrophic Cardiomyopathy. Is this how Tanner knew? Had he seen this letter? Put it here even? But who had put the laptop here? And who had taken it in the first place? Surely not Tanner?

Dad bit his lip. 'I'm thinking we should let the police know.'

Mum nodded while a look passed between Jess and Milla. Milla's eyes were understanding. As though she knew Jess's pain.

'Call Sash,' she said quietly.

Jess nodded, dialling the number. Maybe Sasha could shed some light on all of this madness.

'Jess? Everything okay?' Sasha said, the moment she answered.

Jess bit her lip, knowing it could be the middle of the night in the US. She hadn't had the energy to check.

'Sash, my dad has a heart condition.'

'Oh Jess, I'm sorry.'

'Did you know Toby had it too?' Silence. Jess tried not to cry. 'You knew.'

'I did.' Her voice was low, sad-sounding. Sasha had known the man she loved could die at any moment. That his heart could stop. But none of them had expected the train accident.

'Why didn't he tell us?' Jess asked, pain rolling through her chest all over again, her voice breaking.

'Because he could have lived as long as your father has. We figured we can all die ... at any time.'

'Oh Sash, I'm sorry.'

'It changed our lives,' Sasha said. 'It puts things in perspective. We don't know how much time we have, Jess. Anything we know we should do, we should do *now*. Because now is what we have. That's why we donated so much of our money to Kangon Hill rather than buying a nice house or car. We wanted to have an eternal impact while we could.'

'You knew about Kangon Hill?'

'Yes. It was a joint decision. A ministry we donated to together.'

Jess pictured Rod Green. Everything kept coming back to him. To Kangon Hill. Was God trying to tell her something? And then it hit her. Toby's heart was not beating in someone else, but the Holy Spirit who had worked through him and dwelt within him was living in this Rod Green. Rod shared Toby's heart for those young people. Jess knew there was something she must do while she had the time. She must meet with Rod Green. And she must reach out to those young people with what she had - her gifts and abilities as an occupational therapist and counsellor. She could become their social worker. And whatever else they needed.

She spoke to Dad about it first. She didn't want to abandon the family. They'd already lost Toby and now she knew Dad could go at any moment too. But she didn't feel needed here.

'Go,' Dad said. 'If God is telling you to go, then go.'

'But what about you? What if ...' she couldn't finish.

'What's different now, Jess? None of us know how long we have. Toby taught us that. The thing is, I know where I'm going when I die. Those young people at Kangon Hill don't, and this could be their last day on earth. So if God's telling you to go, you need to go.'

But was he? She still hadn't had a response to her email, so this time she called the number on Toby's brochure.

A professional sounding woman answered. 'Kangon Hill, Beth speaking.'

'Hello, my name's Jessica Cardelle. I'm an O.T. and physio and I'm interested in working with your team there. I wondered if I can speak to Rod Green?'

'He's busy at the moment. Can I get him to give you a call back?'

'That would be great. Thank you.'

CHAPTER THIRTY-ONE

Jess was frustrated. Rod Green still hadn't called back. Should she call again? She heard the door open followed by Tim's uneven steps through the house. He could have stopped that limp if he'd let her help. The sooner she was away from this place, the better. She was tired of the reminders of her pain and failures.

'Anyone here?' Tim's deep voice called.

Jess came out of her room, resisting the urge to ask if she could help him. She knew how that would go down.

'Got a calf with an infected foot,' Tim said.

'Dad's not around?'

'No, he went into town.'

Was he was hoping she would help him catch the calf and hold it down? She wasn't going to offer and risk rejection again. He studied her and she waited. If he wanted her help, he'd have to ask.

He turned around and walked out again and she watched him go. What would he do? Try by himself, or wait for Dad? What if he injured himself? What if the calf trampled him?

She'd better check he was okay. With a sigh, she put on her farm boots and headed out the door.

She found Tim out in the paddock, eyeing off the calf, a deep frown fixed in place.

She shook her head. 'I don't think that's going to make it come to you.'

Tim glanced at her. 'I'm trying a new vet technique. Remote calling.'

'Pardon?'

'It's all about connecting with the calf's mind. My thought waves will infiltrate its brain until it comes to me.'

Was that a joke?

'It's a cheeky little blighter though,' he said. 'It's using its own thought waves to make me want to eat grass.'

He *was* joking. She stared at him and one side of his mouth tilted up. 'Well, aren't you the serious one these days?' he said. 'Where's your sense of humour?'

Defense rose up. She had good reason to be sad. Why was it expected that she would be the one to carry everyone else? She was tired of it. She had nothing left to give. 'Who are you to talk?'

His eyes narrowed. 'Don't turn it back on me. We're talking about you for a change.'

She turned away, focusing on the calf. She could feel Tim's eyes on her and blushed under his scrutiny.

The calf bounded past.

'You might catch him quicker if you keep your eyes on him,' she muttered.

'I'd prefer to have my hands on him.'

Another joke. The calf stopped to eye them warily, and Jess moved forward. 'Cut off that corner. I'll drive him in there.'

Tim moved in to force the calf into the corner. It let out a bellow, but Jess wasn't letting him go. Frustration gave her strength and she held him down while Tim knelt on the ground and studied the hoof. He clipped it and dipped it in some kind of liquid. Normally Jess would have been curious enough to ask him what he was doing, but today she didn't care.

She watched him skillfully handle the calf, and was drawn to his nimble, capable hands. He was attractive. She couldn't deny that. Something stirred inside and she cut the feeling off. She was done here. She forced her eyes away, out to the hills she had once loved. Hills that now looked empty, that threatened to smother her with their beauty. What was wrong with her?

'So,' Tim said when they'd let the calf go, 'going to tell me what's going on? Why you're so out of sorts? Moping around like you've given up on life?' His smile was tight and he leaned forward as though he were a counsellor. Was he trying to be funny again? There may have been a spark of amusement behind those dark eyes, but she wasn't willing to look into them to work it out.

She felt like that cornered calf. 'It's not me who refuses to live the life I've been given, Tim.'

He stepped back, crossing his arms. 'You can't beat me at my own game, Jess. I know what you're doing.'

She frowned. 'What am I doing?'

'You know exactly what you're doing. Attack is the best form of defense, isn't it?'

She looked away.

He let out a grunt. 'I've faced pain and death too, Jess.'

'Yeah, but you're still not making the most of your life. You're alive because my brother died. It hurts to see you wasting the gift you've been given.'

Tim scowled. 'Don't try to make this out to be some parallel to Jesus, Jessica. If your brother had the choice, I doubt he would have given his life for mine.'

'Not if he knew what you'd do with it,' she snapped. It was easier to be angry with Tim than to … feel anything else.

Tim's expression gentled into something close to sympathy. It threw her and she licked suddenly dry lips, guilt niggling. She'd been spoiling for a fight, but she hadn't been fighting fair.

'Tim, I'm sorry. That's not true. If you knew Toby, you'd know he would have given his life to give another person a chance at finding it.'

Tim reached for her hand and she stared at him in confusion. 'I've found life, Jess. I'm doing okay. It's you who —'

She jumped up, jerking her hand from his. Who was this person? 'Since when did this become about me?'

She had to leave. She couldn't handle Tim like this. His pity. His caring looks. She couldn't breathe. He was smothering her. She was the therapist, not him! She was the strong, capable one so why did it feel like it was all slipping out of her control?

She needed a new ministry and she needed it now.

Tim was still studying her, that interested, concerned expression on his face. 'I hear you're going to help out at the place your brother donated to,' he said, as though reading her thoughts.

So Dad had told him her plans. She nodded. 'They need a worker with my qualifications so I'll be on my way as soon as I hear back from them.'

'Good pay?'

'Yes, but no money.'

Tim's mouth tightened. 'So you've totally given up on me.'

Yes. She'd given up. 'When you want to, you'll walk like any other man. If you'd let me I could have made you ready physically, but your heart … that's up to you.'

She turned away, but he tugged at her arm. 'Jess!'

She turned back, eyebrows raised in question.

'Is it because you think you're not good enough? That you don't belong here? That you'll never find someone …?'

His voice faded out at her look. How dare he imply she was going because she thought no one would have her! She could tell him about Pierce's proposal, but that was none of his business. And what did she care what Tim thought of her anyway?

'That's not it at all, Tim,' she said.

She needed to go. Now. She turned and walked away without a backward glance at Tim Bateman. Even as he called her name.

CHAPTER THIRTY-TWO

Kangon Hill was beautiful. Rain had greened the hills and covered them with purple and yellow wildflowers. Yes, Paterson's Curse and Capeweed were despised by farmers, but today Jess couldn't find it in her heart to dislike them. She felt hope and excitement building as she drove up to the main house. She still hadn't been able to speak to Rod, but she was meant to be here, so she would just speak to him in person. She would present herself as Toby's sister in case he had forgotten her, and offer herself for ministry. Her heart beat hard and suddenly fear took over. What was she doing? Really? For the first time she regretted not waiting to hear back. Maybe they didn't want her. Maybe they saw deep down inside where she was insecure and lost.

She made her way cautiously into the office beside the main house. A young woman with a delightful, welcoming smile greeted her.

'Hello. Can I help you?'

Jess nodded, managing a smile of her own. 'I'm after Rod Green.'

The woman looked surprised. 'Is he expecting you?'

Jess shook her head. 'No,' she admitted, 'but he knew my brother, Toby Cardelle.'

Immediate recognition passed over the woman's face and with it, deep respect.

'I'll see if I can contact Rod.'

Jess sat in the waiting room as the young woman tried Rod's mobile. She soon came out with a huge smile.

'Rod will be here as fast as he can. And by how excited he was, I expect it will be faster than he should.'

Jess found out what the young woman meant when a ute tore down the driveway and screeched to a stop outside the office. Rod jumped out and charged in. Once again he wore faded blue jeans and a sport top that somehow reminded Jess of Toby. There was an intensity to his square, determined face as he studied Jess and held out a firm hand for her to shake.

'Jess.'

Jess smiled. 'Good to see you again, Rod.'

He sat down and motioned for her to do the same. 'So what's the deal?'

Jess once again noticed the gold ring in his ear and wondered why she found it appealing. In fact, she found everything about this man appealing.

'After you came to see us about Toby, I emailed you about your position for a social worker, and called a few days ago but didn't hear back. But I just believed it was time, so I came. I'm a physio and O.T. and I majored in mental health. I think I can help you.'

Rod's brow wrinkled. 'You emailed me? When?'

She shrugged. 'Months back, now.'

He shook his head. 'I didn't get it. But I guess it wasn't God's timing.' He shuffled awkwardly for a moment, his eyes meeting hers in a direct, open way. 'We have a social worker now. However, I am hoping to start a chain of rehabilitation houses and I'd definitely consider you for the next one.'

'When will that be?'

Rod shrugged. 'We don't have a location yet, but it should be soon.'

Disappointment knifed through Jess. There wasn't even a position for her. Seeming to sense her despondency, Rod leaned forward, his look intense.

'Jess, I believe this is God's timing. Nothing is chance. I have no accommodation for you because the spare units are taken up by a family helping me out temporarily here. But is there somewhere close by you can stay? I think it would be good to talk more with you about this. You'd be an asset to have around as we plan our future projects.'

He smiled and Jess found herself responding with her heart. Toby had helped this man. Toby shared this man's heart for God and young people.

'I'm sure I can find somewhere.' Whatever happened she didn't want to leave. Her pride and her heart would never allow her to go back home again this soon.

Rod became all business then, his officious movements matching his tough exterior. Jess could see he was the perfect person to work with teenagers and young adults. There was a no-nonsense air about him, yet a firm kindness, too. She doubted many people dared mess with him.

As Rod looked over her resume he seemed deep in thought. Then without even looking at her, he took his mobile from his pocket and dialled a number.

'Phil!' he said into his phone. 'I think we have our next employee for project three here. How soon can you get here?'

PHIL DIDN'T ARRIVE AS QUICKLY as Rod had. The tall, sandy haired man came into the office, a toddler bouncing in his arms. Jess smiled at the little girl with the beautiful green eyes, then looked to her father.

'Phil,' he said, holding out his hand, and Jess knew where the little girl got her eyes.

'Jess,' she said, taken off guard by the joy and warmth Phil exuded. He reminded her of her dad.

Rod, Phil, and the lady who'd first met her, whose name she discovered was Beth, interviewed her. She was impressed by their passion for God and the project and the way they looked through her resume, asked questions and prayed with her. Then they welcomed her to the team.

It seemed Phil was about to leave when he suddenly stopped.

'Rod, my family's staying in the only available house ...'

Rod smiled. 'That's fine. Jess said she can find other accommodation.'

Phil looked doubtful, but Rod seemed to think it was settled. With a final look at Jess, Phil left again with the little girl still happily in his arms.

JESS SCROLLED DOWN HER PHONE, dismayed that there were no rental properties available. She could afford to stay in a motel for a couple of nights, but what about after that? She should have confessed she had nowhere to go.

'You're doing this for God and those teenagers,' she reminded herself. 'Teenagers who have probably slept rough for years, with no home of their own.'

God, show me what to do.

Even as she prayed, she noticed a dirt track that appeared to lead into some bushland. It was like the track her family and the Buckley's had gone down every year on their camping trips.

Why couldn't she camp? She loved the outdoors and she could

afford all the gear, knew exactly what she needed. Some alone time would be perfect, time out in nature with just her and God.

She began to plan. She could buy a decent sized tent, a gas cooker, a solar fridge and she could use the laundromat in town. She had enough savings to cover food, petrol, car rego, and plan for the future without pay as well. She had seen a local gym. If she went there daily she could shower there after a workout. She could also recharge her mobile phone in their powerpoint. Yes, she could manage.

CHAPTER THIRTY-THREE

Tim worked on his exercises, anger giving him strength. What was this Kangon Hill place Jess had gone to? He was sure it wasn't even legal not to pay your workers.

He pushed hard against the stretch band. He didn't need Jess. He'd collected his medical file from Lauren and was working through his exercises himself. He'd also called the surgeon and arranged for more surgery. But Lauren had admitted the practice was struggling without Jess.

And then there was Charlie. He'd given Jess his blessing to go, but now he walked around the farm with his shoulders slumped and such sadness in his eyes that it tugged at Tim's heart. He really shouldn't care, but Charlie was like a father to him. And if he was honest, the whole family had wormed their way into his heart.

Even Milla looked sad despite having Zac with her most of the time. He'd left Bluey with her for a few days, hoping to cheer her up.

Charlie had confessed his concerns about Toby's stolen identity and Tim was sure Kangon Hill had something to do with it, even though they'd been cleared. It was time to do his own investigating. He would discredit the place that had stolen Jess's heart to show it for what it was. Jess had been brainwashed and he had to do something about it. She was as bad as his sister, Clare. Once she'd been drawn into Christianity, she'd lost all reason. He didn't know what was worse – refusing to become a physiotherapist in the first place, or being one and not making any money out of it. He was going to look into this man, Rod Green, and all he stood for.

MILLA MISSED JESS. She missed Toby. And she missed the closeness she had felt to God when life was slower; when there'd been time to notice him every day. She needed to feel alive again, like she had when she couldn't see. With a sigh, she took out the washing basket to bring in the dry clothes. Even the clothesline looked empty without Jess or Toby's clothes hanging there. She looked up into the sky, at the clouds.

'God?'

She knew he was there. And Toby was there somewhere, too. She remembered lying out under the stars on camping trips, talking with Toby, listening as he told her the names of stars.

Dumping the basket, Milla plopped down onto the grass and looked up at the sky. It was so vast. The clothes flapped past as the clothesline rotated in the breeze. She closed her eyes, concentrated on the tickle of the grass beneath her skin, the breeze on her face, the squeak of the clothesline and the clicking noise it made as it turned around, grinding against the rotary mechanism. She smiled at the warmth of the sun on her cheeks. She was alive. So alive.

Something nipped her toe. She jerked up and brushed the ant off her foot. Where had it gone? She turned onto her stomach and focused on the grass, imagining she was as small as the ants down there, noticing the detail in every blade of grass, every stalk as it swayed gently.

'What are you doing?'

She looked up. Zac. He grinned down at her, head tilted, amusement written in the lines of his face.

'Pretending I'm an ant.'

'Really? How's it feel?' He went down onto his knees, and peered into the grass.

'Good. You should try it. Properly. You have to lie down, put your face at ground level.'

He laughed, but did so. 'Hmm,' he said, turning his face to hers. 'Not too bad a view here.'

She shoved his shoulder. 'We're looking at the ants, not each other.'

He grinned wider, but turned, resting his chin on his hands to study the ground.

Milla allowed herself a sneak glance sideways. He appeared absorbed in the activity of the ants scurrying around in the grass. She studied him. Every detail of his face. His strong jawline, his …

He caught her eye and gave a self-conscious smile. 'What?'

She smiled back. 'Just seeing you. Got to remember how you look for if I ever lose my sight again.'

'Wouldn't it be good to never see me grow old and bald and fat?'

She chuckled, but considered his words. She would like to see him grow old no matter how he looked.

'Where do you think Jess is right now?' she asked to change the subject.

'I dunno, but I doubt she's lying on the ground, studying the ants. Come on, let me help you get the clothes off the line.'

Jess had begun to enjoy her lifestyle, as hard as it was. There was a freedom in living rough, in not needing all the comforts of home. It brought her back to those days of camping in her childhood; nature, the bush. And her whole family.

And yet she was so alone. She picked up her phone, desperate to hear her parents' voices.

'We're in the process of planning for a future home for the young people,' she reported to her family. They would never guess accommodation wasn't being provided for her.

Jess thoroughly enjoyed the planning meetings with Rod and Phil. She understood why Toby and Sasha had given so much to the project. Jess's only struggle with those meetings was Phil's caring interest in her. He asked too many questions about how she was going and where she was living. So far she'd managed to avoid them all nicely, but she knew if she didn't start getting a more comfortable night's sleep she was likely to stumble and let her secret out. Tiredness was wearing her down. Her other problem was her dreams of Tim. Rod was right here in front of her, ruggedly good looking, a believer with a commitment and heart for God and an appealing smile. So why was Tim plaguing her dreams at night?

As Jess left the office with Phil and Rod, Beth waved a hand to her from the front desk.

'I'm headed home now. Want to join my husband and I for dinner?'

Beth looked too young to be married, but Jess smiled. 'I'd love to.'

Beth led Jess a few doors down to a simple but beautiful cottage. She opened the door. 'Welcome to my home.'

The smell of roast lamb wafted out. Jess's stomach rumbled.

'Come this way.' Beth led Jess into the kitchen. 'Gus, this is Jess.'

A man turned from the stove where he was placing chunks of pumpkin on a tray. His whole face softened as he looked at his wife. He stepped forward, put an arm around Beth and kissed her soundly on the mouth. Then he gazed seriously at Jess.

'Pleased to meet you. I hear you'll be helping with our next project.'

Before Jess could respond, he'd gone back to the cooking.

Beth didn't bat an eyelid. She left Gus to it and led Jess out to the loungeroom. Jess sank into the sofa. If only her camp chair was this comfortable. Speaking of, she needed to start asking Beth questions. She'd learned that the more questions she asked, the less was asked about her.

'So what brought you to work here, Beth?'

Beth smiled. 'I met Gus at the Kamira Creek project when Clare and Phil were working there. Clare's my sister. Now I have a degree in environmental science so I help with environmental planning for the project. I also teach the guests to care for injured wildlife and help in the office every other day.'

Wow. That was not what Jess had been expecting. 'Guests?' she asked.

'The teenagers in our program.'

'Oh. What about Gus?'

Beth gave a proud smile. 'He does everything. He designed and built these buildings, he does maintenance, computer set-up, whatever needs doing.'

Jess's eyebrows raised. 'And he cooks, too.'

Beth giggled. 'Only when I let him. I mean, I have to be needed somewhere, or I feel a bit useless.'

Jess smiled, liking Beth intensely. There was something familiar about her.

She was happy and well-fed when she headed home to her tent that night. Surely the property for the new project would be found soon? Jess was longing for a comfortable bed, toilet, and running water.

'At least I have a shelter over my head,' she told herself, grateful for her years of camping experience. The rustles on the ground and in the trees above her at night didn't bother her. Most likely bats, maybe a bandicoot or echidna or two and possibly a snake. They all kept their respectful distance while she was awake at least, and whatever happened in her sleep she didn't care so long as she didn't know.

ANOTHER MEETING and this time Rod had invited Jess to dinner. She was flustered by the invitation. It was different being invited to dinner with Beth and Gus. They were married. She had been accepting a dinner invitation and nothing more. So why did it feel more personal when Rod asked her? Because it would just be the two of them, or because she had a crush on the man? She was sure he had no idea. She was practiced at being professional and would continue being that way, dinner invitation or no dinner invitation.

Rod was chatty as he led her down the path to his home. A light had been left on and Jess liked his thoughtfulness. He had known it could be dark when they got there. Jess did, however, wonder at the size of the house. And then she saw the swing set in the yard. And the small bike. For the first time, she glanced at Rod's ring finger. She couldn't see in the dark. Funny she had noticed the gold ring in his ear, but never one on his finger. But then, she had never looked because she had never considered he might be married. And yet he must be the same age as Phil and Gus, and they were married …

Rod opened the door and light flooded her eyes. She squinted and glanced at Rod's ring finger. A spark of gold glinted in the light. And there, coming toward them was his pregnant wife.

Her smile was reserved, almost as though she knew what a threat Jess had been. Shame heated her face and she swallowed hard.

Rod's wife didn't need to worry. Now she knew, she would never think of him that way again. Remorse made her sick to the stomach. How could she have? And yet, how could she have known? Rod had never mentioned his wife. How committed was he anyway?

The answer came when Rod reached for his wife, pulled her fiercely into his arms and gave her a passionate kiss on the lips. She grinned at him.

'Welcome home.'

He grinned back and turned to Jess. 'This is my wife, Toni.'

Jess nodded, pulling herself together. 'I would hope so.'

Toni chuckled and the ice was broken. She offered Jess a seat on the lounge. 'I'll just check on dinner. Won't be a moment.'

She disappeared around the corner after Rod. A few moments later, the owner of the bike and swing set ran into the room. He stopped short when he saw Jess.

She smiled. 'Hello, I'm Jess. What's your name?'

'Billy,' he said. 'I'm five.' Jess couldn't believe how like his father he was. That same determined jaw, intense grey eyes and even the ring in one ear.

'You gunna help with the project?' he asked.

'I hope so.'

Billy nodded. 'Uncle Phil, Aunty Clare and Zoe help too.' He pointed to a bedroom. 'They sleep in there.'

Jess's eyes widened. 'They live here too?'

'Just sometimes. They went to Uncle Gus and Aunty Beth's for tea.' He handed Jess one of his toy cars. 'I let Zoe have it when she's here, but sometimes she sucks on it.' His nose wrinkled up in disgust and Jess grinned, trying not to think of the slobber that might have been on the car she now held in her hand. Billy hugged the better one to himself. 'This one's mine.'

The little guy was so cute. He jumped up and ran back down the hall. 'Just getting my racetrack,' he called over his shoulder.

She sat and waited, wondering how long it took a child to find a racetrack. Was he building it?

She looked around. So Phil and Clare were staying here, too. And there was she thinking Rod lived alone. This evening had turned out nothing like she expected but she couldn't bring herself to talk to God about it. Perhaps because she now knew she had jumped in over her head without turning to him for guidance. She had raced ahead of him and his plan and now she was running. The wrong way.

Her mobile rang. 'Dad.' She answered it with a smile.

'Jess, where are you?'

'Having dinner with Rod Green and his family.'

'Have you got time to talk?'

'Yes. Is everything okay?' There was silence and Jess felt her heart sink. 'Dad?'

'I'm tired.'

'Where's Tim? Isn't he helping out?'

'He has other business to attend to.'

She wanted to ask but told herself not to. Tim was none of her business anymore. 'What about Zac?'

'I don't want to ask him. He's a kid. He needs to be a kid. And he's got school.'

'I'll come home.'

'No, Jess, that's not why I'm calling. You are where God has called you to be.'

Was she?

'I'm praying about selling up, Jess.'

What? Her heart skipped a beat. This was where racing ahead of God got her. 'But Dad, our farm has been in the family for generations.'

There was a heartfelt sigh on the other end of the phone. She knew Dad loved that property more than anyone, but now he didn't have a son to continue it on for him. And she was here because of her own foolish, stubborn hopes and dreams.

'Just pray about it for me will you Jess?' Dad asked.

'Of course.' She heard the dinner plates being put on the table. 'Dad, I've got to go, but I'll be praying.'

They hung up and Jess groaned. This was all her fault.

'Call from your father?' Rod asked as they were eating dinner.

Jess looked at him in surprise.

'Sorry, I couldn't help hearing.'

She smiled sadly. 'He rang to say he may have to sell our farm. He has a heart condition that—'

She stopped at the look on Rod's face.

'Where is this property?'

'Barrawi.'

'Where I came to see you?'

'Yes.'

His forehead wrinkled in concentration. 'Small town about an hour from the city,' he said, his mind clearly working through something. Then he chuckled. 'Perfect. How do you think your Dad would feel about selling up but still living there and teaching some young people how to farm?'

Jess felt her heartbeat quicken. God had this planned all along.

MILLA WATCHED Dad's face light up as he told Mum about Rod Green's proposal.

'The whole project would be built and set up here on our property. We wouldn't have to leave. And we could continue Toby's dream.' His eyes sparkled with life and hope, the way they had before Toby died. 'We would still have the farm and a ministry to go with it.'

Mum caught Dad's excitement and her eyes sheened with tears. 'And Jess would work here?'

Milla caught their excitement. She was missing Jess, but it seemed God might have a plan to bring her back.

'We need to pray about it,' Dad said and Mum smiled, giving him a sideways look.

'Okay. But you already know, don't you.'

Dad held back a smile. 'Know what?'

'That this is God's good plan. His good, pleasing and perfect plan!'

Dad let the smile spread across his face and Milla's heart sang at his joy.

CHAPTER THIRTY-FOUR

im's jaw clenched harder the closer he came to Kangon Hill. By sheer determination, without the help of a physiotherapist, he was not only walking well, he was driving. Jess would be proud of him if she knew. And he was going to make sure she knew, just as soon as he showed this place for what it really was. It should be easy enough to discredit the work done here. He wouldn't be surprised if it was actually a cult. He couldn't understand why Charlie and Lydia Cardelle couldn't see that. They were willing to hand their farm over to this group. He couldn't fathom why anyone would do such a thing.

Gums lined the country road, some arching across both lanes, a guard of honour. Justice would soon be his. He saw the little boy on the road just in time. Standing there, glaring a challenge at Tim's car as though he thought he could hold a bulldozer off. Tim screeched to a stop and flung open his door.

'What do you think you're doing? You'll get yourself killed!'

The little boy lifted his chin and crossed his arms over his chest. 'You nearly hit her!'

'What?' It was then he saw. A toddler, a little girl who mustn't be more than a year old, at the feet of the boy, trying to crawl across the road. The boy moved and attempted to haul her up. 'I can't carry her,' he said, something suspiciously like tears rimming his eyes. 'She's too heavy.'

Tim flipped on his hazard lights, ran back to the little girl and hoisted her up into his arms.

'Put her down!' The little boy beat at his legs. 'Let her go!'

Tim gritted his teeth as a well-aimed kick from the small shoe hit him in a sensitive spot near his shin, just above his prosthetic foot.

'I'm just getting her off the road.' He reached out to grab the boy, but he backed away, eyeing him warily.

'Are you a kidnapper?'

'No. I'm trying to help. To get you both to safety.'

'Why? You're not my friend.'

'How can I be your friend?' Tim demanded, exasperated. 'I don't even know you.'

'Give her back!' He pointed at the little girl in Tim's arms.

Tim looked at her. She was pretty. Huge, green, expressive eyes, a heart-shaped face and dimples that reminded him of … no. How could he be holding a little Clare in his arms? Besides, Clare had brown eyes. But the likeness was uncanny.

'I don't know you,' the little boy accused, using Tim's own argument against him as though that automatically made him a bad man.

Tim glanced at him, but was distracted when the little girl used two hands to turn his face, forcing him to look into her eyes. Then she smiled. Such delight. Such trust. He didn't deserve it.

Bewildered, he looked down at the little boy. 'Where do you live?'

The boy eyed him with distrust. 'Not allowed to tell strangers my address.'

'Look, I need to get you and this little girl safely home.' Maybe he should just call the police. But who knew what the boy would do in the time it took him to call. Neither he nor this toddler were safe out here on the road, that was for sure.

He held out his hand to the boy. 'My name's Tim Bateman. We're not strangers now you know my name.'

The boy screwed up his face and for the first time Tim noticed the gold ring in his ear. 'Uncle Tim?' he asked.

Tim's felt his lips tilting. 'Well, I wouldn't go that far ...'

The boy looked down, studying his leg. 'Where's your pretend foot?'

'Pardon?'

His eyes lit up. 'Uncle Phil said you have a pretend foot. Like a pirate.'

Phil? Something clicked into place. Philip Cairn was his brother-in-law. But Phil didn't have a son. Not one this age, at least. The little girl, though ...

'What's this little girl's name?'

'Zoe Maria Cairn.'

The greatest urge in Tim at that moment was to drop the toddler and run. But how could he when he held his niece in his arms? And who knew who this little boy was?

'What kind of accident did they say I had?' Tim asked. What had his sister said about him?

The boy shrugged. 'I dunno.'

Tim felt indignant and relieved all at once. 'They don't talk about it?'

'Not much, but Aunty Clare talks about you all the time. We pray for you every night because you don't know Jesus.'

They weren't interested in his physical condition, but his spiritual one. Tim shifted the little girl in his arms as she tried to get his attention again. He needed to get them home. Now.

'What's your name, kid?'

The boy stuck his hands in his pockets. 'William Calvin Green. But everyone calls me Billy.'

'Billy, how about I take you home in my car? You can hold Zoe really tight in your lap and I'll drive slowly. Now that you know I'm Zoe's uncle, you can trust me.'

Billy bit his lip, and his lower lip protruded. What now?

'Aunty Clare said you can be my uncle, too. 'Cause her dad and my dad were foster brothers.'

What? That would make Tim's dad and Rod Green's dad brothers. Not likely. He knew about the Green family. Mum had mentioned them. Losers. Drug addicts. He wasn't going to accept any connection to them. But then, when this little boy looked at him like that …

He sighed. Fine. 'I can be your uncle, too.'

The boy beamed up at him and raced to open the back door of Tim's car. Tim followed, carrying Zoe.

He put the little girl down on the back seat and she scrambled across to the other side. He kept a close eye on her. She moved fast. She fiddled with the seat belt and he breathed a sigh of relief. So long as she didn't work out the door handle he'd be right.

'Here,' Tim said to the boy, 'I'll help you get your seat belt on.'

'But I'm s'posed to have a booster seat.'

'Yeah, well, sorry but I don't have one. How far is your house?'

'Just 'round the corner.'

'Okay, well we'll use this seatbelt and you can hold Zoe tight and we'll be right for a little bit.'

He clipped the seatbelt into place. It sat across the little boy's face. He moved it out of the way, peeking over the top. 'I can't see.'

Tim sighed. 'Okay, let's leave the seatbelt off, and you just sit real tight, holding Zoe.'

Billy nodded, and Tim watched the boy gently pull Zoe toward him. She beamed and settled right into the little boy's lap. With a sigh of relief, Tim shut the door and jumped into the driver's seat. Hopefully Billy could hold the squirming toddler long enough to get them home.

'So which way?' he asked, turning in the seat to look behind at Billy. He was doing a good job of holding Zoe firm.

'That way.' He pointed, then quickly grabbed Zoe's hand when she reached her fingers towards the window button.

Tim drove, glancing behind as often as he dared. 'How much further?'

'There! See. In the gate.'

Tim squinted. He could see something ahead. A gate? And some buildings. That must be it. A sign greeted him as he drove over a cattle grid.

Kangon Hill.

No. His heart pounded. Seeing his sister for the first time in two years was not what he expected when he made his way here to discredit the place.

He turned in the drive. A man charged toward them. He had to be Billy's father. He had the exact same eyes and jaw, although his chin was hidden by a goatee. He even had the gold earring. His eyes were wide, his face pale.

The back door of the car opened and Zoe tumbled out, into the dust. She let out a wail and Billy scrambled out behind, lifting her from the ground and brushing off her hands. 'You're okay, Zoe. You're okay.'

'Billy! Zoe! Oh, thank God!' The man charged at the two, looked back to Tim then at the still-screaming Zoe.

'Who's meant to be taking care of these two?' Tim asked pointing to the toddler and the poor little boy trying to calm her down.

The man swept Zoe up into his arms. 'What happened? Billy, where was she?' Then he looked wildly around. 'I have to let everyone know we've found them.' He tried to settle Zoe down while fumbling for his phone.

'Phil, we've got them!' His voice was breathless. 'Yes, both here. Call everyone back. Oh, and can you call the police – let them know we don't need them anymore? Thanks.'

He put the phone back in his pocket, then let out a huge sigh as he looked at Tim. 'Someone left the gate open. And Zoe … she's so quick.'

'I tried to get her to come back, Daddy, I tried.' Billy's bottom lip quivered, and the man squatted down to his level. 'It's okay, Billy. It's not your fault.'

'She was too heavy. She didn't want to come back. I followed her.'

The man looked to Tim.

'I found them in the middle of the road,' he said. 'Billy was guarding her like a bull terrier.' He looked down at his leg. 'His kicks felt like a terrier bite, too.'

The man shot a proud look at Billy, then smiled. 'God is good.'

Tim didn't know about that, but he had to admit he was thankful he hadn't hit them.

The man hesitated. 'I'm Billy's father. Rod.'

'Tim.'

'Thank you, Tim.'

Billy ran to the verandah of the house, picked something up and raced back to Tim, holding it out. A toy car.

'For you,' he said.

Rod frowned. 'Billy, that's your favourite.'

'Yes, but he saved us.'

Tim shook his head. 'You keep it, mate.' At Billy's wounded look, he changed his mind and reached to take it from his small hand. He didn't deserve it, but Billy clearly wanted him to have it. 'Thank you.'

It wasn't easy swallowing his pride and accepting a gift from such a little boy, but what else could he do?

Roaring engines came toward them. Rod raced over, Zoe still in his arms. A ute screeched to a stop first, followed by a sedan. So many people piled out Tim couldn't keep track.

A dishevelled looking woman ran to Billy and shook his little shoulders. 'What did you think you were doing? You're supposed to look after Zoe!'

The fear and remorse Tim saw in Billy's face was too much. 'Hey,' he said, pulling the woman's hands away. 'He saved Zoe. He's a hero.'

He couldn't let this woman put such a heavy load of responsibility on such a little boy. He knew the burden of that weight. The woman spun around and Tim took a step back. That's when he saw the fear in her eyes. She'd been worried.

'I'm Tim,' he said, holding out his hand. 'I found Billy protecting Zoe in the middle of the road. I hate to think what would have happened if he hadn't stood in front of her, refusing to move. I might not have seen her.'

Billy's lip quivered. 'She was too heavy, Mummy. I tried to look after her like you said. I tried.'

The woman's face softened. 'Thank you, Billy. You did well.'

Billy's smile lit up his face.

The woman reached for Tim's hand. 'Toni,' she said.

He shook her hand at the same time he saw the other woman standing there, frozen, her face pale. Clare.

Clare came forward almost hesitantly, and he could see she was holding a surge of emotion at bay.

'Tim, you're really here!' she whispered in disbelief.

With a smile, he opened his arms and she came to him, half crying, half sobbing. She had almost lost her little girl, and now here she was, crying her heart out because he was here. For the first time he understood the depth of pain he had caused his family by keeping away.

'Hey, Clare, it's okay,' he said, surprised by the old protectiveness that surged through his veins.

She stepped back from him. 'Tim look at you!' She wiped at her red eyes and smiled through tears. 'You look amazing!'

Last time she'd seen him he'd been in a hospital bed, refusing help, wrapped up in bitterness and turning away everyone who had ever loved him.

'I prayed ...' she stopped short, and he knew she was afraid of making him angry. 'I so badly wanted you to come.'

'It's okay,' he said. 'Billy already told me I'm prayed for.'

She nodded. 'Every night.' Her eyes looked hopeful. 'You're okay with that?'

He shrugged, giving her a wry grin. 'Do I have a choice? Now tell me what you're doing here.'

'Just helping out until it's all set up.' She reached over to take Zoe from Rod's arms. To his surprise, the toddler reached for him, instead. Feeling awkward, he took her while Clare grinned as though seeing her daughter in his arms was the best thing that could have happened to her. 'It's a part of the project we began back at the Cairns' farm on Kamira Creek,' she explained. 'Phil's parents are keeping that going while Rod and Toni - the managers, and Beth, Gus, Phil and I are all getting this place going.'

Tim's eyes widened as he heard his youngest sister's name.

'Beth's here?'

Clare nodded. 'She really misses you.' She looked at Zoe now snuggled against his chest. 'You're the one who found her?'

'On the road. Billy was guarding her.'

'Oh Tim,' Clare said, 'what if ... what if it had been anyone but you?'

Tim winced. 'I don't know that I'm any better than anyone else.'

'You're family!' She flung her arms around him again, squeezing Zoe against his chest. Zoe giggled and the sound did something to his heart. Protectively, he held the little girl closer. Was this how it would feel to be a father?

Clare pulled on his arm, eyes dancing with joy. 'Come and see Beth.'

Tim glanced over at Phil. His gentle smile as he watched Clare touched something inside him. Phil adored Clare. He caught Tim's eye as he was dragged past and winked. No doubt he'd been on the receiving end of Clare's coercion many times.

Tim's heart pounded at the thought of seeing Beth. His little sister had always looked up to him with admiring, loving eyes. She had never rebelled like Clare and Dan, and for that reason he had felt greater responsibility for her.

'Beth!' Clare called, still dragging Tim by the arm.

Beth came out of the house, saw him and gasped. Her face drained of colour, then her eyes filled with tears.

'Tim?' Her voice broke, then she flew at him, flung her arms around him and clung. 'Oh Tim, you missed my wedding. We didn't know when we would see you again. Oh, I wanted you there so badly.'

She sobbed there in his arms and Tim knew deep regret for his selfish actions. He shouldn't have shut out his family. He'd thought he was saving them the burden of his condition, but he'd hurt them. Deeply.

'I'm sorry, Beth,' he choked out.

'No, no, I'm just glad you're here. So glad!' She stepped back and stared at him as though afraid to believe he was real. Then she gave him her gentle wide-eyed smile, the one she'd given him as a child. Despite him being an amputee, she still admired him. Loved him. And oh, but he knew he didn't deserve it! Beth had the biggest heart of anyone he'd ever known.

He swallowed hard at a memory that had never quite left him. Beth had only been five years old when she saw a little girl on the news who needed a heart transplant. Her eyes had sparkled with tears.

'I want to give her my heart,' she had declared.

'You can't, Beth,' Mum said, horrified. 'You would die without your heart.'

She had lifted her chin. 'I still want to.'

Tim's heart had broken. His little sister's compassion was beyond his understanding. She would give her life for another!

Did she really think so little of her own life, or was her compassion and selflessness so deep that she would sacrifice her life for another?

'It doesn't work like that,' Grandpa then explained. 'She will have the heart of someone who has already died.'

Beth had looked relieved and devastated at once.

Tim shook his head at the memory, his heart hurting. Transplants. They required someone to die so another might live. It *was* a good parallel to the story of Jesus, despite him declaring to Jess that it wasn't so.

Jess. Where was she? She was, after all, the reason he was here. He would have asked except that Beth's husband —so hard to take it in—came out to see what was going on. Gus strode to Beth's side, his protective gaze assessing the scene before him. Then his eyes met Tim's in a steady, open challenge. And Tim knew his little sister didn't need him as her protector anymore. Gus would not let anyone hurt Beth. He was her hero, now. Tim had abandoned her but another had stepped in to take his place.

CHAPTER THIRTY-FIVE

Tim didn't ask about Jess. They were so overjoyed that he had come to see them, he didn't want to burst their bubble by admitting he'd come for another reason. Instead, he asked about the project, the staff, the guests, the future plans. He was surprised not to hear Jess's name mentioned, and felt guilty about how delighted his sisters were with his interest in the place.

But as Tim listened, he couldn't find fault with any of the methods used by the team of workers. He could find no underlying motive that was suspicious. This place truly seemed to be run with concern for the youth in mind. And yet, Jess was needed more at home than she was here. This was one big, happy family. They didn't need Jess like her family did.

'How long are you here?' Phil asked as they ate together in the Green's dining room. Beth and Gus had joined them for tea. Tim knew they would ring Mum and his brother Dan as soon as he was out of earshot. Let them. Perhaps he had been selfish cutting them off the way he had. He hadn't realised how worried they'd been; how much he'd hurt them. He'd planned to surprise them one day by turning up their doorstep walking like a whole man. Now that he'd accidentally done it, he saw how unfair it was.

'I have no plans, really,' Tim said. 'I've recently had surgery and rehabilitation and I'm having a break.'

Phil grinned. 'Maybe you can stay here for a couple of years and teach some of the guests some vet skills.'

Anger flared. 'I don't think so.' Already they were trying to involve him in their little project. Couldn't they see he was not one of them? They were as different as black and white. As dark and light. Tim could feel his darkness when he was with his sisters. They glowed with life and contentment. They had a happiness he couldn't remember them having as children. All that he'd invested in them had done nothing. They'd gone and found joy elsewhere. Because he hadn't been able to pass on what he didn't have.

Phil shot Tim an apologetic look and changed the subject. At least he was astute. The family talked about the new residents of the program, but Tim wasn't listening. He studied his youngest sister, Beth, relieved to see the change in her. Last time he'd seen her she'd been thin and sad, struggling with depression. At the time he'd felt helpless and as though he'd failed at being the father figure he needed to be. He had wanted to blame Beth's faith for her struggles, but her expression became animated and full of hope whenever she spoke about God. She now appeared healthy, though definitely not plump. And her eyes lit up as she talked about the work she and Gus were doing for God. And Gus sat with his arm around her, a strong and silent support. Tim had been replaced.

TIM SLEPT on a mattress in the loungeroom of Rod and Toni Green's house. They had all insisted. Phil, Clare and Zoe were staying in the spare room and Tim tried to tell them they already had a full house, but they wouldn't listen. And so here he was. He rested his head in his arms, listening to the sounds of Zoe settling to sleep. Clare and Phil were expecting again, he'd discovered. They hoped to head back to Kamira Creek in the next couple of weeks.

Zoe was the most content baby he had ever known. It wasn't normal. Could happiness and contentment be a disorder? It wasn't safe to take to strangers the way she did. It did strange things to his heart, having her delight in him for no reason at all, except that he was there. The way she snuggled into his chest after dinner, smiling up at him with those huge, dark-lashed eyes and dimpling at him, and the way she'd fallen asleep there in his arms, completely trusting him, warmed him and made him uncomfortable in equal measure. He didn't deserve her trust. Didn't deserve the trust or love of any of them.

A noise from the next room had him sitting up. That baby even giggled in her sleep? Definitely something wrong with her.

Or was this the way it was meant to be? Is this the way God originally planned the world before humans made such a mess of it?

He heard Phil and Clare talking quietly as they readied for bed and he settled back down. He hadn't realised how lonely he was until now, and for the first time he longed for a family of his own. If he ever had a daughter, he wanted her to be like Zoe. And if he had a son, he'd like him to be like Billy.

He smiled, thinking of the boy. He was like him, in some ways, taking on responsibility for a little girl when it wasn't his to take on. His heart jarred. Was he listening to himself? What if his siblings had never been his responsibility in the first place? He'd never expect a little boy like Billy to take on the care of younger siblings. So why had he expected it of himself? Why had Ms Schneider required it of him? She had no right.

TIM AWOKE in the night with a start. Something had startled him. A noise. There it was again. A helpless, terrified cry. Soft, but intense. Small footsteps wandered through the house. He jumped up from the lounge and tiptoed into the hall. He saw the shadow of little Billy, then saw the boy himself. The soft cries followed by sniffles were heart-wrenching.

'What's wrong, Billy?' Tim whispered. The weeping stopped.

'I was scared,' a little voice answered.

'Of what?'

'The dark.'

Tim came and took his hand. 'Do you want to sit with me on the lounge for a bit?'

He felt the boy's small hand clasp his. When they were settled on the lounge, Billy still held tight to Tim's hand.

'There's nothing to be afraid of,' Tim said in a low voice. 'The dark can't hurt you. All it means is that you can't see. Everything's just the same as it is in the daylight, but you can't see it.'

To his surprise, Billy chuckled and rested his head on Tim's shoulder. 'I don't mind it now,' he said. 'I'm not by myself anymore.'

Tim put his arm around him. 'You weren't really alone, anyway,' he said. 'Your mum and dad are here, even though you couldn't see them. Baby Zoe is asleep with Phil and Clare in that room over there. And I was here.'

Billy nodded. 'I know, but I thought Mummy wouldn't hear me. And she didn't, but God did. He sent you.'

Tim nodded, resting his hand on the little boy's head. Something in his heart and mind was stirring. Billy was scared of the dark because he was afraid no-one would be there to hear his call for help. Was that why he was so afraid to call for help? Because if he finally admitted he might need help it was possible there would be no-one there to help him?

TIM AWOKE to morning light filtering into the room. Little Billy leaned against him, fast asleep. Gently, he tried to move him, but Billy's eyes opened.

'I'm glad you're still here,' he said, giving Tim a bear hug. 'I thought you were just a dream.'

Tim smiled, rubbing his eyes. He had thought the same thing, but here he was.

'Maybe you should go back to your bed now it's light and get a bit more sleep,' he suggested. He was still tired, even if Billy wasn't.

'Okay.' Billy gave him one more beaming smile and headed down the hall. He swayed a little, still half asleep and rubbed his head, making his hair stand on end. Tim smiled.

CHAPTER THIRTY-SIX

Jess didn't know why Tim was on her mind this morning. She moved aside the bag of dirty clothes ready to take to the laundromat.

'I can't do anything else for him, Lord,' she prayed, wondering why it was so much easier to pray for someone other than herself. 'You know he needs a heart transplant. He's so angry and self-reliant. Replace his heart of stone with a heart of flesh.'

She glanced around her tent. She had once thought she could happily live outdoors, but she was missing the comforts of home. Her savings were almost gone and Toby's estate still hadn't cleared. Thankfully, Rod and Toni had invited her to dinner that evening. She was desperate for another warm meal and company.

TIM WAS SHOWN around the farm by Clare and Phil. He watched for any sign of Jess. None of the cars that came and went down the road looked like Jess's Toyota. He looked up at the sound of another engine. The four wheel drive belonging to Beth and Gus came through the gate. And then a Commodore that looked like his brother Dan's. He stiffened.

'Did Clare tell Dan I'm here?'

Phil followed Tim's gaze, squinting. 'She did.'

Panic surged. He wasn't ready to face Dan. Desperation seized him. He needed to hide. To escape. His gaze darted left and right before he bolted into the bush. No one would know he was an amputee, the way he ran, but he felt trapped. Which way should he go? His breaths came in short gasps, his chest tight. Had all reason left him? He must appear like a madman, but all that mattered was his escape. He charged forward, shoving branches of the undergrowth out of the way. His prosthetic foot caught on a fallen branch and he found himself falling.

Now he lay flat on his face in the dirt, all dignity gone. His heart did one final tumble and he was back in the train carriage, fighting to get free. Pain and fear consumed him as the carriage rocked and the seat captured and mangled his leg. Nausea and panic rose up as he realised this could be his last living moment. Why did his father's face flash through his mind? Failure threatened to suffocate him. His whole purpose in life from the age of eight years had been to be there for his mother and siblings. He'd always been strong and in control, despite Clare and Dan rebelling against his care.

As he had now done to them. He breathed in the smell of damp earth and eucalyptus. He had survived that accident. He was alive. So what was he doing running from his own brother? His own family?

What if he'd never met Zoe? And Billy? That little boy had stood in the middle of the road and risked his life for a toddler who wasn't even his responsibility. Caring for a toddler was an adult's job.

Was he listening to himself? Who made it his job to care for his siblings? The truth was, he wasn't capable. Even now. Look at him lying here on the ground, breathing in dirt and eucalyptus leaves. He'd been forced to face his weakness with a foot that would never exist again. There was nothing he could do to be physically complete again.

It had cost Toby's life to save him, and yet he didn't deserve to be saved.

'What kind of life am I living anyway?' he demanded through clenched teeth.

'Tim?'

Phil's deep voice called through the bush. He sounded worried.

Tim entertained the thought of remaining quiet and hidden, but he doubted Phil would give up searching. There was something genuine and strong about Philip Cairn. He couldn't help liking him. Trusting him.

He lifted his head. 'Over here.'

He heard the pounding of Phil's feet through the bush as he rushed over, then looked down at him in concern. 'Are you okay? Are you hurt?'

Tim turned his face, lifting himself up onto his elbows. 'Only my pride, I think.'

Phil's lips twisted. 'I know what that's like.' He held out his hand. 'I'll give you a hand up.'

Tim allowed Phil to help him up. But what did Phil know of damaged pride? He was whole. Capable. Useful.

Phil helped Tim to a rock, then sat down on a broken branch close by. Phil didn't speak. Just sat there. Tim would have wondered if their silence was some kind of power struggle had he not seen the compassion and understanding in Phil's gaze.

'I came here under false pretenses,' Tim finally said. 'If I'd known … if I'd known Clare and Beth were here …' He swallowed. 'I can't see Dan as well.'

Still, Phil sat silently, waiting.

'I have Toby Cardelle's kidney inside me, Philip. A very loved, very capable young man who had a fiancée.' His words were heavy with the shame he felt. 'I didn't even want a transplant. I wanted to die.'

'I know.' Phil said. 'We've been praying for you. Every day.'

Tim studied the ground. 'But I don't want to be prayed for. I want to be respected. I've lived my whole life trying to protect my family, trying to do the right thing,' he clenched his teeth. 'And then my brother has to save me from a train carriage and a family gives up their beloved son's body organ so I can live.'

Phil nodded. 'There's no shame in that. We all need help sometimes. That family wanted good to come from their sorrow. That's why they donated his organs.'

'You don't understand. Dan risked his life to save me that day! He stayed with me while the carriage burned, just so that I wouldn't be alone. And Toby … '

Phil nodded. 'His death saved your life. There are times we can't save ourselves, Tim. That's just the way it is.'

Tim stared at him. He couldn't save himself. Why was that so hard to accept? Was it pride? Fear? This tall, capable man before him accepted it so easily.

'It's okay for you to say. You are strong and whole.'

Phil shook his head. 'Not true.'

Tim glared a challenge at him.

Phil sighed. 'It's not.' At Tim's questioning look, he pulled a leaf off a nearby branch and twisted it around his finger. 'I used to help on the family farm at Kamira Creek. That farm has been in my family for generations. But as soon as I finished school I went on a mission trip to the Madorean Islands. A tsunami hit and I nearly died.'

He gazed past Tim into the bushland. 'I don't even remember most of it, but my travelling companion died. He wouldn't have been there if he wasn't my guide that day. I was knocked unconscious, and when they found me, I was fighting an infection and virus of some kind. They thought that was it for me. My body organs were shutting down.'

'In the times I was conscious, part of me was excited about going to heaven, but another part of me wanted to stay … for Clare. God saved me, but I haven't been the same since. My body lets me down. That virus has left me with chronic fatigue syndrome. Some days I can hardly get out of bed. I hate it sometimes. I fight against it. Us men like to be so in control and strong.'

Tim hadn't known about that. He followed Phil's gaze into the bushland, then looked back at him.

'But you're so … content.'

Phil let out a dry laugh, his direct gaze connecting with Tim. 'Believe me, Tim, it's been a long struggle. I battled and fought with God at first. Still do, sometimes. But if this hadn't happened, I'd still be chasing all the manly, physical things in life. Instead, I'm doing something that really matters. I'm writing music with messages of hope and helping set up homes to save young lives damaged by crime and drugs. Maybe I can't round up sheep and cattle like I used to, but because of that accident and my permanent physical weakness, I've found my purpose. In accepting my weakness, I've connected with God on a much deeper level. And there's no greater joy than that.'

Tim shook his head. 'I can't see how me missing a part of my body can have a purpose Phil, if that's what you're trying to say.'

Phil didn't answer. Didn't try to explain it. But as they sat there together, Tim felt less alone. Phil understood him. Perhaps even more than he understood himself.

He mulled over Phil's words. *There are times you can't save yourself.* He gave a grim shake of his head. Phil had accepted that and now lived life to the full.

And sometimes, recognising you can't save yourself can save your life.

He shook his head at the thought. He'd almost refused the kidney transplant. Pride had almost cost him his life.

Christianity had been so foreign to him, but maybe he was beginning to understand. It was about recognising you couldn't save yourself. About letting God do what you couldn't. Accepting your weakness.

He looked over at Phil. His eyes were closed.

'Are you praying?

Phil's head jerked up. 'Yes,' he admitted quietly.

'For me?'

'Yes.'

'What are you praying?'

Phil searched his face before he answered. 'I was pleading with God to break down the walls around your stubborn heart and open your eyes to the truth. I'm begging God for your life.'

Tim's eyebrows shot up. He should be offended, but he felt a laugh welling up. 'Well, at least you're honest.'

Phil's smile was sad. 'I can sense the fight going on inside you. It's like a spiritual war raging.'

He was spot on. Tim could feel it. It was as though a small beam of hope shone through the darkness but he was too scared to reach for it. He remembered what Jess had once said. That light was more powerful than darkness. He was tired of the smothering darkness he felt deep inside. Yes, he did want God to take the darkness of his heart and fill it with light. If that were possible.

Phil leaned his hands back to support himself on the branch and shuffled to get comfortable. His head bowed again and Tim stared at him, wrestling his thoughts. Phil knew what really mattered. He lived for someone and something greater than himself. His face shone with light and life and joy.

Could Tim really have that, too? Would believing in God do that? And if he didn't, would he continue to die inside?

All it took was a laying down of his pride.

His heart resisted. It had been humiliating enough having to accept the kidney transplant. But it had saved his life. He had a choice before him. Life or death. Light or darkness?

What was he going to do? This wasn't just a matter of his earthly life. There was more at stake.

God, if you're real, you're going to have to help me. Part of me wants to believe, but I still doubt it. Every bit of it.

And yet he'd just asked a God he didn't believe in to help him believe. He chuckled. That was one positive step forward, wasn't it? Or was he losing his mind?

Maybe he was. But something inside felt lighter.

He stood, found his balance and faced Phil. 'Let's go and see Dan.'

CHAPTER THIRTY-SEVEN

Tim could hear Dan's voice as he and Phil entered the house. A female voice joined Dan's. Tim's heart tripped and pounded in his chest. Was Fleur here, too? She was a friend of Dan's. She'd been in the hospital the day of the accident. She'd challenged him to accept a transplant. He couldn't remember her words exactly, but he remembered the way he'd had to shut off his heart to the pleading expression in her brilliant blue eyes.

He wasn't ready for this, but for once he was going to do something he wasn't ready for. He had to let go of the fight to be strong and in control because it was killing him. Darkness had smothered him.

He stepped into the room. They were all here. Dan, Clare, Beth …

Dan looked up from where he stood beside his friend, Fleur. Dan, the rebellious, scornful little brother who despised weakness and trampled on it. He'd been different after the accident, but still Tim prepared himself for his old smug, self-satisfied smile.

Instead, he found himself thrown off balance when Dan threw his arms around him. 'Tim!'

He lost his balance and stepped back into the wall. Dan pulled away, expression sheepish. He looked down at Tim's foot. 'Sorry. I forgot.' His looked back at Tim, eyes fixed on his face. There was only concern in his usually mischievous brown eyes. Dan really had learned to care, Tim realised. He'd learned to love someone other than himself. Was it because he was a Christian too? Tim shook his head. Why had he been fighting this? He should just join them; see what it was like to believe in their God.

God, have my heart because I've totally messed it up. Change me. I need your help.

Unexpected tears filled his eyes. He turned away to hide them.

'Tim?' Dan's voice was troubled.

Tim looked back and their eyes locked. Connection and understanding flowed between them.

'Let's go to the loungeroom,' Phil suggested.

When they were all seated, Tim looked around at his family gathered there. They looked at him with hesitant but hopeful expressions.

'I've been a bit of an idiot,' he confessed, looking from Clare to Beth and back to Dan. 'I thought I had to be the strong one. I've been so ashamed of my weakness, the way I've let you all down.'

Heads shook, rejecting his claim. A single tear tracked down Beth's cheek and Clare turned her head into Phil's shoulder.

'It was us who gave you a hard time, Tim,' Dan said, his voice catching. 'You tried. You really did.'

'Yes, but it was never enough. It never could have been. In my stupid pride I think I was trying to be God for you.'

Dan bit his lip. 'And all I ever wanted was for you to be my brother. I wouldn't care if you never walked again.'

Tim could see he meant it.

'I think that's why I wanted to donate a kidney for you,' Dan said. 'You tried to meet our needs for so long. I wanted a chance to give back.'

Tim's throat closed over. Why hadn't he allowed his family to meet his needs the way he'd tried to meet theirs? He was weak, but they weren't despising his weakness the way he was. They loved him. Just the way he was. The way God loved him.

It was too much. He buried his head in his hands. Arms came around him and he could hear weeping. He realised it was his. And his family wept with him as the bitterness of his heart rolled away. He hadn't expected it would be like this to surrender his pride. So powerful. So healing. So liberating.

JESS WAS LOOKING FORWARD to dinner at Rod and Toni's. Phil and Clare would be there too. An unfamiliar car was parked out the front, but that wasn't unusual. Rod had been known to invite strangers home at the last minute. She smiled. He was like Dad that way. Poor Toni. She didn't seem to cope with it as well as Mum did. Still, the Green's home offered warmth and friendship.

She rapped her knuckles on the front door, enjoying the sound of Zoe's little girl giggles coming from the loungeroom, followed by Billy's excited chatter. A deep, pleasant voice mingled with theirs. Perhaps the owner of the vehicle she didn't recognise.

Clare opened the door, inviting her in and Jess rounded the corner into the loungeroom. A dark-haired man sat cross-legged on the floor with Zoe in his lap. He turned.

Jess froze. No, no, *no!* Was she dreaming? Her heart felt as though it has jumped into her throat.

'Tim, this is Jess Cardelle,' Clare introduced him. 'Jess, this is my brother, Tim.'

Tim's eyes locked with hers and he smiled.

'Hello Jess.'

So much meaning in those two simple words. She couldn't speak. Thoughts tumbled over each other, searching for solid ground. Clare. The sister Tim wanted to become a physiotherapist, but who refused to fulfil his plans for her. How could this be?

God, help.

'Come through and chat with me while I finish the vegies,' Clare said, seemingly unaware of the war going on inside Jess.

Jess followed on wooden legs, unable to look back at Tim. She needed to think. What was he doing here? Was he here to find her? Or to see his sister? And what about the way he was seated on the floor? He couldn't be sitting that way so comfortably unless he'd had more therapy.

Clare chatted as she peeled and cut up potatoes but Jess couldn't focus. If she noticed her distraction, Clare didn't call her out on it. Once dinner was served, Jess was grateful to be seated beside Tim rather than across from him. That way she didn't need to look at him. However, she had forgotten how this family said grace. Hands reached around the table and Tim reached for hers. She hesitated. Things had changed. Her relationship with Tim was no longer professional. But they were just saying grace. What was her issue? His hand wrapped around hers, warm and manly, comforting and frightening all at once. There was strength in his grip, and she felt desire that confused and flustered her - the desire she had been running from when she left home.

'Jess's family are going to be involved in Rod's next project,' Clare said to Tim as the group made conversation around the table. 'Their property will be used, and Mr. and Mrs. Cardelle will be the house parents so to speak. Jess will be a part of it, too. She's a physiotherapist and occupational therapist so she fits in perfectly.'

Jess felt Tim's eyes on hers. She glanced at him but was unable to read the look he was giving her.

'I know,' Tim said, still looking at Jess. 'I know Jess and her family.'

'You do?' Clare's eyes lit up. 'Wow, how -'

Jess stood abruptly, fork clattering to her plate. 'Um, excuse me. Do you mind if I use your bathroom?'

She saw the looks passing between those around the table. Toni cleared her throat. 'Of course not. Down the hall, first on your left.'

Jess escaped while she could. She splashed cold water over her face, tried to pull herself together. She heard the hum of conversation resuming around the table. She could do this. She just had to get through dinner, then she'd escape and try to sort out what was going on.

She came back to the table. People kept talking. She felt Tim's eyes on her, but she focused on the food in front of her. Thankfully, no one drew any attention to her.

Zoe's chatter subsided as she put her arms out toward Phil. 'Down peas.'

Phil lifted her from her highchair. She toddled straight over to Tim and pulled at his trouser leg. Tim chuckled and picked her up, settling her in his lap. She grabbed at his cutlery and he gently prised her fingers away from his knife. He was a natural with her, Jess realised. He would make a good father. For a reason she couldn't explain, her face warmed at the thought.

TIM FELT tension radiating off Jess beside him. He could see she was troubled. How much could he ask her in front of his family?

She stood, reached into her pocket for her keys. 'Well thanks for dinner, everyone, but I'd better get going.'

'Wait.' He hadn't meant to blurt the words out like that. She looked at him, startled. 'Where are you staying?' he asked more gently.

She swallowed, looking at Clare, rather than at him. 'Not far away.'

'In town?'

'Not exactly. I need to go.'

As soon as the front door closed behind her, Clare turned to Tim.

'What was that about?'

He knew it was time to confess, as much as he hated the disappointment he might see on Clare's face.

'She was my physiotherapist. In Barrawi.'

'What?' Clare's eyes widened. 'Why didn't you say?'

'Because I came here to discredit this place. To bring her home. I've been living in her hometown and working with her father on the property Rod plans to buy for the project. I actually came to Kangon Hill, not knowing you would be here.'

Clare stared, then let out a slow breath. 'I wondered how you knew where to find us.'

Tim shook his head. 'I didn't.'

Clare's smile lit her face. 'Wow, God's clever isn't he? He had this whole thing worked out.'

Tim had to admit it seemed like a pretty huge coincidence. But now he had to find Jess. He was worried about her.

'Do you know where she's living?'

'I don't.' Clare turned to Phil. 'Do you know where?'

Phil shook his head. 'She's been a bit secretive about it. She said she's found somewhere adequate and not too expensive. I didn't want to pry. She said she was fine.'

She wasn't fine. Tim had heard it in her voice, seen it in her eyes.

CHAPTER THIRTY-EIGHT

Tim needed to speak with Jess, but she had ignored his calls for three days. Rod said she'd asked for time off. She was even ignoring Clare's calls. How could he find her? He'd called her parents and made discreet enquiries. They clearly thought she was staying at Kangon Hill. So where was she really? Nearby, she'd said. How could he run into her? Obviously, she would have to go shopping, but there were several local shopping centres and he could easily miss her.

'The gym,' he thought, but then shook his head. Jess liked to powerwalk on her own. She was a farm girl who liked wide, open spaces so she wasn't likely to exercise in town. However, there was the possibility she'd gained herself a job as a physiotherapist.

Tim began his search. No physiotherapist had heard of her and it seemed no one knew Jessica Cardelle. He had soon ruled out all the caravan parks, boarding houses and motels.

'It's hopeless,' Tim told his sisters, but Clare smiled.

'Nothing is impossible for God.'

She was right. It was such habit for him to think himself the only solution for any problem. He had never had anyone else to call on before and it hadn't occurred to him to ask for help.

'So please help me, God,' he prayed.

'Have you tried the gym? Beth asked. 'She was late here once because she had been to the gym.'

Tim shook his head. If only he had listened to that thought earlier. Perhaps God had given it to him but he had rationalised it away. He headed to the gym. His heart pounded as he walked through the glass doors and to the counter where an older lady sat drinking a can of Coke.

'I'm after Jess Cardelle,' he said when she gave him a questioning look from behind the Coke can still raised to her lips.

'And you are?'

'A friend.'

The lady put down the can and studied him suspiciously. 'She's not here.'

'She's not coming in today?'

The lady shrugged. 'It's not my business to share a customer's business.'

Tim got the message. He would just have to wait. From what he knew of Jess, she exercised every day and it used to be after work, so it was likely she was still keeping her routine. He would come back around five and see what happened.

'Find anything out?' Clare asked when Tim returned from the gym.

'She wasn't there and the lady wasn't keen on me asking questions. I'll go back later.'

Clare nodded. 'We'll be praying for you.'

Tim frowned. 'What for?'

Clare grinned. 'Oh, I don't know. The right words, maybe. A peaceable meeting where neither of you get hurt feelings.'

Tim nodded. He hadn't thought of that. He had just planned on going in there and taking control of the situation. But that hadn't worked in the past, so why not let God take control, now?

TIM STOPPED at the traffic lights a few blocks from the gym. Clare was right. The last thing he wanted was to hurt Jess's feelings and from his past record, he more than likely would. It took a moment for him to register that the vehicle stopped in front of him was familiar.

Jess! What a coincidence. He gave a wry smile. Then again, maybe not.

'God, did you arrange this?'

He followed her car, surprised when she headed out of town rather than to the gym. He kept his distance as she drove down less used roads. Then she slowed and turned down a track he would have missed. He desperately wanted to follow, to make sure he didn't lose her again, but he forced himself to drive past, knowing she would notice if he pulled in behind her. He watched as she headed down the bumpy track and her car disappeared from sight. After waiting five minutes, he u-turned.

'God, I need you to show me the way.'

JESS SORTED her washing into her suitcase. It had taken way too long at the laundromat today. No one seemed to think it mattered if they left their clothes in the machine and disappeared for a few hours. She'd missed going to the gym, but her phone battery should last. A shower would have been nice, though. She sighed. She was tired of living rough, but she wasn't ready to go home. If she was honest, she was tired of the solitude, too. She'd tried fishing yesterday and caught nothing. She'd tried talking to God, but her prayers were stilted and formal. Why couldn't she feel him? Hear him? Was it punishment for deceiving her parents?

They rang her each evening, but so far she'd managed to head off questions about where she was staying. If they knew Tim Bateman was here, they hadn't said anything about it.

Jess stopped to listen. Was that a car engine? No one had come down this road yet. Up until now she'd been left to herself and felt perfectly safe. Was she trespassing? There were no signs to indicate she was. Her heart hammered inside her chest. She should have checked if it was okay to camp here. Why had she kidded herself it was? She glanced through the open screen of her tent. Should she run to her car in case she needed to escape? Or should she just wait? Perhaps the person wouldn't care that she was here. She knelt inside the tent door, frozen in place, listening and watching every movement.

A car door opened. 'Jess,' a deep voice called.

Tim.

Intense dismay unfurled inside. How had he found her? She forced herself to crawl out of the tent and came to her feet.

Tim stood by his car. He smiled. A full, complete smile that said he was delighted to see her. It transformed his face. Her breath caught. He walked toward her, his gait firm and steady as though both legs were perfectly intact.

Her eyes stung and she blinked, swallowing hard to keep tears at bay.

'I've been looking for you everywhere!' he said, in a voice she hardly recognised, the voice she'd heard a few nights ago as he played with his niece. It was just as deep, but no longer harsh or angry. His look was almost gentle. 'I thought I'd have to chase you forever.'

She couldn't take her eyes from his now expressive, handsome face. 'How did you find me?' she choked out.

He chuckled, tilting his head. 'I have my ways.'

He stopped a few metres away. Neither moved and she studied him, trying to make sense of her heart and mind. Why was he here? What did he want from her?

'I had to get away,' she said hesitantly. 'From home, from ...'
She shrugged, eyes burning.

'I know.'

'I couldn't bear the ... the ...'

'Darkness. Me either.' He stepped closer, close enough to reach out and touch. 'I have a lot to tell you.'

His heart was in his eyes, but she couldn't read what she saw there. 'About?'

He shook his head. 'Now is not the time.' His gaze went to the tent. 'You've been living here? This whole time?'

She shrugged, but tears welled in her eyes. 'I had nowhere else.'

'Yes, you did. You have home. You need to go back there.'

Despite his words, his tone was gentle. He reached out a hand and she backed away. He didn't know what she needed, what God wanted.

'You know you want to.'

She bit her trembling lip. 'You have no idea what I want, Tim Bateman. Nobody does. Nobody ever asks me. Jessica Cardelle is just there to meet everybody else's needs, to do what they expect her to do, what they want her to do.'

He studied her, head tilted, squinting into the sun. 'So tell me, what do you really want?'

As if she'd tell him.

When she didn't answer, his expression softened. 'I really think you should go home – back to your parents. You're not needed here. Phil told me they don't need you until the next project begins. But your family need you. They're missing you.'

Her face contorted with her tears.

'Jess? What's wrong?'

His concern undid her. She collapsed into the camp chair she'd set up beside her campfire. 'Please go, Tim. I'm too tired to fight you.'

'I'm not looking for a fight, Jess.'

'Then what do you want?'

His eyes captured hers. 'I want you to be happy. Whole. I want you to let me help you the way you helped me.'

'I didn't help you.' He'd clearly managed very well on his own if his strong walk and posture were anything to go by.

He hunkered down in front of her, his soft expression doing strange things to her heart.

She jumped up from the chair. She wouldn't be manipulated. Wouldn't let him win this power game or whatever it was he was playing. He didn't love her. He didn't love anybody. He was stubborn and cold and hard.

Only he wasn't. And she didn't know what to make of him; of this strange fluttering inside when he looked at her this way. Unable to take it any longer, a sob escaped. Followed by another and another. She turned away.

Then Tim was pulling her into his arms. She was so sad and confused. His hand came to the back of her head, stroking her hair, cradling her against his chest. She sobbed into his shirt. He stood there, a man, tall and strong on two legs, holding her and caring, but not loving. She needed love.

'Will you come home, Jess?' he asked. 'You have a family who need you.'

She stepped back, glaring up into his face through her tears. 'Did that stop you running from yours when you needed to get yourself together?'

He flinched and stepped back. Did he think she might slap him again?

'Jess ...'

'Go away, Tim. You aren't family. You aren't my therapist. I'm not even yours.'

She stared straight ahead, unable to meet his gaze, afraid of what he might see in her eyes.

'If that's what you really want,' he said.

'It is!'

He searched her face. Then, 'Goodbye, Jess,' he said quietly, resignedly, turned and walked steadily back to his car.

Jess didn't want to watch him go, but she couldn't keep her eyes off him. He walked so smoothly that even she, a physiotherapist, would never guess he was an amputee.

Once he was gone, she sank onto the ground and cried. She couldn't go back home. The truth was, she couldn't stand the thought of watching her family members die. If this heart condition claimed Dad, what would be expected of her? They'd all depend on her, but she had nothing left. And what if Milla had it, too? God hadn't spared Toby, so how could she depend on him to spare the rest of her family?

'I can't live this way God,' she cried. 'I can't do this anymore. What do you want from me?'

She looked up into the sky, above the trees. 'God?'

Nothing.

What if something had already happened to Dad? With trembling hands, she took out her phone and called Mum. What if that's why Tim had really come to convince her to go home?

The moment Mum picked up the phone, all Jess could do was cry.

'Jess?' Mum asked in concern. 'Take slow, deep breaths. That's the way. I'm here when you're ready to talk.'

Jess drew in deep, shuddering breaths. 'Mum, is everyone okay?'

'Yes. Why, what's happened?' Mum sounded calm.

'Oh Mum, I've made a complete mess of everything.'

Silence. She knew Mum was waiting.

'They don't even need me here. And every time I try to do something for God I make a complete mess of it.'

Mum was silent for a long time, then she spoke, her voice tender. 'Jess, do you remember how you used to help me with the washing?'

Jess managed a tremulous smile. 'Yes.'

She'd loved helping Mum. Mum would lift her up to reach the line and she'd hang the clothes in a haphazard fashion. Mum would help straighten them. And Toby would take the peg bag and drag it along the concrete path. 'I'm going on a holiday,' he'd say, while she and Mum worked hard to hang the clothes.

'Do you remember the day you decided to do it all by yourself?' Mum asked.

Jess remembered. She'd pulled a chair up to the clothesline and tried to hang the clothes. She'd even chosen matching coloured pegs for each item. But it was harder to hang them without Mum's help. And then she'd fallen from the chair, knocking the clothes basket of clean, wet clothes over into the dirt. She'd cried and cried, but Mum had brushed off her dirty knees, rewashed the clothes, thanked her for trying and then worked with her to re-hang the lopsided clothes on the line.

'God doesn't need us to do things for him, Jess, just like I didn't need you and Toby to help. But I loved you helping. The time we spent together, the way we chatted as we worked, the way it helped you learn and develop ...'

Mum considered Toby's holiday-making 'helping' too? Jess smiled. They went through so many peg bags the way Toby wore holes in them, dragging them along the concrete. But she'd always felt she was the one helping. She was the one who actually did it right ... or was she?

Did God really allow them to help in their own, flawed human way because he loved them; enjoyed being with them?

'Jess, what if you stopped trying to do everything right and just basked in God's love? What if you were to lift your face for his kiss every morning and know that he loves you? What if you trusted that he would cover all your mistakes?'

'But Mum, I hate making mistakes.'

'I know, sweetheart. But when you do, Jesus is still there. He loves a broken and contrite heart. It's all about him, Jess. He died because he knew we couldn't do it. He did it all. Don't throw that back in his face by trying to do everything on your own.'

Jess drew in a deep, shuddery breath. 'Mum, I think I might come home.'

Mum laughed gently. 'We'll be waiting with open arms.'

Tears streaming down her cheeks, she stood, picked up the camp chair and folded it up. Then she fell to her knees.

'Oh Jesus, I can't do it anymore. I'm sorry I tried to be so independent, so good, so perfect. I'm broken and I need you. Please take my life and make something of it. Your way, not mine.'

Tears still streaming down her cheeks, she packed up her tent. She was going home.

CHAPTER THIRTY-NINE

'Jess has come home,' Charlie Cardelle announced when Tim came back out to the farm after his week away.

Tim smiled at Charlie's joy. He'd thought his pleas to Jess had fallen on deaf ears. His trip to Kangon Hill had been way beyond his expectations.

But how was Jess really going? Did Charlie know she'd been sleeping in a tent?

He walked beside Charlie to the paddock of new calves. 'Did she say anything about her time away?'

Charlie frowned. 'Not much. I think she's still reeling from the news about my heart condition. And the fact that she might have it, too.'

Tim felt the blood drain from his face. He hadn't thought of that. 'Has she been tested?'

Charlie kicked at a clod of dirt. 'Not that I know of. I'm leaving it up to her.'

Was that why Jess had run? Because she couldn't bear the thought that she might have a heart condition? How would she cope if she had it? She prided herself in her health and fitness. He of all people knew what it was like to lose your strength and independence. Milla knew, too.

'What about Milla?'

'She's already been given the all-clear. To be honest, I'd have been surprised if God healed her of myasthenia and then allowed her to be held back by a heart condition.'

Tim agreed but didn't say so. Charlie didn't know about his new-found faith. And it seemed Jess hadn't told her family that he'd turned up at Kangon Hill, either.

What would happen if he told Charlie everything? He felt so different, but did it show? He wished he'd told Jess about his change of heart, but he hadn't been able to. Not after the look that came over her face when she'd crawled out of her tent and seen him there. She was clearly shocked but there was something else. Fear? Revulsion?

He got it. He really did. Jess was used to fixing people and making them whole. Then she went back to her own, comfortable life. She couldn't fall for someone like him; someone wounded, who would never be whole physically, even if God had begun healing his heart. Wait. *Fall* for him? What was he thinking? He didn't want her to fall for him. Did he?

'Where is Jess today?'

Charlie smiled. 'At work. Typical Jess. She's gone back to the clinic to help Lauren and she's there morning till night.'

Tim's eyes slid closed. Obviously she was trying to lose herself in her work. And neatly avoiding him at the same time. He would pray for her. Clare told him that bringing things to God was a lot better than worrying about them or trying to fix them himself. And he had to admit he was worried. Jess had become a part of his life and he couldn't bear the thought of losing her. He admired her. Liked her determined spirit, her quick mind. She was probably the smartest girl he'd ever met. And it didn't help that he'd liked the feel of her in his arms. That her hair was way softer than it looked.

Stop it.

'Where are these calves?'

Charlie gave him a strange look, but he'd needed to change the subject; direct his thoughts elsewhere.

'Still in paddock with their mothers. Too early to separate them.'

Tim nodded. He knew that. Charlie knew he knew that. What he didn't know was how he was going to react when he finally did come face to face with Jess again.

Charlie put his hand on the gate to the paddock, but then stopped. He looked steadily at Tim.

'We're having our first planning meeting for the farm project in a couple of days. I'd like you to be a part of it.'

Tim was surprised. 'Why?'

'You have a lot to offer. I'd love to see you involved with the project. It's all about –'

'I know what it's about.' It felt wrong to let Charlie wrongly assume otherwise. 'My sister Clare and her husband are heavily involved with it.'

Charlie's eyes widened. 'The Kangon Hill Project?'

'They live at Kamira Creek. But yes, they're all connected.'

Charlie blinked a couple of times. 'You mean Phil and Clare Cairn? Clare's your sister? Did you know they're coming? For the meeting?'

'Yes, actually. I thought I might ask them if they'd like to stay with me.'

Again, Charlie blinked and Tim wanted to laugh. 'Well, … well, that would be good,' he finally said. 'I was wondering how we'd fit them all in. Rod and his family are staying in Toby's room. Jess offered to sleep in Milla's room, but this is even better.'

'I think it works well,' Tim agreed.

Charlie's mouth opened and closed a few more times so Tim opened the gate for him. 'Let's check these calves.'

Tim opened his front door a few days later to find Phil, Clare and Zoe on his doorstep.

'You're early.'

Clare dimpled at him and drew him into a hug. 'Good to see you too, big brother.'

He opened his mouth to respond, but before he could, little Zoe threw her arms around his trouser leg.

'Up,' she said.

As soon as he lifted her, she put her hands either side of his face and planted a slobbery kiss on his chin.

'Thanks, Zoe,' he muttered as he wiped it off, but he couldn't help grinning.

Clare laughed. 'You'll get used to it. Good practice for when you have your own.'

Tim pulled a face, placing Zoe down on her feet. He kept an eye on her as she charged down the hall, toward Blue. It wasn't Zoe he was worried about. It was poor Blue.

'I'm not planning on having my own,' he said, waving Clare and Phil inside.

Clare's smile fell as she walked down his hall. 'It doesn't have to be the way our family was, Tim. I never dreamed being married and having children could be so … special. Leave room for love and marriage if that's what God has for you.'

He didn't answer, but he had to admit he wouldn't mind a little Zoe of his own someday. And he wouldn't mind the kind of marriage Clare and Phil had, either. Their mutual respect and love for each other, the way they supported and enjoyed one another's company, made his heart squeeze with a longing he had never experienced before.

Did he know anyone he could respect that way? Someone he could enjoy spending time with, getting to know? Jess's face flashed through his mind. He shook his head. He'd caught glimpses of her occasionally, but hadn't been able to talk with her. It seemed she was determined to either put on a professional façade that kept him at a distance or avoid him altogether.

'Sorry we're early, but we thought we'd dump our bags here, then head over to the Cardelle's for the meeting,' Phil said as Tim showed them to the spare room. 'Thought maybe we could all go over together.'

Tim smiled. 'Sounds good.'

TIM HELPED Charlie and Rod drag out some extra seats to fit everyone in the Cardelle's loungeroom. Rod called everyone together and Charlie opened in prayer.

'First on the agenda is the name for this project,' Rod said. 'Phil and I have talked with Charlie, and we agree we can't use the name of the farm.'

Tim tried to think if he knew the name of the farm. He didn't think so.

'For those of you who don't know, the real name is something like Wontatocumbagandra,' Rod said, 'but it's never used. For obvious reasons.'

'Wandobagalandra,' Charlie corrected and the group chuckled.

'That,' Rod said with a sheepish grin. 'But if I can't say it, how is anyone else going to be able to say it?'

No one answered and Tim hid his smirk. Rod could be intimidating, but surely no one here was scared of him? He glanced over at Jess. She carefully looked away. Still avoiding him.

Lydia placed a plate of cup cakes in the middle of the table. She was in her element, welcoming everyone who came through the door, cooking up big meals and soaking up lively conversations around the table.

'What about if we call it El Roi?' Milla suggested.

All eyes turned to her.

'Why?' Rod asked.

'Because it means, "The God who sees me".' Her beaming smile was alive with joy.

'I like it,' Rod said.

And everyone else nodded.

It was decided. The very next afternoon, work began on a sign for the front gate.

Tim held Billy's hand, keeping a safe distance from Buck and his chainsaw. Zac and Milla supported the huge chunk of wood as Buck cut, shaping it into a rustic sign. Then Zac took a chisel and began carving out the words, 'El Roi'.

'Can I cut too?' Billy asked Tim. He'd become his little shadow, following him and Bluey around the farm.

Tim chuckled, holding Billy's hand tighter and taking a step back from the chainsaw and chisel.

'Not until you're older. But Milla said we can help paint.'

Billy beamed up at him and Tim smiled back.

'Can I play with Bluey then?' Billy asked, eyes looking hopefully up at Tim.

'Sure, but maybe we should move away from the noise.' And the sharp tools.

Billy nodded, let go of Tim's hand and ran to the other end of the driveway, Bluey at his heels.

When Tim caught up, Billy regarded him with big grey eyes. 'Can I stay at your house tonight?'

The boy switched from one subject to the next faster than Tim could think. 'Not tonight. I still have Phil, Clare and Zoe staying with me. Maybe another time?'

'But they're going home soon. 'Cause Aunty Clare has to have another baby.'

Tim smiled. 'Yes.' Clare was looking more pregnant by the day.

'Will she have the baby at your place?'

Tim chuckled. 'No.' He certainly hoped not, anyway. He handed Billy a stick. 'Here, throw this for Blue.'

Tim supervised as the two of them played fetch with a stick. Bluey was happy to fetch the stick and bring it back, but refused to drop it.

'You need to be firm with him,' Tim said as Billy attempted to wrestle the stick from Bluey's mouth. 'You need to tell him to drop it.'

Billy hunched down, looking seriously into Bluey's eyes, hands still on one end of the stick.

'Bluey, let go of the stick,' he ordered. 'Let go.'

The dog dropped it and Billy spun to face Tim. 'Did you see that? I got him to drop the stick.'

Tim grinned. 'I saw. Good job.'

Billy beamed, the words of praise lighting up his face. He was a bright kid, but so intense. He reminded Tim of himself as a child.

He looked up to see Rod striding down the drive toward him. He never knew what to expect from Rod. Like father, like son.

Rod was frowning when he came to an abrupt stop beside Tim. 'Have you told the Cardelles about what happened at Kangon Hill?'

Tim tensed. 'No. I haven't even told them I was there.'

'Well sorry mate, I might have put my foot in it.'

His heart quickened. 'How?'

'I suggested to Charlie that we have a bonfire night here to talk to everyone about the project. I thought it might help get the local young people involved too so they're ready to support the guests once they start arriving. But Charlie said we can't do that because it's bushfire season. So I said we could have a 'bon night' and leave out the fire. You know, like, just sit around a pile of wood.'

Tim chuckled. 'That's certainly an original idea.'

Rod shook his head. 'Charlie said we can't. The mozzies would eat us alive. But I don't want it in the church because I know how I felt about churches at that age. Anyway, we've changed the plan so it's not in the main building. It'll be in the church hall instead.'

Tim failed to see how that involved him. 'And?'

'And I said it would be good if you share your testimony on the night.'

'My testimony?'

'Your story. You know, what you've been through, what God's done in your heart and life. What happened at Kangon Hill.'

Tim winced. 'Charlie doesn't know about ... he still thinks I'm like I was.'

'No, he doesn't. He knows you're different, just doesn't know why.'

'Did you tell him?'

'No. That's your story to tell.' He gave Tim a look. 'But I think it's time you told him.'

Maybe it was, but if he was honest, he didn't know where to begin.

Rod crossed his arms and gave Tim a sideways look. 'What about Jess? Does she know how you feel about her?'

'Pardon?'

Rod shrugged. 'I see the way you two dance around each other. Trying not to look at each other.'

Tim frowned. The guy had no boundaries. 'You don't know what you're talking about.'

Rod smirked. 'Fine. Keep telling yourself that.'

Rod didn't get it. He didn't know the full story. Hadn't seen the way Tim had treated Jess. What would Jess think of him if he told her what had happened in his heart? Would she resent that he who had persecuted her for her faith, now shared it? Would she feel it was unfair, that he was undeserving? Tim swallowed hard then looked away.

'Actually, Rod, having me speak to the young people might not be the best idea.'

Rod shrugged. 'I'm happy either way, Tim. But I want you to find out if God is.'

TIM WRESTLED with Rod's idea. Everything in him balked at the thought of making himself vulnerable and sharing his heart. He'd kept it hidden in the dark for so long it was hard to bring his pain, his struggles, God's healing and redemption to light.

Finally, he threw up his hands. 'God, what do you want me to do?'

There was a part of him that felt fickle for changing his mind about Christianity. And yet, he knew it wasn't him who'd changed his mind. God had. It was silly to keep saying the sky was red when you'd discovered it was blue. That was pure stubbornness. And immature and unhelpful and untrue …

'Okay God, I'll do it, but you're going to have to help me!' His stomach knotted at the mere thought of what he would say. But with God's help he'd do it. And leave the fallout with Jess to him.

CHAPTER FORTY

Jess looked around at the group filling their church hall. Milla stood talking with her friends, bouncing with restored energy, full of life and joy, but also a new depth of perception. She stopped to listen to something her friend Kirra was saying. Maybe teenagers like Kirra would come to understand more about God through the El Roi Project. Maybe even make a commitment to him. Like she had so many years ago in this hall.

And yet she'd blown it. Time and time again. It was in this same room she'd hurt Sasha so deeply, speaking thoughtless words to Pierce after Toby's funeral.

Who did she think she was, inviting herself to be part of the El Roi Project when her life was such a mess?

Rod Green sauntered down the front and invited people to take their seats. He suited his role perfectly with his goatee, ripped jeans and leather jacket. Cool but classy. Tough but authentic.

Jess took a seat near a side door, giving herself the option to escape. Being here reminded her of her distance from God. It reminded her she couldn't control the world or life and death.

However, at the same time she thirsted for the spiritual intimacy with God she'd once had.

Rod presented a video. Jess watched as story after story was shared of teenagers whose lives had been changed by God through the Kamira Creek and Kangon Hill projects. She'd tried so hard to have that kind of impact, but had never had any success. Tim was proof of that. Who did she think she was, inviting herself to be part of it? What if she ruined it? Turned people away?

'We're excited about what God is going to do through El Roi and all of you who are willing to support the project,' Rod said as the slide show finished. 'We'd love each of you to partner with us in ministry in some way. Whether it is to be a friend to a teenager who comes to live at El Roi, whether it's providing finances, or more importantly, supporting us in prayer. We need you.'

He was persuasive. Just the right person for the job.

He smiled. 'And tonight I have a special guest here to share some of the ways God has already used El Roi and the Cardelles.'

He nodded at someone down the back of the hall and Jess resisted turning as the person stood and made their way down the front. She heard the steady, even gait of a young man. He walked past. Jess started.

Tim.

What was he doing? She tensed, heart pounding as he walked right up onto the stage. Rod stepped aside to let him have the microphone.

Tim turned to face the crowd. He was wearing jeans and a casual t-shirt and looked … friendly. Approachable.

People clapped and Tim smiled but looked tense.

'I've been asked to share with you tonight,' he said as the applause faded. He drew in a deep breath. 'Those of you who have known me for a while, know I have been bitter. I was living in darkness. Angry at life, but more angry at myself than anyone else.'

His hands shook slightly and he shoved them in his pockets.

'My father died in a car accident when I was eight. At the funeral, someone told me that God needed my father more than I did. That was the worst thing she could have said to me.'

His eyes scanned the room. Jess tried not to stare. Tried to make sense of what she was hearing, what Tim was saying. Her heart was with that little boy, feeling his pain and confusion, wanting to comfort him, to take it away.

'I couldn't believe that if God was real, he'd need my father more than I did. From that day, I felt it was my responsibility to take my father's place. To be there for my siblings. But then they became Christians. And I thought they'd been brainwashed. I was angry that they wouldn't let me help them.'

He drew in a deep breath and looked up into the lights. 'And then I was in the train accident that Toby Cardelle lost his life in. I lost my foot, but I might as well have lost my life. Until I moved here and began seeing Jess Cardelle.'

He looked right at Jess and smiled a full, complete smile. Her breath shortened. The walls seemed to be closing in. Nothing felt real. She could still hear Tim talking, but the words were a blur in her mind. They floated around the room, unable to sink in. Something about his donor's family. About God. About her and how she'd never given up on him.

God knew she didn't deserve a mention. She'd failed. She stared at Tim, remembering the day he'd first walked into her office. She remembered her first impressions. Tall, dark and handsome. But also angry and bitter. Tonight his handsome face was filled with light and life. Was this real? Had God really transformed his heart of stone into a heart of flesh? Her vision blurred.

'I don't feel the need to be a father figure to my siblings anymore,' Tim was saying. 'They have the same heavenly father I do. The God who takes away the darkness of our hearts; who gives us a heart transplant. And God does a much better job of being a father than I ever did.'

Jess's mind filled with the image of Tim holding Zoe in his

arms, of him holding Billy's hand and even carrying the little boy on his shoulders around the farm. The pain burning in her chest was like her heart was breaking and bursting with joy all at once. Overwhelmed, she drew in a shuddery breath. It was real. Tim knew God now. And it had nothing to do with her trying to convince him to believe.

She couldn't take her eyes off him. Could this be the same man she had dreaded facing each day at work? A smile played about the once so serious mouth when his eyes met hers again. There was a depth to him she could never have imagined possible. How could she have missed the change?

She knew how. She'd been avoiding him. Wallowing in her own pain and fear. She sank further into her seat. She didn't want him to see her, to realise what she had become. But there was nowhere to hide. His eyes met hers again and his gentle, concerned look shook her more than his anger and bitterness ever had. It was as though he saw beyond her professional façade to the person she really was deep inside. She looked down.

'Whatever you're going through,' Tim said into the microphone, the deep timbre of his voice stirring her, drawing her in, 'Know that God knows. He sees you. He wants to be your father. Your God.'

Jess couldn't take anymore. She pushed past the person beside her and crept out the side door, glad for the first time ever that she was invisible. She drove straight home, climbed into bed, pulled the covers over her head and cried until she had no tears left.

JESS AWOKE to the familiar sound of activity in the house. Her throat felt scratchy and she desperately needed a shower. Rod talked to Dad in a loud, enthusiastic voice nearby. Mum bustled about, rattling cutlery and plates as she prepared breakfast. Buck's raucous laughter filled the kitchen and Jess knew Milla and Zac would be there too, sharing breakfast, then catching the school bus together. Maybe it was time she found a unit in town. That would allow space for more people in the house while the new accommodation quarters were built. Maybe it was time to make some decisions. And yet, look how her last decision had turned out. Rod hadn't expected or needed her. She'd thought God was leading her there. Now she didn't know and she didn't trust herself or her heart.

She waited until the noise died down, then crept to the shower. She was tired of sharing the bathroom. Tired of sharing what was left of her family. Tired of always being on guard, trying to make the right impression and be who she was supposed to be. Her whole world had been turned upside down.

She showered, dressed and went into the kitchen. And stopped. Tim had just walked in the door. Mum dumped the dishes she'd been carrying to the sink and ran to give him a hug.

'You're an amazing young man, Tim Bateman,' she said, beaming from ear to ear. 'Oh, you had us all in tears last night. Look at you!' She stepped back, then threw her arms around him again. 'We thank God for you.'

Jess couldn't look at them.

Tim cleared his throat and stepped back from Mum's hug. 'I know I've caused a lot of pain and heartache and I'm sorry for that. I'm hoping you'll forgive me.'

Mum gushed over him. 'Oh Tim, of course you're forgiven. We're just so delighted. You're like a son to us. Charlie has loved having you around, working with you, and I love it when you walk in this door and share meals with us. You're part of our family now.'

Tim was silent and Jess knew he was looking at her. She forced herself to meet his gaze.

'I guess I have to prove things to you, Jess,' he said. 'It's funny how things turn around, isn't it?'

She swallowed hard. 'I don't understand.'

He smiled but didn't offer any explanation. There was an awkward silence, but nobody offered to fill it. Tim left with a brief wave and Jess breathed a sigh of relief. She needed space.

Only Mum wasn't going to give it to her. She stood in front of the cupboard, blocking Jess's way to the toaster.

'You need to forgive him, Jess.'

'For what?' Tim was the one who'd been so angry with her, not the other way around.

'For not being Toby.'

Jess blinked hard. What was Mum talking about?

'You need to leave room in your heart for Tim. God knows that young man could do with someone like you in his life.'

Jess frowned. 'Mum, Tim doesn't have feelings for me, if that's what you're thinking.'

Mum touched her shoulder. 'I know you don't want to believe it because you've lost so much and you're afraid, but he cares about you deeply. I would even say he loves you. Just don't stay afraid too long or by the time you realise the truth, it might be too late.'

Had her mother gone mad? Did she think Tim was on the lookout for a wife and someone else would snatch him up if Jess didn't? How had the world become so off-kilter?

'He's not a cow for sale, Mum,' Jess snapped. Ignoring her stomach's cry for breakfast, she escaped to her room. If Mum was trying to be a matchmaker she needed to give it up. She didn't know all that had happened between her and Tim. Jess stretched her shoulders, trying to ease the tension there. She needed to go for a run. Escape. Billy Can Hill was the best place to go. The kangaroos no longer worried her. With all the activity on the farm she rarely saw them now.

With each step up the hill, Jess's confusion grew. What did Mum think she was seeing between her and Tim? Didn't she realise her eldest daughter wasn't pretty? That her achievements meant nothing? That her confidence was all show? After the way she'd snapped this morning she wasn't even the nice Christian girl everybody thought she was.

She reached the top of the hill, breathing hard. She bent over, hands on her knees. No matter how far or fast she ran, there was no escape from herself.

She wasn't angry with Tim for not being Toby was she?

She felt to her knees. 'Oh, Toby,' she cried. 'I miss you. I just need to talk to you.'

What about God? Why couldn't she talk to God? Why did he feel so far away? She buried her head in her hands. Nothing made sense anymore.

The crunch of sticks beneath someone's feet alerted her that she was not alone. She looked up and there was Tim. He walked toward her, carrying a coffee travel mug. He held it out to her.

'Jess,' he said, his eyes uncertain. 'Your mum said you missed breakfast.'

Heat flooded her face. What else had Mum said? She took the mug from his hands. Tim lowered himself down beside her. His movements were smooth and lithe. No one would guess he was an amputee. And no one would guess he had been eaten up with bitterness and pain only months ago. Jess breathed in the smell of the coffee, then took a sip. She crossed her legs beneath her.

Tim didn't speak, just looked out over the hills at the land now given to God for ministry. She was so aware of him; of his silent strength and confidence, of his heart. His new heart.

'Tim,' she managed. 'I ... I thought ... I didn't know ...'

To her frustration and embarrassment, tears filled her eyes. Tim's face softened and he reached over and took her hand. His grasp exuded strength and warmth and she tried to think. What was he doing? Mum couldn't have been right about his feelings for her, could she?

He smiled. Warm and tender, and her heart missed a beat.

'Thank you for never giving up on me,' he said. 'Thank you for trying to reach me, even when I made it as hard as I possibly could.'

How could he say that? She'd slapped him! And she'd run away. From God. From him.

'I actually took that slap as a compliment.'

Her eyes flew to his face. She'd said that aloud?

His expression softened. 'It showed you consider me an equal. In that moment I wasn't some poor, fragile patient you had to treat with extra special care. And I deserved it. We both know that.'

Her breath caught.

'Jess,' he said, his voice whisper soft, eyes capturing hers. 'I know I can't replace the brother you lost and I don't want to, but I want to be a part of your life.' He threaded his fingers through hers. 'I want to be there for you the way you were for me. Will you let me see you?'

She looked at the strong fingers entwined with hers, confused. 'You mean as a patient?'

He laughed and the sound was warm and free. 'No. We've done that and it didn't work so well. I want to see you in a personal capacity.'

This couldn't be happening. Couldn't be real. She couldn't make sense of it.

'You don't mean that.'

'I do,' he said, but a smile played about his mouth.

'You're being sarcastic.'

'No.'

'Tim, don't ...' she pleaded. 'You know what I'm lacking ...' He knew she wasn't pretty. He hadn't respected her intelligence or capability. And now she'd discovered she couldn't even be the composed professional she'd tried so hard to be.

'I know what you're *not* lacking. And it's all the things that count.'

She looked up into expressive, warm brown eyes. Filled with light and life.

With a small laugh, he stood and reached a hand, pulling her to her feet. She stumbled, and he steadied her, the warmth of his hands sending tingles up her arms.

He stood directly facing her, his hands still on her arms, his gaze capturing and holding hers. 'What do I have to do to make you believe me?'

She tried to step back, but he held her firm, gaze tender. Then he lowered his head and his mouth brushed with hers. Just gently, but definitely a kiss. She gasped, eyes wide.

'Do you think you could ever have feelings for me?' he asked, his voice whisper-soft. 'Do you think there's a chance you could ever love me?'

Heat rushed to her face. She already had feelings for him. Her pounding heart and the strange fluttering somewhere deep inside was testament to that. But could he ever truly love *her*, was the question.

Tim's smile wavered at her hesitation. She saw the hurt that filled his eyes. That's when her heart took over. God help her, she'd overthought everything enough in life and it had never worked in her favour. She threw her arms around him, burying her face in his neck the way she longed to.

'You know I have feelings for you,' she whispered.

His arms came around her waist, drawing her closer, and he chuckled, a relieved sound. 'I didn't. I never dared presume. Until in the hall last night when I saw the way you looked at me.'

She pulled back to see his face. 'How did I look at you?'

A dimple she didn't know he had appeared in one cheek. 'Like you love me. Like you accepted my disability long before I did.'

She brought her hands to her face, covering her embarrassment. Was she so easy to read? With a chuckle, he pulled her hands away, and held them in his own.

'Hey, it's a good thing.'

'I know. It's just … I'm so used to having it all together. Being the strong one.'

'You *are* strong. Probably the strongest person I know.'

'No, Tim, I've made such a mess of things.'

'Haven't we all?'

'Not like I have.'

'I don't know about that. But God forgives.'

'Maybe, but I'm having a hard time forgiving myself.'

He shook his head. 'That's ridiculous.' His tone took the sting of his words. He tilted his head. 'Are you saying that you expect more from yourself than God does? That your standards are higher than God's?'

She winced. When he put it like that …

'You know what I think?' His tone was gentle but his warm brown eyes were intense. 'I think you have unreasonable standards for yourself. I think you need to wake up each morning and give yourself permission to make a mistake. And know that God has taken the fall for it. And still loves you.'

Why did her heart cringe at the thought? 'I don't want God to have to take the fall, Tim.'

'And yet he already has.' Tim drew in a deep breath. 'It must hurt him to see you beat yourself up for what he's already paid for.'

Jess couldn't look away. Who was this man? She was the one who had been a Christian for years. The one who helped others. The one who had it altogether. Except, now she knew she didn't. 'Tim, I don't know what to say.'

He nodded, drawing her back into his arms. 'And that's okay. But one day I hope you can be so comfortable with me that you'll just blurt out whatever you're thinking without even thinking about it.'

A laugh bubbled up inside. 'Like Milla does?'

He grinned and that dimple showed again. 'Yeah. But from your heart. In your words. It's you I want to know, not her.'

'I'm not pretty like her.' Why had she said that? She looked away but was drawn back when his fingers traced the scar the kangaroo had left on her forehead.

'That's not true. If you could see the way your eyes sparkle when you laugh, the way they shine with compassion when you're helping someone, the way your smile warms a room, you would never say that.'

She closed her eyes. She needed to tell him. 'Tim, I might have the heart condition Dad has.'

'So? I'm missing a foot. That doesn't make me half a man any more than having a heart condition would make you half a woman.'

She let out a long, shuddery breath, and looked up at him, taking in his dark features now filled with light and life. He was so different.

He shuffled uncomfortably. 'What?'

'I.. I just never dreamed I'd see you this way.'

His brows raised in question and she smiled. 'Your light and joy is infectious.'

He nodded, pushing a strand of hair back from her face. 'It always is. Bitterness can only contaminate those who don't have joy. Those who live in the darkness and don't know the Light.'

'You mean God.'

His eyes lit with warmth. 'Yes.'

Still, she hesitated.

He took her hand. 'It's okay, Jess. I really want to take our relationship further, but we can wait until you receive your results if you like.'

Was that what she wanted? She really didn't know. He didn't push for a response. Instead, he picked her coffee mug up from the ground and reached for her hand. 'Your coffee's cold. Let's go and get a refill.'

And so she walked down the hill with him, mind and heart full, trying to comprehend all that had just happened between them. It seemed Milla wasn't the only one God had gifted a miracle.

CHAPTER FORTY-ONE

Tanner knew what he needed to do, but still he fought it. He felt as though a rope was coiled around him, tightening with every step he took. He'd heard Tim Bateman's testimony, though he'd hidden at the back of the hall. He'd seen the healing of Milla Cardelle. Witnessed the protection God had placed over those who believed in him and the way he worked quietly, gently, lovingly in peoples' lives. No way would Tanner work to destroy the work God was doing, changing lives of foster children, giving them a future, a hope and a place to belong. It was futile, anyway.

He'd wrestled with God day and night for close to a week. Joel was his brother. By blood. But he had a dark heart and he refused to let the light in. He wouldn't be betraying Joel by going to the police. He'd be giving him a chance to turn his life around, take a different path, repent as those Christians said. The way Joel chose to go would be his choice.

Tanner knew all about mind games and manipulation and he knew the power Joel had held over him from the day he was born. He didn't want it any longer. He thought he'd been so intelligent but now he saw clearly the way his brother used him. The way he had been drawn in, pushed away, then drawn in like a yo-yo so that he had become dependent upon Joel for his very identity.

But now Tanner Elliott was a child of God. He believed. Jesus was real. How could he not believe after the miracles he'd witnessed? After God had spoken into his heart? But it was so hard to disentangle himself from the person Joel had helped him become. And he still had doubts. Maybe talking with Joel would help. More likely it would make things worse. He walked towards the prison doors. He put his hand on the buzzer to be let in, then stopped. Reached forward again, then with sigh, let his arm drop to his side.

'Can I help you?'

A man stood behind him, balding and grey, with an open, honest face. And yet there was a shrewdness to his eyes. He read the man's name badge. Stephen Coleman. Prison Chaplain.

'Yes,' he breathed a sigh of relief. Surely God had sent this man? 'Have you got a few minutes?'

The chaplain smiled. 'Of course. Let's go in and find somewhere to sit.'

They went through security, leaving behind their phones, keys and personal possessions. Stephen led him to a seat overlooking the lawn. He turned to face Tanner. 'You're troubled.'

It wasn't a question. There was understanding in the man's eyes. 'That might be an understatement. I'm wrestling with God.'

Stephen nodded then waited.

Tanner's heart started a more insistent thumping. It had been doing that too often lately. No more could he distance himself and present a calm, cold façade. 'I met a family,' he told Stephen. 'They believe and they live for God every moment of their lives. Even when they lost their son in an accident, and then when their daughter developed a serious autoimmune condition and lost her vision, they still believed. And then they prayed and asked God to heal their daughter. And he did. I wouldn't believe it except that I saw it myself.'

'You believe in the Lord Jesus Christ now? You're saved?'

Tanner sighed. 'Yes. But I still have questions.'

'About?'

How to explain? 'I guess emotion bothers me. When the girl's family were praying for her there was so much emotion. No reason.' He shook his head. 'And my own commitment happened in a moment of high emotion. I went to a huge church in Sydney on Sunday. It was an excellent, professional production. And so authentic. And yet, the commitment I made was during a moment of high emotion, after being carried away in worship music, my heart so full it wanted to explode, my hands unable to help lifting in surrender to God. I meant every word of surrender I prayed, but when I think on it all without emotion, in the light of day I still have my doubts.' He bit his lip. 'I mean, what I felt in my heart was so real, but when I sit down and rationalise it, it just doesn't all quite fit.'

'Fit what exactly?'

'Reason. Common sense. I've always highly valued my mind and I like to rationalise everything. I guess I'm just not used to living with my heart when my mind is fighting it so strongly.'

Stephen smiled. 'Your mind will surrender, too. When you get to know God more you will start thinking like God.'

Tanner frowned. 'And yet that scares me. Why am I so afraid to let go of the way I have thought for so many years?'

'Because you have always depended on yourself and your own intelligence. You're still learning about faith. Faith comes from the heart, not the mind. It's about believing in what you can't see or understand even when you don't have answers.'

'But didn't God give me this mind and the ability to think? Doesn't it defy reason to then go against the mind God supposedly gave me?'

Stephen looked out across the prison grounds, and Tanner

guessed he was seeking God's wisdom; listening on another level like the Cardelles had appeared to do. 'God created our minds, but he allows us free choice,' he finally said. 'That free choice is affected by selfishness, human weakness. There are verses in the Bible where God says his ways are not our ways, and his thoughts aren't our thoughts. And that the wisdom of humans is foolishness to God. His ways are so much higher than ours. I'd show you on my phone except that I'm not allowed to bring it into the prison. I recommend you look it up for yourself.'

Tanner studied the man. How much could he trust him?

'My brother is in here.'

Stephen's eyes expressed compassion. 'My sister was in gaol a few years back too.'

'What for?'

'Grievous bodily harm. She was high on drugs at the time.'

Up until this point, Tanner had considered Joel a step above those whose crimes were due to addiction, passion or emotion. He'd considered them weaker and looked down on them. Joel was here because of his intelligence and power. For being a master manipulator who could make the world do what he wanted. He considered being in prison a mere hiccup in the journey as he worked to mould the world and its people for his own purposes. Now Tanner saw it for the weakness it was. The sin and pride that had entangled his brother and that had entangled him, too.

On Sunday night he had been pulled from the evil clutches on the devil. Now he needed to be completely free from his brother's hold as well.

He looked at Stephen. 'My brother is a master manipulator. He has plans to get out of jail and to defraud the Cardelle family of their money and their son's identity. I've been helping, but I need to tell him I'm not having a part of it anymore and that I'm going to tell the police, but I'm afraid I won't have the strength to do it. Joel will know exactly what to say, how to make me back down.'

Stephen pursed his lips, looking away, then up at the clouds before settling his wise grey eyes back on Tanner.

'You need to go to the police first. Sometimes we need to recognise our weakness and put guards in place to protect ourselves. Recognising our weakness is what allows us to accept God's strength.'

'It feels dishonest to go to the police first. Like a betrayal.'

'And yet you'd be doing the right thing. For everyone. Deep in your heart you know that.'

'I do.'

Stephen stood and held out his hand. 'Would you like me to come with you?'

Tanner let out a shaky breath. He was about to give up his freedom. His brother's freedom. *God, help me.* The tightness around his chest loosened. With every step he took, Stephen by his side, the ropes fell, one by one until the lightness of his heart made him want to dance and sing.

IT WAS DONE. This time as Tanner entered the prison's visiting room, he knew guards were watching, listening, ready. The law was on his side. Still, he was shaking inside as he approached his brother.

Joel lounged back in a chair, dark eyes glittering, watchful, picking up every nuance in the body language and facial expressions of those around him. When his eyes met Tanner's, there was a brief flicker. Confusion? Question? Could he see the difference? Tanner could feel it in his spirit. Was it also visible on the outside?

'Good to see you, little brother.'

Tanner nodded. Joel always reminded him of his place. His responsibility as the younger, loyal brother. Well, no more.

'I'm still here, as you can see.'

Tanner didn't look away at the accusation. He was supposed to have had Joel out of here by now, changed his identity, accessed Toby's account.

'A lot has happened, Joel.'

'And yet, here I am.'

'I met someone.'

The slightest movement of Joel's eyebrow indicated his displeasure. 'A girl?'

'No, God.'

Joel's whole body jerked back. His chair legs scraped along the floor and fury filled his eyes. His jaw ticked and Tanner knew he was working to calm himself.

'So,' he finally said, his voice a dangerous monotone, 'what are you saying?'

'I believe. And I won't work against him. I've seen his love and protection of those who believe. You'll never win against him.'

Joel let out a long hiss through his mouth, almost like a snake, and an ever-watchful guard tensed and took a step closer.

Joel's eyes shot daggers. 'I can't believe you would betray me like this. Of all the people to go against me.'

'I'm not against you, Joel. I want what's best for you.'

'Stop it!' Joel held up a hand. 'Just stop it. You know what I think of this. God is on the opposite side to us. He's against us. He's our enemy. Get that into your thick head.'

'What if he's not against us, but for us, Joel? Have you ever thought of that? Maybe he's stopped you making a big mistake. He's foiled your plans because he loves you, not because he hates you. He wants your attention. He wants you on the winning side.'

Joel lunged forward, grabbing Tanner by the throat. Tanner heard the pounding of feet, but wondered if the guards would be too late. Joel knew how to kill. Quickly. His mind grew fuzzy. He gasped for air. Yet peace filled him. He'd done the hardest thing he'd ever done in his life, but he'd done the right thing. The police knew all about Joel and his plans. Tanner would be a key witness and his own sentence would be lenient. If he ever lived to face the judge.

God?

Joel's hands loosened as he was pulled back and Tanner clutched his throat, coughed, tried to catch his breath.

'Slow, deep breaths,' the guard by his side instructed. 'Help is on the way.'

Tanner looked to the side. Two guards held Joel down, face to the floor, but still he lifted his head. His eyes bore into Tanner with hatred and unsuppressed fury.

'You're going to die, little brother. I would have liked it to be at my hands, but don't you worry, someone is coming for you.'

Tanner wanted to speak, to beg Joel again to give up the fight, to hand his life over to God, but thanks to Joel his voice wouldn't work. He would need to leave that to God. He would now be put into witness protection. Maybe even sent to another country with a whole new life. That was okay. He *was* a whole new person now. He felt it. God had given him a new heart, a new hope and new life.

The Cardelles, Cairns and Batemans would never need to worry about Joel Elliott again. God had seen to that and protected them in ways they would never know.

CHAPTER FORTY-TWO

Boots scraped against the front door mat. Jess pretended she didn't hear the door open, but she knew who it was. Tim was the only one who wiped his feet so thoroughly before entering the house.

Mum looked up from dinner preparations with a beaming smile. 'Tim! I hope you're staying for dinner?'

'I'd love to.'

Jess could tell Tim was looking over at her, but she kept her eyes on the cutlery she was taking to the table. It was hard to have Tim look at her the way he did. There was a tender concern that touched her so deeply it made her ache. She didn't deserve to be loved. And yet he loved her.

She now understood what he'd said. Things had turned around. So, was she going to allow him to minister to her, the way she had ministered to him in his pain and fear? God had sent him to help her and she'd be foolish to refuse that help. At the same time, she wrestled with her mind and emotions.

For years she'd told herself she didn't need a man, that through God alone she was whole.

It was true, but if she was honest with herself, the real issue was that Tim added a dimension to her life she wasn't ready to face - the fear of losing another loved one. There was security in a relationship with God. He was always there. The relationship was eternal.

And what if Tim became a distraction? What if he took the place God should have in her life? She wanted to give her whole self and life to God.

Another concern was the fact that she hadn't received her heart test results back yet. What if she didn't have long left? She refused to put Tim through that. She wouldn't let him go through another loss.

She set another place at the table, then stopped. Tim had moved directly in front of her, blocking her way. She couldn't really ignore him now. She looked up. He stood, hands in pockets, smiling at her. Had he always been this tall?

She dropped a fork onto the table with a clatter. And watched as he bent to straighten it, bringing his face closer to hers. His eyes softened, almost as though he knew she was nervous and unsure.

'Jess, I was wondering, would you be interested in coming to a concert with me?'

Was he asking her on a date? 'What kind of concert?'

'Philip Cairn's.'

'Your brother-in-law?'

He nodded and Jess tried to understand. 'What does he do? Is he a musician?'

'He is. From what I've heard he's a very gifted singer and songwriter in Christian circles. He's been invited to a church in the city to perform and I thought it would be nice if we went.'

She shuffled the cutlery in her hands. 'Isn't Clare due any day?'

'She still has another month to go. The concert is on Saturday so I thought we could travel on Saturday morning, go to the concert and stay in a motel that night, then travel back Sunday.'

She tensed and her voice shook. 'I'm not staying in a motel with you, Tim.'

His eyes darkened and he stepped back. 'Not the same room. Or same bed. I know Christian morals, Jess.'

She'd offended him. She bit her lip. How was she supposed to know what his standards were? 'Sorry. I'm a bit off-centre today.'

He nodded, then rested a hand on each of her shoulders.

She drew in a shaky breath, cutlery still in her hands. 'What are you doing?'

'Helping steady you. The way you helped steady me.' He smiled and it was so filled with warmth and reassurance that her eyes filled with tears.

She stepped into his space. 'I need a hug,' she whispered.

He looked at the cutlery in her hands and chuckled. 'I'd feel safer if you put the knives down first.'

She plonked them onto the table and his arms came around her, strong and secure.

After a few moments he rested his cheek against her hair. 'Does this mean you're coming to the concert with me?'

'Yes. I'll come.'

His arms tightened around her. 'Thank you. We can bring Milla and Zac as well if it makes you more comfortable.'

Jess thought about it. No, Milla and Zac were studying for school exams. She wouldn't be selfish and interfere with that.

'It's fine.'

Tim stepped back and raised his brows. 'Just fine?'

Why did she keep saying the wrong thing? Why was she still so self-protective? She drew in a deep breath and tried for honesty.

'I want to go with you. Just you. Milla and Zac would change the dynamics.'

His face lit up into a smile and his dimple showed. 'My thoughts exactly.'

MILLA WAS STRESSED. Her heart was pounding, her mind racing and her body wouldn't allow her to stop moving. Exams had never been her favourite time of year, but these ones were important. They could shape her future. The teachers had stressed over and over how important these exams were. She sighed.

God, I never wanted to come back to this place. I've lost the rest, the peace I had in you when I lost my vision.

She loved being able to see again, but she hated this busyness, this feeling of being driven. Not being able to see gave her permission to slow down, to choose what she did. Did she still have that choice? She plonked her pen down on her maths notebook and let her head fall into her hands.

The front door opened. 'Mill?'

She looked up at Zac. He was carrying his maths textbook. Her heart lightened at the sight of him and she grinned. 'I never imagined a knight in shining armour would be carrying a maths textbook instead of a sword.'

He tipped his head to the side and studied her. 'Looks more like I needed to bring the sword of the Spirit.'

He could read her so well. She sighed. 'I hate studying. I hate the pressure, never knowing if I should have put in more effort and studied every hour of the day or if it was okay to do the things I love, to be outside, helping develop El Roi …'

He set his books on the table beside her. 'I know what you mean.' He sat and put his elbows on the table. 'Has Jess heard back about her heart yet?'

'No.' And that was another thing. Why was it taking so long? Was it because there was something wrong?

Zac's hand came over hers, pulling it from her mouth. She hadn't realised she'd been biting her nails. He studied them.

'Leave some.'

'Why? You hungry?'

He chuckled, turning her hand back over but still holding it in his. 'No. I just happen to like your hands the way they are.' He stood. 'You can't sit still, can you? Let's go for a walk.'

'But—'

'God will take care of our marks. Our lives. He healed you, Milla! Let's go and take a walk and look at this amazing world he made for us to see and enjoy.'

She followed him out the door. He pointed up at the hills. 'See. Look! Feast your eyes on that view!'

She would, except she couldn't draw her eyes away from Zac. Her friend who had been there as long as she could remember. The one who understood her, supported her, loved her. Yes, loved her. She loved him too. So much it hurt.

'Milla,' he said, turning to find her looking at him. His eyes locked on hers and he gave a half smile. 'Out there,' he said, pointing, but he didn't move his eyes from hers.

'Yeah.' The word came out breathless. 'I know.'

'So what are you doing staring at me like you've never seen me before?'

'Maybe I haven't. Not really. Not before I lost my vision.'

His smile faded. 'What do we do, Milla? From here, I mean. You know I love you. But … kissing and stuff, well, it's …'

'Scary? I understand.'

He laughed and she knew it wasn't what he was going to say. 'Oh I love you Mill,' he said, affectionately. 'But how do we navigate this … this relationship without messing up? How do we keep it God-honouring? Holy?'

Yes, how? Into her mind came the picture of him walking into church each Sunday with his Bible. 'By fighting temptation with the sword of the Spirit. With the Spirit of Jesus. And by allowing him to fill us with the fruit of his Spirit. Love, joy, peace, patience …' She screwed up her nose. 'What are they again?'

He grinned. 'Kindness, goodness, faithfulness, gentleness and self-control.'

'Yes.' She reached for his hand. 'And that just proves why God brought you and I together. You fill in the gaps in my life. Together, with God, we're whole.'

He bit his lip. 'Milla—'

She watched his mouth, his lips as he said her name. She was tired of talking. She was the action type of girl. On impulse, she reached her arms up around his neck and plied her lips to his.

His eyes widened, and he let out a muffled laugh, before he pulled her close and kissed her back. It wasn't what she expected, though she wasn't sure what she'd expected. She'd have to get used to the warm, wet feel. But no doubt he would, too. Although his enthusiasm now suggested he didn't mind the feeling at all. His eyes were closed. She closed hers, too. And allowed herself to drown in the feel of him, of all her senses awakening.

Suddenly Zac stepped back. 'Self-control.'

She grinned. 'Yes. Right. Sorry.'

'Don't know that I'm sorry.' He put both hands on her shoulders. 'We need to do this with God. Pray with me?'

She nodded. She didn't shut her eyes. She wanted to see Zac, to see the world, to feel God with them. He bowed his head, dropping his hands from her shoulders and taking her hands in his instead.

'God, you've given us this love. We want to honour you, live our lives for you. We know we'll mess up and make mistakes, so please help us. Help us love you and love each other more and more every day.'

'Amen.' Milla smiled. Peace had been restored into her heart. Her eyes were open and she had full vision, physical and spiritual. God saw her. Saw them. And loved them.

JESS WALKED into the concert hall beside Tim, shaking inside. Music blared from the speakers and lights glared down from the stage. People moved about, trying to find their seats, shouting to be heard. The atmosphere was exciting and alive but overwhelming. Having Tim standing tall beside her, holding her hand, added to the unfamiliar sensations bombarding her heart and mind.

'Here's our spot,' Tim said, leading her down a row of seats.

She sat down beside him, staring ahead and watching as sound equipment was given final checks and lighting was tested. She had never heard Philip Cairn sing before, let alone known his music was so big. But then, music wasn't something she had much time for.

'Tim!' An excited voice whisper-shouted from the end of their aisle. Clare stood there looking more pregnant than ever, little Zoe in her arms. 'Come and sit with me in the front row.'

Tim frowned. 'Are we allowed?'

'Of course. There are extras reserved for family.'

Tim smiled then glanced at Jess with raised brows. 'Coming?'

Jess followed him past the people who made way for them to exit the row. Clare moved down the aisle at a surprising speed for one so obviously pregnant. She stopped at the front row where seats were marked 'Reserved.'

Jess felt awkward. She wasn't family. 'You sure? I can sit where we were. Tim can stay here ...'

Clare laughed. 'Don't you dare. You belong here with us.' She patted the seat. 'You sit right there and don't you dare move.'

Jess couldn't help her grin. 'I wouldn't dare.' Her voice softened. 'Thank you.'

'No, thank you.' Clare leaned over to let Zoe slide into Tim's arms. The little girl had been reaching for him from the moment she'd seen him. 'I don't like sitting here all alone while Phil's up there.' She glanced at Tim. 'You have no idea how much it means to me to have family and friends here.'

Jess could see the sincerity in Clare's eyes. There was no pretense there. No saying the right thing for the sake of being nice and meeting expectations. She could learn a lot from Clare.

She settled into her seat, amused by the way Zoe put her hands both side of Tim's face and popped his cheeks while he blew raspberries at her. It was a sight that warmed her heart.

The concert began. A worship band came on before Phil, and they were good, but she was here to hear Phil. If this band was the standard, she was impressed. Could Phil be even better?

Phil walked on stage strumming his guitar and the crowds went wild. They quieted and he began to sing. Jess's heart missed a beat. She had never heard a voice like his before. Pure, deep and strong. It rose up in worship and devotion. Soon the audience joined in. It had to be a taste of heaven. Jess's heart was so full it wanted to burst. And like the rest of the audience she felt her hands lifting of their own accord, unable to help responding and joining in the worship. She sensed when Tim raised his hands beside her.

And then Phil went down on his knees and the audience joined him in full surrender to God as he sang. Jess couldn't stop the tears filling her eyes. She'd never experienced anything so moving and powerful. Nothing else mattered but this moment in God's presence.

'I surrender, God,' she found herself mouthing to him. 'Everything. My fears. My hopes, my dreams, my future. If I have a heart condition, I leave even that in your hands because my heart is yours. Everything!'

As they drove home the next morning, she glanced over at Tim. He looked a bit pale but he'd still insisted on driving the first leg of the journey.

'You doing okay?' she asked. He walked well with his prosthesis, but she worried he might overdo it.

He nodded. 'I am. I think I'm just a bit drained. I mean, the concert was incredible and it was an experience I'll never forget, but …' He shrugged. 'I guess that kind of high isn't sustainable.'

Jess knew what he meant. 'Yeah. It's easy to be on a spiritual high when you're listening to moving music in an environment like that, but I do think what really matters is how we live our everyday life.'

His mouth tipped up and he glanced over at her. 'You mean in the mundane, day to day life like walking in cow pats, birthing calves … or listening to unreasonable patients go off at you?'

Jess laughed. 'Exactly. We need to be able to continue living for God, heart and soul, whatever happens.' She bit her lip. 'Even when things get tough. When things happen that are worse than we could ever have imagined.'

Tim's hand came out to touch her arm briefly. 'Yes,' was all he said, and she knew he understood.

She focused on the road in front of them as Tim indicated and turned on the highway. She was still overwhelmed by all she had experienced last night. Being at a Christian concert with Tim Bateman had felt surreal. He truly knew and loved God now. It was more than she'd dreamed possible.

She studied him as he drove. His strong masculine hands rested comfortably on the steering wheel. His arms were well-toned, his chest and shoulders broad. His dark hair curled slightly as though he'd run his hands through it. Her hands itched to reach out and smooth it down. Desire for him welled up inside so strong it shook her. Tim brought about feelings in her she'd never experienced before. Until now, she hadn't thought she was the marrying type. She'd been so proud of her self-control and the strong grip she had on her feelings.

Tim looked over at her and a slow smile filled his lips. 'What's that look for?'

It was as though he knew. And yet, she didn't need to feel guilty. Natural desire experienced in God's way, in his time, was a beautiful thing. Her parents were evidence of that.

She needed to talk to Tim about her heart. About the change. She needed to do it now, before she lost courage. She dove in.

'You know how I said I want to get my heart results back before I decide about us?'

'Yes.' He glanced over at her, then back to the road.

'Well, something changed last night. My heart, it's God's. All of it. No matter what. And yours is, too.'

He stiffened. 'What are you saying, Jess?' Tension lined his mouth and eyes. 'You don't think God wants us to be together because it might stop us giving him our whole heart?' He tapped the steering wheel. 'Because I think he gives us enough love for both.'

Her heart sank. She'd messed this up just as she'd feared. 'No, that's not what I'm saying.' She blinked back tears. 'I've said it all wrong. Can we pull over?'

He gave a curt nod and pulled in at the next rest area, beside some picnic tables. He got out of the car and sat down on the picnic bench.

Jess sat across from him and he watched her intently, chin in hands, expression cautious.

God, please give me the words. She took a deep breath, wringing her hands on the table in front of her.

'Tim, what I'm trying to say is that I don't think it matters if I do have a heart condition. I mean, in the Bible it says that God planned out every day for us before we were born.' Words spilled uncontrollably from her mouth. 'I'm not going to die before his perfect time for me. Toby's death wasn't a surprise to God. He knew it would happen. I can't stop living because my life might or might not end earlier than I thought it would. I might as well be dead if I did that.'

A spark of hope lit Tim's eyes, though he didn't move. 'And what does living mean for you, exactly?'

'It means grabbing every moment of life with both hands. It means trusting, giving up the habit of second-guessing everything and never doing anything in case I make a mistake. It means telling you what's in my heart, without watering it down, without being afraid of the consequences.'

'So what's in your heart?'

She couldn't read his expression now, but it didn't matter. She reached both arms across the table, letting her hands rest either side of his face the way she'd seen Zoe do. She felt the stubble of his jaw beneath her fingers and moved them up until they settled in his dark, wavy hair.

'Love. For you. Love so strong it scares me half to death. A dream of marriage. And children. Of giving myself completely to God, then to you.'

He glanced away and her heart sank. She'd dared open her heart and it was terrifying. She let her hands slip from his face, drawing them back and crossing her arms over her chest. She felt cold.

'Jess,' he said, sounding sad. 'I can't offer you what you're offering me.'

Her throat ached and she couldn't speak.

'You're a good, Christian girl,' he said. 'Always have been. But I … I haven't lived such a pure life. Before my accident there were … girls.'

Was that it? She'd already guessed that. She reached for his hand. 'You're a new person, Tim, with a new heart. Your mind is still being transformed to be more like God. Whatever is in your past is forgiven, and it's not like I'm perfect. You know my pride, my independence, my foolishness.' She blushed. 'And I understand how hard it can be to fight desire now I've felt it.'

His shoulders relaxed and he leaned across the picnic table, a smile tugging at his lips, dimple in full view. 'Really?' His hands came over hers, his thumbs gently caressing her wrists, dark eyes capturing hers with burning intensity. 'Desire for who?'

He knew exactly what his touch was doing to her. The feelings he was stirring in her. He was enjoying this way too much. Still, she forced herself to say it. 'For you.'

He continued smiling and her face grew warmer. She pulled her hands from his and covered her face. He chuckled and she peeked through her fingers at him.

'You're not playing fair.'

He grinned wider, but then it faded. 'I have to admit I understand why Clare and Beth got married so young now, with God's rules as they are.'

She reached for his hands again. 'But do you understand that God's rules are only for our good? Because he knows what we need most? That relationships are way more fulfilling when there's commitment and faithfulness to one person?'

He nodded. 'Yeah, I get that, now that I understand God's heart. I used to think he was being restrictive and wielding his power. Now I understand he doesn't tell people what to do to prove his authority. He's giving instructions from a caring, Father's heart – a father who knows what's best for his children and wants to give us the best.' He stood, came around the table and took her hand, pulling her up. He drew her into his arms. 'I think this is pretty good, if not best.'

Jess smiled up at him, heart full. 'I can't imagine it being much better.'

But then he kissed her and she knew the best was yet to come. In God's good time.

CHAPTER FORTY-THREE

Jess looked up from her breakfast as Tim barged into the house, grinning from ear to ear.

'Clare and Phil have another daughter,' he announced. 'Melody Clare. 7 pound 6, healthy, blonde and Zoe's new favourite doll.'

Jess dropped her piece of toast, jumped up and threw her arms around his waist. He lifted her up and swung her around.

She laughed as he set her feet back on the floor. 'Anyone would think it was your daughter.'

'Yeah. Speaking of which …' He dropped to one knee there in front of her in the kitchen, took a box from his pocket, opened it and held it out to her. A ring sparkled inside.

'Will you marry me?'

She stared at him, trying to take it in. He was proposing? Here, in the kitchen? Not exactly the most romantic place, but his dark eyes drew her in. He was romantic even if the location wasn't. A bedroom door opened and Milla screamed in delight. Jess covered her ears.

'Oh Jess, have you said yes?' Milla squealed. 'You have to say yes!'

Tim laughed. 'Be quiet, Milla. You're ruining the moment. Just be patient and step to the side for a minute and let your sister speak.'

Milla didn't look the least bit offended as she tilted her head, watching them with a big grin.

'Jess?' Tim drew her attention back. 'This isn't the most comfortable position for me.'

Of course it wasn't. His prosthetic foot made it harder for him to keep his balance. She reached out her hand to help him up.

'Yes. Yes, I will marry you.'

Milla let out a whoop. Jess and Tim turned in unison to see her give a little spin and bounce of joy. She stopped and made a hand waving motion at them.

'Don't look at me, you two. You're supposed to be kissing or at least hugging.'

Tim gave her a bemused smile. 'You're a bit distracting, Milla.'

She gave him a cheeky smile. 'Fine.' She flounced around the corner. Jess knew she was still peeking at them, but she didn't care.

'Do you think it's safe to hug now?' She opened her arms wide.

Tim didn't answer. Instead, he threw his arms around her and kissed her like he'd never kissed her before. Then he smiled down into her eyes.

'I love you, Jessica Cardelle.'

'I love you, too.' More than she'd ever dreamed possible. God had given her more than she'd been able to ask or imagine. He'd given her a man who shared her heart for God. She tried to put words together. 'Tim, I don't know how long I've got or even if I've got the heart condition Toby had, but I do know I want to be with you as long as I live.'

A blast of music coming from the table jarred them both. Her phone. She glanced over. It was the specialist's number.

Tim moved toward the phone. 'You going to get it?'

'No. It doesn't matter what the results are. It won't change anything now.'

His brows shot up, then he chuckled. 'They'll keep calling until you answer.' He lifted the phone off the table. 'You want me to get it?'

'Nah, I will.' She took it from his hands and smiled as his arms came around her shoulder, protecting her, sheltering her from whatever news might come.

'Hello?'

'Jessica Cardelle? It's Dr Samuel here. I'm sorry it's taken me so long to get back to you. Your results were misplaced in our surgery and we had to send through for them again. Good news. The result was negative. Your heart is perfectly strong, whole and healthy.'

'It is?' Tears filled her eyes. She smiled up at Tim through them. 'Thank you.'

'You're welcome.'

She placed the phone back down on the table, trying to comprehend what she'd heard. To realise she was free from the concern of a heart condition; free to give herself heart, body and mind to this man in front of her. 'My heart is fine, Tim.' More than fine. Although it did feel like it could burst with joy right at this moment.

His eyes lit up. 'All clear?'

'All clear.'

He laughed with delight, then sank down into a chair, resting his elbows on the table, his head in his hands. 'I can't quite believe it.'

'Me either.'

He looked up, his eyes taking on a mischievous glint. 'So we can climb mountains together? Jump out of planes together? Have kids?'

She felt herself blushing. 'I hope so. Some people can't have kids, though.'

He chuckled. 'I know. But even if we can't have any of our own, we can always adopt some of the foster kids who come here.'

Jess smiled. 'You have a father's heart, haven't you? First there were your own siblings, then Billy and Zoe. Now you want to take on the foster kids of the world as well as our own if we have them.'

He screwed up his nose. 'Yeah, maybe. You know what I've been thinking?'

'I wouldn't dare guess.'

'Clare and Dan rebelled against me trying to help them, but I never even considered disowning them. And Beth, when she was little, she tried so hard to please me – too hard sometimes – but I love that she tried, even though she didn't need to. And that's how God is with us. I'm far from perfect. I'm a mere man. But that's okay, because God is the one who loves us so completely. Anything I have to offer is only a bonus on the complete love God already offers.'

She laughed. 'A pretty good bonus, I reckon. I have the love of God, but I'm not going to say no to having the love of a good man, too.'

Tim reached for her hand and studied the diamond ring now sparkling on her finger. Then he lifted his gaze to meet hers.

'How did I not see you?' he asked quietly, gazing into her eyes. 'That first day I came into the office I was so blinded by anger, frustration … but how did I not see you?'

She knew the answer now. 'It was too dark.'

'So you shone the light of Jesus.'

'I tried. And I prayed. But it was all God. He softened your heart, gently, slowly, and let the light in.'

'And made room for you.'

She sighed a happy sigh, looking up into Tim's warm, brown eyes. Touching the dimple in his cheek. 'Yes.' That man she dreamed about ... the one who held Toby's heart, it was Jesus. Jesus who also held her heart and Tim's heart safe for eternity. God had blessed her beyond belief. He had seen her pain, seen her struggle, seen *her*. And he'd given her more than she'd ever dreamed. He was the God who healed broken hearts and made them whole.

'Thank you Jesus,' she whispered. 'Thank you.'

And she felt the love in his gaze and the warmth of his smile.

A NOTE FROM THE AUTHOR

I woke up one morning a few years ago with blurry vision. As the morning went on, I realised my sight was getting worse to the point that everything appeared out of place. I looked at my son, and his elbow appeared to be coming out the side of his head. It was a strange experience.

A neurologist diagnosed me with Ocular Myasthenia, and later, Myasthenia Gravis. I needed to wear an eye patch to stop the world jumping around me, and had to walk slowly to avoid bumping into things. I struggled to look at screens which was a problem because my publisher was waiting on Book 3, *Framing Fleur* at the time.

I prayed for healing, but I also rediscovered a beautiful stillness. It was as though my spiritual vision was heightened because my physical eyesight could no longer be a distraction.

One day, four months later, I felt a strong sense that God wanted to heal me. Within a week, my vision had returned. My neurologist couldn't explain it. I still get blurry or jumping vision when I'm especially tired, but it's mild and manageable.

God reminded me He does heal. And sometimes He just wants

our attention. He wants us to slow down, to rest, to listen to Him and allow our spiritual sight to be restored.

May you walk with Him by still waters today, and allow Him to heal all that needs healing within you.

Jenny xx

"And I will give you a new heart, and I will put a new spirit in you. I will take out your stony, stubborn heart and give you a tender, responsive heart."
Ezekial 36:26 (NLT)

"He alone is your God, the only one who is worthy of your praise, the one who has done these mighty miracles that you have seen with your own eyes."
Deuteronomy 10:21 (NLT)

"For this is how God loved the world: He gave his one and only Son, so that everyone who believes in him will not perish but have eternal life."
John 3:16 (NLT)

If you enjoyed *Seeing Jess*, please check out my website to find out more about me and my writing. www.jennyglazebrook.com

Reviews help other readers find new-to-them authors, so I'd really appreciate it if you can spare a moment to write a quick review on Goodreads or your place of purchase.

ACKNOWLEDGMENTS

Thank you to my teenage beta readers: Eleanor Wood, Tirzah McKenzie, Nadia Broekman, Michaeli Broekman, Clarity Glazebrook and Merridy Glazebrook. As always, your suggestions have improved this story. You are priceless!

Thank you to Theo Broekman for inspiring some of the fatherly words of wisdom spoken by Charlie Cardelle in this story. And Cate, Michaeli and Nadia, your love of the Bateman Family and enthusiasm to read each new manuscript spurs me on.

With special thanks to my fellow writer, Michelle Dennis Evans. Thank you doesn't seem enough for all you do. Your proofreading and suggestions are spot on and you always make me think about every word and its impact. You offer your time, your gifts and your skills with such a generous heart. I thank God for you.

Once again, thank you to my husband, Rob. What would I do without you? Thank you for sharing this journey with me, for encouraging me to use the gift of writing God has given me and supporting me every step of the way. I love you.

Above all, thank you to God who brings these stories to life in my heart and mind. You bring purpose, hope and joy and have given me life beyond all I could imagine. Thank you for loving me, for bringing light in my darkest times and for healing my sight.

ABOUT THE AUTHOR

Jenny Glazebrook lives in a small country town in Australia. She and her husband Rob have four young adult children who fill their lives with joy.

They also have many pets and rescue animals including a sheep who thinks she's a dog, and a goose who thinks he's a human. Life in the Glazebrook household is never boring.

Jenny writes stories that capture what it means to know Jesus and live for Him in a broken world.

She has a Diploma of Theology, is a qualified chaplain and experienced inspirational speaker. She loves to encourage others to understand God's love, see His hand in their lives, and walk with Him each day.

www.jennyglazebrook.com

ALSO BY JENNY GLAZEBROOK

The Aussie Sky Series (YA fiction):

Blaze in the Storm

Heart of Thunder

Clouds of Prayer

Mist of the Morning

Clinging to Rainbows

Forgiving Sky

The Bateman Family Novels (YA/new adult fiction):

Daring Clare

Saving Beth

Framing Fleur

Seeing Jess

Living Melody

Loving Zoe

The Trinity Lakes Series (Christian romance)

Where Our Hearts Lie

In Truth and Love

Like Stars that Shine

Other books

How The World Turns

Molly the Dog-Sheep and other true pet parables (coming soon)

Collaborative works:

Wellspring Devotional Journal

Dear Jesus Diaries

More about Jenny and her books can be found at

www.jennyglazebrook.com

LIVING Melody

It's not easy being the ordinary sister.

Melody Cairn has two beautiful, talented sisters who are making their way up in the Christian music world. It's hard not to question why God created her with an embarrassing lisp that disqualifies her from performing with her sisters.

When a grown-up Billy Green arrives at the farm, Melody wishes more than ever that God had chosen to create her with an extraordinary gift. Then maybe Billy Green would see her as more than his cute little sister.

But what if the greatest gift she has to offer is her heart for God and her joyful, loving personality?